What critics and scholars have said about
CASTANEDA'S JOURNEY

Intense, intelligent, and witty. Starting point for any serious discussion of the Castaneda phenomenon.
—Publishers Weekly

Though not antagonistic toward Castaneda and his literary achievement, proves pretty conclusively that the entire don Juan series is a hoax.
—Denver Post

Evidence strong enough to sow seeds of doubt in the firmest bedrocks of belief.
—Los Angeles Times Book Review

Should satisfy anyone still in doubt.
—New York Times Book Review

Surely Castaneda is caught here flagrante delicto!
—Human Behavior

Totally convincing.
—San Francisco Bay Guardian

Provocative and witty. De Mille is a diligent detective.
—Daniel Noel

Reads like a highbrow detective story.
—Oakland Tribune

Has blown the whistle on what may be the biggest hoax in academia since the Piltdown man.
—Fate

The authenticity of all of Castaneda's works has been seriously challenged.
—Parapsychology Review

Provides the strongest critique to date from a social scientist.
—Contemporary Psychology

The most devastating part of de Mille's analysis is his chronological ordering of the events said to have occurred during 1961-1962.
—Contemporary Sociology

A brilliant investigative study. Required reading for anyone interested in the social realities behind both Castaneda's books and the academic follies that seem to have accompanied them.
—Zetetic

CASTANEDA'S JOURNEY

The Power and the Allegory

Second Edition, Revised

by

Richard de Mille

Graphics by Frederick A. Usher

CAPRA PRESS   SANTA BARBARA

Copyright© 1976, 1978 by Richard de Mille
All rights reserved
Manufactured in the United States of America
First published, October 1976
Second printing, January 1977
(Pages 11, 180, 188-91, 196, 201 revised)
Second edition, revised, December 1978
(Pages i-xiv, 48-51, 84, 86, 112, 115, 154, 165, 174-177
180, 195-197, 205-206 revised)

Library of Congress Cataloging in Publication Data

De Mille, Richard, 1922-
    Castaneda's journey.

    Bibliography: p.
    Includes index.
    1. Castaneda, Carlos. 2. Anthropologists—United
States—Biography. I. Title.
    F1221.Y3C374   301.2'092'4 [B]   76-26030
    ISBN 0-88496-067-6
    ISBN 0-88496-068-4 pbk.

CAPRA PRESS
631 State Street
Santa Barbara, CA 93101

CONTENTS

'La Catalina,' 1962

Preface to the Second Edition

This book tells the story of a rank newcomer to the field of anthropology gradually discovering how a brilliant pretender named Carlos Castaneda had brought off the greatest science hoax since the Piltdown man. Borrowing Castaneda's mysterious tone, the account often imitates his narrative sleight of hand, thereby testing the reader's ability to separate the plausible from the implausible—a test much like the one imposed by Castaneda's books.

Some readers of this book whose view of things was rather more solemn and literal than mine hated the test, but others enjoyed being fooled occasionally by a quasi-Castanedic chronicle. A few fans were positively transported by a gleeful suspicion that the book had been written by Castaneda himself, playing his most convoluted trick. This illusion was strengthened by minor coincidences such as both writers being scholars, of about the same age, having wives named Margaret, living in California, speaking Spanish, and providing (in my case) no personal history and (in Castaneda's) no credible personal history. Delighted as I was with that reaction, I must state for the record that in spite of common interests in social science, religion, metaphysics, magic, ESP, visions, and trickery, Castaneda and I are definitely *not* the same person. Let me also certify that I am not playing any more tricks on the reader, and point out that when I did play them I also furnished plenty of clues, mostly in the notes, to what was straight and what was twisted. Of course, not everybody reads notes or picks up clues. To start things off right, I assure all readers past and present that the UCSB library door *did break* exactly as Chapter One says it did.

During the two years between editions popular critics flatly proclaimed the don Juan books a hoax—a belated illumination provoked chiefly by the outrageous extremes their generally dense credulity or timid skepticism had driven Castaneda to in *The Second Ring of Power*, published in 1977. Like many another hoaxer, Castaneda had worked hard to give himself away, only to be frustrated volume after volume by man's capacity for self-deception and media's enslavement to fads.

The same interval saw the anthropological profession openly acknowledging the hoax at last, and I think it would be fair to say *Castaneda's Journey* was the main source of this newfound readiness to announce in public what most anthropologists had been saying in private since *A Separate Reality* appeared, in 1971.

Luckily for detective-story buffs, general recognition of the hoax did not spell the end of the Castaneda plot but barely the beginning. Writing in *Religion* (Autumn 1977), Stephen Reno said de Mille's exposé had merely changed the question from "Did it happen?" (*it* being Carlos's strange adventures) to "How could it have happened?" (*it* now being the academic ratification of Castaneda's fantasies, particularly UCLA's covert acceptance of a retitled published novel as a dissertation in scientific anthropology).

The puzzle persisted. Ralph L. Beals, one of Castaneda's early professors, complained at length in the *American Anthropologist* (June 1978) about his former student's evasiveness, improbable trips to Sonora, and invisible fieldnotes, but Michael Harner—from four of whose published works (Chapter Five proposes) Castaneda sequentially adapted some two-dozen ideas for don Juan—indignantly declared he was not familiar with any evidence of that borrowing (*New York Times Book Review*, 7 May 1978).

Given such persistence, the Castaneda plot remains largely intact. Don Juan still appeals to new-age consciousness as a fountain of wisdom and a model for personal growth. Likely sources of his lore await detection in obscure corners of the UCLA library. Of the hoaxer's personal history meager details have been restored, while the depths of character from which the hoax arose go mostly unplumbed. Though speculations in Chapter Four are proving close to the mark, we are still not sure what happened at UCLA. Accumulating information fails to banish the specter of Sonoragate, an appalling scenario in which certain eminent academicians knowingly tolerate or enjoy a hoax, as others carelessly indulge what (to them if not to the general reader) should be a transparent imposture. Five years into the plot, when *Time* began the first skeptical inquiry, the academy closed ranks to cover up what had been done, thus provoking eventual accusations of fraud and demands for investigation and censure from scholars who were not so amused as I.

Such shenanigans (don Juan would dub them) made it possible for a complete novice and utter outsider to write not only this book but an explanatory sequel to be titled *The Don Juan Papers: Further Castaneda Controversies*, a unique opportunity for which I am grateful and because of which—without intending any more irony than is already inherent in the situation—I rightly and gladly call Castaneda my teacher and don Juan my benefactor.

The Piltdown comparison is far from superficial. Though *Eoanthropus dawsoni* (Dawson's dawn man) clung to the evolutionary tree for 41 years (1912-1953), whereas don Juan walked Sonoran sands no more than eight (1968-1976), the hoaxes are alike in several ways. This is particularly true if we compare them in the framework of Ronald Millar's theory (broached in *The Piltdown Men*, 1972) that the hoaxer was not after all Charles Dawson, a Sussex solicitor and amateur geologist who found certain skeletal fragments in a local gravel pit, but Grafton Elliot Smith, a brilliant man of science given to playing mordant jokes on his colleagues.

In Millar's closely reasoned speculation, Smith championed a theory of prehistoric cultural diffusion which would be well served by any discovery in English soil of a missing link between ape and man, an evolutionary gap now filled by *Australopithecus*. Preoccupied by his unfashionable thesis, Smith conceived a trick to draw attention to it. Over a period of several years, he deposited fragments of a modern human skull, suitably antiqued, and parts of an orang-utan's jaw, stained to match, where the unsuspecting Dawson would be likely to find them. This was no careful forgery meant to stand the test of time but a clever concoction meant to explode in laughter at the expense of Smith's scientific adversaries. Filed to resemble human teeth, the orang-utan's molar surfaces bore tell-tale scratches of artificial abrasion. Much to Smith's dismay (reasons Millar) nobody looked for those signs of fabrication. Since he could not openly question Dawson's discoveries without risking exposure, Smith supplied new evidence of their spuriousness, to no avail. Instead of betraying the fakery, parts of a single skull planted at different sites gave rise to a second Piltdown man, and only untimely death kept the discoverer from being knighted. Despairing of exhibits preposterous enough to disillusion his credulous colleagues, the hoaxer went to his grave without confessing. Not until 1953, when he had been dead for two decades, did anyone scrutinize the Piltdown relics as a possible forgery.

In light of Millar's theory, let me now list the features these hoaxes have in common:

Each could have been exposed at once by a competent skeptical inquiry—into the shape of Piltdown's teeth, into the existence of Castaneda's voluminous Spanish fieldnotes, never offered for examination and now, alas, destroyed by convenient flooding of Castaneda's basement.

Each was the product of a clever prankster who was very knowledgeable about the relevant science.

Each provided superficially plausible support for a particular scientific tendency—Smith's cultural diffusion, the ethnoscience and ethnomethodology Castaneda encountered at UCLA.

Each was hailed by some as a giant step in science but was doubted by others.

Each wasted the time of or made fools of some trusting colleagues.

Each cast suspicion on an innocent party—Piltdown on Dawson, don Juan on Theodore Graves. When Don Strachan was reviewing *Castaneda's Journey* for the *Los Angeles Times Book Review* (6 Feb 1977), a UCLA anthropology professor, who requested anonymity, told him "Graves was the prime mover" of Castaneda's doctoral committee. In fact, Graves did not sign the dissertation but had left the country for New Zealand a year before it was signed by five other professors.

Each hoaxer presented ever more extravagant material in an apparent but long unsuccessful attempt to unmask the imposture.

Neither hoaxer confessed. Castaneda, of course, can still do so, but frank confession would be quite out of character for him. His flagrant fourth and outlandish fifth books constitute a sort of implicit confession.

In certain other ways, the hoaxes are dissimilar. Grafton Elliot Smith seems to have had no accomplices, but credence is strained by the optimistic proposal that *not one* of Castaneda's faculty sponsors knew what was going on during the five years in which he presented his suspect, unsupported, self-contradictory writings for academic approval.

The scientific cost of Piltdown man was high, of don Juan low. Some forty years Sir Arthur Keith played dupe to Piltdown; a quarter of a century Arthur Smith Woodward hunted additional fragments of him; countless lectures and articles expounded his evolutionary significance. In contrast, few anthropologists subscribed to don Juan; no pits were dug to find him or monuments erected to him; trifling research funds were diverted by him. The spate of Juanist writings has been literary, philosophical, or occult, seldom scientific.

Piltdown did more harm than good, his only contribution a warning against further frauds. Even within the confines of science don Juan may do more good than harm, for he reveals the condition of anthropology, disclosing a widespread confusion between authenticity and validity—a false inference that don Juan must exist because some of his lore agrees with what Indians say—and manifesting the rift between those anthropologists who (in Colin Turnbull's words) "regard anthropology primarily as a humanity and those who regard it primarily as a science."

In 1955 J. S. Weiner convinced the world of Dawson's apparent duplicity and Piltdown's undeniable illegitimacy. Four years later, when Weiner's *Piltdown Forgery* was galvanizing anthropology students much as *The Teachings of Don Juan* would electrify them ten years thence, Castaneda began his studies at UCLA. Reflecting on his subsequent career, dare we entertain the fantastic notion that the Piltdown hoax not only foreshadowed the don Juan hoax but also inspired it? I believe that if we do not entertain such fantastic notions we shall never understand Carlos Castaneda.

In *Second Ring of Power* Castaneda soared to his fifth level of incredibility, thus disillusioning a legion of don Juan's disciples. As don Juan's loyal debunker, I am not entirely pleased by this turn of events. Though fewer naïve followers survive to accuse me of sacrilege, a small cadre determined to exonerate UCLA have seized upon Castaneda's wild fourth and fifth books not as an implicit confession of hoaxing but as an abandonment of factual reporting. "Anyone reading the later books," snorted one academic legitimizer, "would naturally conclude he was a fraud." My considered judgment is that anyone carefully and skeptically reading the *early* books would also conclude he was a fraud. Castaneda's first book, published by the University of California Press with faculty approval, and his third book, accepted as a dissertation, cannot both be factual accounts, because they contradict each other. Possibly under a spell cast by don Juan, I carelessly omitted a telling example of that contradiction. Let me add it here.

During the first two years of Carlos's storied apprenticeship (narrative 1961-1962) don Juan speaks standard English one day, in *The Teachings,* slang the next, in *Journey to Ixtlan,* a remarkable counterpoint which can, of course, be laid to don Juan's professed translator, Castaneda. Harder to explain away than this counterpoint of speech or translation is a corresponding counterpoint of mood.

The Teachings tells a gloomy, somber tale, in which excitement tends toward fear or wonder, seldom toward joy or amusement. When, in narrative-1968, the legendary Carlos takes up the second part of his apprenticeship (recounted in the second book, *A Separate Reality*), he finds "the total mood of don Juan's teaching . . . more relaxed. He laughed and also made me laugh a great deal. There seemed to be a deliberate attempt to minimize seriousness in general. He clowned during the truly crucial moments of the second cycle."

The text bears out this description, and when we get to *Ixtlan,* the third book, don Juan is a regular cut-up, a walking koan, a Zen buffoon, notwithstanding that *Ixtlan* is set back in the early period, of the somber *Teachings.* So we are asked to believe that "the total mood of don Juan's teaching" changed from day to day during 1961-1962 in perfect concordance with our reading of either the first or the third book. Now I grant don Juan is a versatile fellow, and no doubt prescient, but I do not deeply believe he could infallibly assume the proper mood each day to fit the tone of one of two books in which his mood would be contradictorily described seven and eleven years later. Nor can I think of any authorly excuse for this contradiction. If don Juan's chronicler could not distinguish smiling from frowning, or brooding silence from roaring laughter, throughout two years, or if he didn't care which way he reported them, why should we credit his report? I judge this one systematic flaw, all by itself, unsupported by numerous other contradictions described in Chapter Three, to be fatal to Castaneda's supposed fieldwork and to his nominal dissertation, now standing cheerfully on a shelf in the UCLA library.

Having erred once in don Juan's favor, I also erred once against him. Chapter Three of the first edition argued hilariously but incorrectly that "pulling your leg" could not have been translated from Spanish; the Spanish, Juan Tovar has shown, is *tomándote el pelo.* My conclusion, however, remains unchanged: Except for occasional details, the conversations with don Juan were originally composed in English, by Castaneda alone. In this edition, leg-pulling gives way to an inquiry into the name Mescalito. Chapter Four adds a new view of Goldschmidt's "allegory." Chapter Six restores Barbara

Myerhoff to her rightful place at the waterfall and digs up Michael Harner's missing reference to Yaquis using *Datura.*

Further research has traced additional sources for don Juan's wisdom and Carlos's exploits. The fieldwork of just one of Castaneda's fellow UCLA graduate students, for example, offers the following Juanist ideas: the spiritual warrior, the shields of the warrior, the warrior's strange left eye, death threatening from the left, the soul-defender's special fighting form, the spirit catcher, the head that turns into a bird, and the name Ixtlan (taken by Castaneda for Mazatec Genaro's home town, though there is no Mazatec Ixtlan). Such details await publication in *The Don Juan Papers,* but one thing must be told here: the origin of 'la Catalina.'

How Chapter Nine scrambles to explain that name! And what an odd name it is: 'the Catherine'—in quotation marks! Though I think my previous guesses still have peripheral merit, I now believe I have found the central source of the only significant female figure in Castaneda's first four books.

'La Catalina,' you may recall, was a beautiful but fearsome witch, who trapped Carlos's soul and interfered with his hunting for power. A worthy opponent, don Juan called her. To restore her personal history we have to go back to a rather surprising place, the *Saturday Evening Post,* where John Kobler's article of 2 November 1963 was the first to name her.

In those early days, I have come to believe, Castaneda was an avid reader of the *Post,* where in October 1958 he undoubtedly read an article, "Drugs that Shape Men's Minds," by one of his favorite writers, Aldous Huxley.

"Stimulators of the mystical faculties" like peyote and LSD, wrote Huxley, "make possible a genuine religious experience" by which "large numbers of men and women [can] achieve a radical self-transcendence and a deeper understanding of the nature of things," which will constitute a religious revolution.

Castaneda was not the only spiritual revolutionary to take inspiration from Huxley. When professors Timothy Leary and Richard Alpert (later Baba Ram Dass) got into trouble at Harvard with their psychedelic evangelism, they set up a research and training center for members of their "International Federation for Inner Freedom" in the Mexican fishing village of Zihuatanejo, up the coast from Acapulco. There "If-If" found a shoreline sanctuary in the charming little Hotel Catalina.

"I sat transfixed all evening before a tree, feeling in it the very treeness of trees," said one chemico-spiritual tripper in Kobler's account.

"I sensed it was a tree by its odor," a drugless Carlos would recall in *Tales of Power* (200). "Something in me 'knew' that that peculiar odor was the 'essence' of tree."

"Our favorite concepts are standing in the way of a flood-tide," Leary and Alpert warned. "The verbal dam is collapsing."

"I *saw* the loneliness of man as a gigantic wave . . . held back by the invisible wall of a metaphor," Castaneda would write in his drugless *Ixtlan* (267).

If-If proposed to liberate its members from their "webs," so that they might soar through the infinite space of consciousness. Carlos's be-mushroomed head would fly among silvery crows; his undrugged eyes would see a range of mountains as a "web of light fibers" (*Ixtlan* 202).

Though If-If adopted *The Tibetan Book of the Dead* as a drug-taker's manual, don Juan would tell Carlos the book was a "bunch of crap" (*Reality* 194).

Dashing the hopes of some five-thousand acidophile applicants, the Mexican government, on 13 June 1963, "gave the 20 Americans then staying at the Catalina five days to clear out of the country."

"If anybody can show us a better road to happiness," the notorious Leary challenged, "we'll drop our research. But we don't think they will."

A better road was already running through the unknown mind of Carlos Castaneda—don Juan's path with heart—which would carry future readers away from what Castaneda saw as the haphazard drug-fiendery of the Catalina, toward a disciplined and eventually drugless mysticism. In this unproclaimed competition for the hearts and minds of self-transcenders, Leary soon came to grief and Castaneda triumphed. The impact of a worthy opponent would elicit a warrior's best efforts, don Juan said; the opponent he thought worthy of Carlos was 'la Catalina.' In the fall of calendar-1962, If-If flourished in Zihuatanejo; in the fall of narrative-1962, Carlos survived six hair-raising encounters with his worthy opponent in Sonora.

A startling photograph in Kobler's article shows a formidable young woman in a leopard-skin bathing suit wading into the Mexican surf after taking LSD, her long left hand extended downward toward the water. She is, the caption tells us, "feeling the power of the ocean." That remarkable image, I believe, incubated four years in Castaneda's brain, emerged in 1968 as a *black bird*, "a fiendish witch" who wanted to finish don Juan off—before Castaneda's mythogenic power could be felt in the world through the don Juan allegory.

1. THE DAY OF THE COYOTE

In Dr. Wills' full sight, at a distance of about four feet, a saucer . . . hovered for a split second, then with a loud report snapped in two and fell straight down. *

Rumbling sounds were heard and the glass broke in a wall picture of Jesus.

One night in 1973 Margaret Castaneda was in her living room waiting for Carlos to call from Mexico, when a sound "like a gunshot" came from the kitchen. Rushing in, she found a crystal dish shattered into a thousand pieces. Neither the dish on top of it nor the one beneath had moved. Next day Carlos did call, explaining that her line had been busy. He had placed his call, he said, just when the dish had shattered.

I can't vouch for the details of Margaret's story, but I have no reason to question them. Unaccountable breakage is firmly established in serious literature (like the quotations above) though its causes can only be guessed. Often it seems to come and go with angry feelings of some person on the scene. Whether the shattering dish was a sorcerer's greeting from Carlos or a mental stamp of Margaret's foot when the phone refused to ring, such perplexing events do keep bursting into our ordinary reality, if we are willing to notice them.

A story I can vouch for is the following. On 6 September 1975 I sent a letter to anthropologist Carlos Castaneda saying I was working on this book, asking for some technical information from his dissertation, and suggesting we get together for lunch.

*see notes beginning on page 177.

11

Castaneda had written four best sellers about his 12-year apprenticeship in the Sonoran desert under a Yaqui Indian sorcerer named don Juan Matus. There his head had turned into a crow and flown away, he had become brother to the coyote, and he had learned to erase his personal history. That erasure was making it difficult for me to write a well rounded book. Knowing his reputation for being elusive, I didn't really expect him to meet me for lunch, but I hoped he would answer the letter.

On 1 October, having heard not a word from Castaneda, I visited the library at the University of California, Santa Barbara, to see a rare book called *Mushrooms Russia and History,* which I thought might have influenced him. Arriving a few minutes before closing time, I could make only a cursory inspection of the work, but what I saw convinced me I was on the right track, and I said I would come back in two days to examine it again.

Two days later I was back, but the book was not to be had. The night before, library assistant Howard Rankins had been startled by a noise "like a rifle shot." Searching the deserted reading room, he found nothing amiss at first, then froze in his tracks as he caught sight of the plate glass door to the rare book room. No longer transparent, the glass was mottled like marble. Stepping closer he saw long cracks radiating from a pinhole about five feet from the floor.

In the morning, workmen boarded up the ominous slab to keep glass from falling into the reading room. No possible trajectory for a missile could be found, so the door was deemed to have shattered spontaneously. With a sheet of plywood safely in place nobody could get his hands on the mushroom book for a week or two. Department head Curtis Brown hoped the delay would not inconvenience me too much.

"I'd like to get Rankins's description of what happened," I said. "I might be able to use it in my book."

"Surely," Brown said. "We can give you his number."

"I don't suppose he noticed a coyote around at the time."

"A coyote?" Brown smiled indulgently.

"Or a crow," I said. "A coyote or a crow when the door broke?"

"This is the eighth floor," Brown said kindly. "We never see any animals up here."

It was a silly question, because a coyote stands only two feet tall, and that pinhole was at eye level for a sorcerer five-foot-five. I could see the whole pattern of radial cracks through the window on the opposite side of the rare book room. If Carlos was warning me to keep my nose out of the history he had erased, what should I do? Don Juan, I knew, would deflect a worthy opponent's magic bullet to a target of his own choosing. In telling this story, I believe I have followed his teaching.

Sifting rumors was a major task:

Castaneda was killed in a Mexican bus crash.

Castaneda is alive and well at his grandfather's farm in Brazil.

Castaneda's next book is the biography of an old Yaqui furniture maker.

Castaneda confessed to a Harvard class that his don Juan books were a hoax.

Castaneda is controlling other people's dreams in a UCLA research project.

Castaneda lived for several weeks at the house of a lady in central California. Then he was asked to leave. It seems he wasn't the authentic Castaneda.

Castaneda spent months in 1966 as a psychiatric patient at the UCLA Medical Center. George Olduvai was a UCLA student at the time and he knew all about it. Did George see Castaneda in the hospital? No. Did he talk to the doctors? No—but it was common knowledge.

Benita Zorro knows the man who introduced Carlos to don Juan. Benita lives at no particular address in the Topa Topa Valley. I call the man who knows Benita, and he takes my number. She doesn't call back.

Al Egori has a photo of don Juan. I call him in Los Angeles.

"I understood don Juan didn't allow pictures."

"That's right. This picture was taken surreptitiously."

"Who took it?"

"I can't discuss that."

"Could I publish it in my book?"

"No, no. It can't be shown to anybody."

"Who has seen it besides you?"

"Nobody."

"You must have taken it, then."

"I can't discuss that."

Al goes on to say I shouldn't even *begin* to write my book until I have taken *at least* 500 LSD trips. I tell him I'm fighting a deadline.

Reactions to Castaneda and his works (see page 24) range from visionary enthusiasm, through angry rejection, to complete lack of interest. My own opinions are just as well balanced but not so extreme. I bring some good news and some bad news, some praise and some blame, some affirmations and some refutations. While I have not joined the Castaneda Idolaters' Club, neither can I claim membership in the League of Outraged Skeptics—and I certainly do not belong to the Committee to Stamp Out Sorcery. Far from it. Sorcery lives. Magic is all around us. Swedenborg *sees* a fire burning 300 miles away. D.D. Home floats in and out of hotel windows. A vacuum-physics experiment implodes just as the Subatomic Jinx is passing through town on a train. A soldier is wounded and his mother bleeds. Mild-mannered bumpkins turn into murdering satanic beasts. A sexy dolphin tries to make it with an off-duty restaurant hostess. Lionel Tiger prowls Manhattan shoulder to shoulder with Robin Fox. And crows haunting the Irvine campus are taken for don Juan and Carlos Castaneda. This is a deep, multifaceted subject, having both comic and sober sides. Like the dreamer and the dreamed, I expect to be on all sides at once.

To begin with, Carlos Castaneda must not be mistaken for Margaret Mead, J.R.R. Tolkien, Swami Vivekananda, P.T. Barnum, Plato, or the Great Pretender—though he has something in common with each of them. Castaneda is an original: there is nobody else quite like him. And he is controversial, no doubt about it. I will not waste any time trying to be neutral about him: but I will not be for him or against him either: I will be for him *and* against him simultaneously.

In that contradiction, I shall not be alone. Legions betray mixed feelings about Castaneda. Those he has tricked laugh wryly at his slyness. Those he has betrayed forgive him through their tears. Critics boo him for one thing and applaud him for another. Myriads adore him, but no one simply despises him. His former wife told me with cheery regret: "Carlos is one of those people you can love and hate at the same time." Exactly. One ferocious, bearded fellow, whose name escapes me now, told me a tale of Carlos Coyote, Trickster Teacher.

"I had this kilo of grass," he said, "and my stupid cat pissed on it. Carlos was there, and I asked him what I ought to do. He said to take a sharp knife and carefully cut out just the part the cat had pissed on—and save it. He said to throw the rest away. Well, he got that peyote-chewing grin on his face, so I knew he was kidding. But then he came around later when I was separating the seeds (which I keep) from the stems (which I throw out).

'Hey!' he said, 'Don't throw the stems away. Don Juan told me they're the best part for *seeing.*' Hell, *everybody* knows better than *that,* but I was really into *The Teachings* at that time, so I thought, don Juan must know a lot more about grass than the rest of us. 'Okay,' I said, 'I'll save them.' 'Just make tea out of them,' says Carlos, 'You'll be surprised.' Right. But that time he wasn't smiling. So I made tea out of them. I didn't *see* anything, but I sure got a helluva headache." Chuckling through clenched teeth, my friend refilled his shot glass, till it ran over on the table. "Carlos is one funny falcon coyote," he said.

Not being addicted to best sellers, pop mysticism, drug trips, cactus, or Indians, and having too many other things to read already, I had survived well into the spring of 1975 without reading a word of Castaneda. Of course I had admired the mesmerizing black crow on the cover of his first (Pocket) book, the flash-faced levitator on his second, the fleet white falcon on his third, and the ten-foot moth on his fourth, but I had resolved not to be seduced by any of those entrancing symbols. Having seen no book reviews, I felt pretty well insulated from Castaneda—whoever he was—but still his far-flung silvery web entangled me. One after another, various weighty academic articles I was reading kept mentioning him in passing—with respect, with admiration, even with awe—and gradually the feeling grew that I ought to check out his books just to see what was going on there. Perhaps he did know something I didn't know but needed to know.

And then there was my niece, a most enthusiastic young woman. She kept harping on Castaneda. "What's the general theme?" I asked her. "Nobody can *describe* don Juan to you," she said. "You have to read the books yourself." One day she dumped all four of them on me. "Start at page one," she said, "and go straight through. Don't skip around and don't leave anything out." "I heard you could get the message," I said, "just by reading a few pages in *Tales of Power.*" "Forget that!" she yelped. "You can't fool around with don Juan. You have to take the whole trip."

For months the books stayed in a pile on the table where she had put them. Every time I walked by, that fanatical crow fixed me with his angry eye. "What are you waiting for?" he cawed. I shuffled him down into the pile, but then Old Glowhead kept walking toward me out of the sky—and where was that spout of water coming from, anyway? I shuffled them down and got the white falcon. He was okay at first, but then he turned into a flying fish, which reminded me of the loneliness and seasickness of childhood, so I balanced the hardcover on top of the three pulps and was relieved to see the two dusty chums sitting peacefully back to back in the moth-fanned purple twilight. Eventually I began to wonder what they were talking about.

It is true (as don Juan says—and Michael Polanyi said before him) that once you learn something you have learned it. Never can you go back to where you were before you learned it. For better or worse, it has become a part of you. One thing I learned from reading Castaneda was that there were two funny little old guys out there in the desert who were a real kick in the head. I wanted to go out there and talk to them—which I could easily have done, since both of them spoke excellent Spanish, a language I can understand tolerably well if people don't speak too fast. I hadn't learned any Yaqui yet, of course—*hupa hu'upat kateka upaupatia* (skunk sitting on a stump making a noise like a skunk)—but that wasn't necessary. The only obstacle between me and Carlos's playmates was Carlos himself. He wouldn't give out their address.

Another thing I learned was that Castaneda was kicking some very big true ideas around: There is more than one kind of reality. There is magic that is not illusion. The world is what comes out of what can be. The world we know is something we are doing. Part of you is not in this world. Part of you knows what the rest of you doesn't. If you trust your silent self, your talking self won't have to stay so ignorant. A wise man knows his time to act is short. Say hello to Death: he has some good advice for you. Responsibility gives power. But greater than power—is knowledge.

Wow! I thought. This young UCLA anthropologist is plugged into the right channel. But he has a very noisy receiver. Along with the good stuff, it keeps giving out interference like: On the other hand, greater than knowledge—is sometimes power. A man with a past is weak and helpless. Woman is the scariest thing on earth. Nothing really matters. Nobody can be happy. Nobody can get close to anybody. You can love the world but not the people in it. Laughing is always better than crying. If your kid is dying, see him as a fog of crystals, and you'll feel a whole lot better. A man of knowledge walks on the river of life without getting his feet wet. And there is no way to tell one kind of reality from another.

What a mess! The wisdom of the ages folded into an omelet with the neurosis of the century. It didn't help that Carlos was always badmouthing himself as a neurotic. I had to agree with him. Like the psychiatrist who told his patient: Don't worry about having an inferiority complex. You're inferior.

But he was superior too. I mean—how many anthropology graduate students would have the gall to tackle the world outside the world and the man inside the man while leaping into oblivion and bouncing back a celebrity? You have to give Castaneda plenty of credit for effrontery.

And for talent. Joseph Conrad grew up speaking Polish and became a master of English prose. Vladimir Nabokov did the same from Russian. Castaneda started out with Spanish (or maybe Portuguese or Italian—we'll get to those later) and wrote 1,000 pages of quite readable, mostly entertaining colloquial American narrative and 70 pages of utterly unreadable but logically self-consistent social-science jargon. That's pretty good.

One fervent follower of don Juan told me: "The reason you can't grasp the fact that don Juan really exists is that you can't believe a Yaqui Indian could express himself with clarity and elegance. What you don't realize—and what many anthropologists don't realize—is that the oral tradition of sorcery cuts across tribal cultures, going back for thousands of years and displaying an eloquence far above the local cultural level." "Shamans everywhere," Gwyneth Cravens wrote, "have been found to have unusually large and poetic vocabularies." I admit don Juan often waxes poetic, but his shamanistic vocabulary also supports discourses that sound like this:

To recapitulate my teachings, little Carlos—I first taught you the routines of the game we were hunting, then I taught you to test your traps against those routines. When you indulged in your self-pity, I taught you to assume responsibility for the acts that brought you to the state that elicited that self-pity. By altering your use of those acts or elements, you changed the façade of your *tonal*. But changing the façade meant only that you assigned a secondary place to a formerly important element. After that I taught you to stop your internal dialog and to account for everything that was accountable.

Other shamans, not so well traveled or educated as don Juan, sound more like this:

I am the mushroom that speaks, it says. I am a mouth awaiting the voice of heaven. I am a wind that blows on the mountain, it says. I am star, moon, cloud, and dew on the grass. I am the one that goes to meet the day, it says. I am the one that holds up the world. I search out sickness, it says. I am the one that cures. All things that should be together I bring together and all things that should be apart I separate. I am the one that speaks in the silence, that shines in the darkness, that talks with those who live in the sky. I am the one that brings truth to the asker, it says.

Castaneda was lucky to find a shaman who could lecture like a university professor and not one of those monotonous mountain poets. We have to score a big plus for his finding such a sophisticated informant—or for inventing one, if it turns out don Juan doesn't really exist.

I began my trek into don Juan's desert with an open mind. Sure, I had heard rumors. Castaneda wrote his field notes in a motel room, and so on. But I thought: If I were a struggling graduate student or an obscure professor, and some guy came along and wrote four best sellers in a row while I was trying to finish my dissertation or get some puny five-page paper published in the *American Anthropologist*, I might have some snide and unfair things to say about him, too. Let's just read what the man wrote and see if we believe it.

Sociologist Harold Garfinkel says people try very hard to make sense out of random signals. Often they succeed, but the sense is theirs, it's not in the signals. Castaneda's outpourings are not random, but they are sufficiently and artfully disordered to make the reader work hard pulling the whole thing together into a coherent picture. That's what novelists do, of course. They drop you right into the middle of the fun house and let you try to find your way out. You're not supposed to escape until the last page.

Castaneda goes them one better. He never lets you out. Even when you reach page 1000, you still aren't sure what happened when Carlos and Pablito jumped off the edge of the plateau, you still don't know where don Juan took his degree. Reading the first book, *The Teachings of Don Juan*, one gets a strong and consistent impression that this is a factual report of what went on in deserts of Arizona and Mexico between June 1960 and September 1965. Every entry is dated, and the dates check out on the perpetual calendar (except for 8 April 1962, which is called Saturday instead of Sunday—a perfectly ordinary error that proves absolutely nothing). My nephew, a suspicious analytical type, told me he had caught Castaneda in logical errors, such as being in two places at the same time without benefit of magic. Hah! I thought. A sitting duck. Forget it.

There are no such errors anywhere in 1,000 pages. Castaneda leaves no fingerprints, no laundry marks, no cigarette stubs, no roaches, no seeds, no stems, no nothing. His tracks fill with sand before he is over the next dune.

One man I talked to had spent a week with Castaneda. "If you could sum up your impression of him in a word," I said, "what would it be?" "Egnimatic," he said. "What do you mean by egnimatic?" I asked. "The story he tells. I couldn't get things straightened out." "The chronology?" I said. "That's it," he answered.

Castaneda's time track is like a ball of string. The reader gets utterly confused about what-happened-when. We're going to straighten that string out later on till it twangs like a spirit-catcher, but I can assure you that we are not going to find any simple concrete contradictions like having lunch in Mexico City and Los Angeles on the same day. Castaneda's contradictions are on higher levels of abstraction.

When I finished *The Teachings,* I was still going along with the proposition that Castaneda had met an old Indian in an Arizona bus station who had fed him various poisonous plants, had taught him a lot of intricate rituals, and had put him through trials of endurance and tests of sanity not all of which he had passed with high scores. Like most readers, academic or amateur, I wanted to believe what I was reading no matter how strange it might be, and so I was glad that the University of California had already put its stamp of approval on Castaneda's report. "It has been assumed," the merchandising voice of the University Press had intoned in an early ad, "that the West has produced no way of spiritual knowledge comparable to the great systems of the East. The present book is accordingly nothing less than a revelation." Whoever wrote that could not have read Rudolf Otto's *Mysticism East and West,* but never mind, the point is subsidiary. Castaneda's five-year apprentice-ship, the ad went on, and his strangely beautiful narrative would assure his book "a place in the literature of ethnology." To back that claim, *The Teachings* carried a laudatory foreword by a senior professor of anthropology at UCLA acknowledging our debt to Castaneda for his patience, courage, and perspicac-ity in seeking out don Juan and reporting the details of the experience. "In this work," the foreword said, Castaneda "demonstrates the essential skill of good ethnography—the capacity to enter into an alien world." Such authoritative cre-dentials could not be lightly dismissed.

The ethnological gourd began to leak, however, when I got into *A Separate Reality*. I don't know just how it happened. The writing was better, but the effect was not so good. One reviewer—after finishing the fourth book, I read some thirty reviews—one reviewer said: "The story no longer seems to have the same quality of objectivity that marked the first book." Quite so. I found myself asking: What kind of Yaqui Indian talks like this? And what exactly was Carlos doing to those unfortunate reptiles back on page—where is it anyway?—it's impossible to find anything in these books—but was that lizard caper a dream or a practical task?

Realizing before long that such ruminations would ruin the adventure for me, I stopped my internal dialog, stepped heavily on the intrusive foot of doubt, reasserted my will, and pressed forward hopefully into the new reality. Literary license, I told myself, and Carlos's many psychotropic detours would surely account for the vagaries of his tale. Nevertheless, the seed of dissent had fallen on fertile soil, where it would silently grow for another seven-hundred pages, steadily accumulating power like a lonely *Lophophora*.

Vincent Crapanzano, an expert on shamans, wrote a scholarly article about five works of "popular anthropology"— "works which may be admired for their literary quality but which for professional anthropologists are not to be taken too seriously." Three of the five were by Castaneda. Though the article starts out with cool academic detachment, it winds up complaining that Castaneda has let us down—has in fact let Crapanzano down personally. "He once told me that [*Journey to Ixtlan*] was to be his last book on the subject," but now (the complaint continues) he is compulsively writing more and more books, clowning for the public, playing coyly with his image, showing a lack of courage, a weakness of vision, falling dupe to his own tricks, dallying oddly with the media, and cheapening the quest. There is something inauthentic, something desperate about his act. He has not passed the test of the warrior. He has betrayed the teachings.

Anyone who ever wanted to believe in don Juan (and that includes most of us) can sympathize with Professor Crapanzano's disillusionment. "The books," he says, "should not be read . . . as an accurate description of Castaneda's apprenticeship, however accurate his reportage may be." What an oddly inconsistent statement! Is the reportage accurate or not? Surely that matters. Crapanzano thinks there must be "many" embellishments added to the tale of the "somewhat" dubious Yaqui sorcerer, but still he does not find the tale wholly incredible or even definitely dubious. One suspects he found it wholly credible in 1968, when the first volume came out, but has been gripped by misgivings in the meantime and is hiding his embarrassment in a fog of ambivalence.

Castaneda's opus, he laments, will suffer the fate of popularized texts. "It will be worked up, exploited, made into a movie, simplified beyond recognition," and resurrected later as a mere social phenomenon by cultural historians. "Meanwhile the text that is Castaneda's will be lost." With a million copies in existence, the text that is Castaneda's will be *lost*? But this lament has a deeper meaning. Something truly has been lost already: the text you and I and Crapanzano thought we were holding in our hands when we confidently accepted Castaneda's first innocuous sentence: "In the summer of 1960, while I was an anthropology student at the University of California, Los Angeles, I made several trips to the Southwest to collect information on medicinal plants used by Indians of the area."

While the general reader does not have to endure public embarrassment like the duped expert, he does suffer the private wound of betrayal. For each of us, public or private, professional or amateur, critical or gullible, the faith elicited by Castaneda's bland beginning was at least partially betrayed somewhere along the way. Whether in book two or book four, whether spontaneously or at the urging of Castaneda's many critics, the realization finally came that, to some extent anyway, we were being had. Though I have found many appreciators, subscribers, followers, and defenders, I have not found anyone who expresses complete and unqualified confidence in Castaneda. At the same time, I have found very few who roundly condemn him. For most of us, he begins as an ingratiating stranger and ends as a family delinquent, the sort of person you have to make allowances for but can't get rid of. The best thing to do with such a fellow is to try to understand him as well as you can.

My contribution to understanding Castaneda will be a sorceredelic trip up the long road from obscurity to fame, winding back and forth between record and rumor, truth and fallacy, lessons and tricks, literature and mythmaking, scholar and shaman, imp and saint, power and helplessness, love and isolation. It will be a rough ride for believers, not because I want it that way but because the road is full of holes. Just the same, it won't be a free ride for skeptics or cynics, who will have to hang on to their hats when we sight the same Navy diver on both sides of the road at once or nearly fall into the void out of which everything comes.

Keep an eye peeled for love in the separate reality. You could miss it altogether. "What else can a man have except his life and his death?" asked don Juan. "We are all born for love," Disraeli would have answered. "It is the principle of existence and its only end." Though don Juan told Carlos to be an unflinching warrior, not a whimpering child, he gave his apprentice tender, loving care, teaching him how to walk, putting him down for his nap, washing him when he soiled himself, soothing him with a voice like warm water, calling him "my little friend," cooking for him, setting food in front of him, urging him to eat, smiling at him like a fond parent, forgiving his foolishness and enjoying his childish ways. When a mothering Matus pushed a bowl of soup gently toward him, Carlos couldn't take the warmth and kindness in that gesture. It made him feel "idiotic." Unable to relax and let the old man love him, he had to disrupt his mood by rummaging for his spoon and asking intellectual questions.

At some point, I believe, Castaneda forsook human companionship for a separate reality where he could substitute ideas for love. Ideas he juggles like oranges, dropping hardly any. Love he finds too hot to handle. Well, who can handle love? One of Castaneda's favorite writers, San Juan de la Cruz, noted the difficulty:

> Since thou hast wounded this heart,
> Wherefore didst thou not heal it?
> And wherefore, having robbed me of it,
>   hast thou left it thus
> And takest not the prey that thou hast spoiled?

Castaneda labored 49 years to become the complicated, superficially inconsistent, deeply constant man who wrote *Tales of Power.* I have labored one year to unfold him. The contest is clearly uneven. Where I have gone astray, others will stay on the path. Where I have hit the nail on the thumb, many whose thumbs are throbbing will stoically deny it. Though this study of the man and his works is necessarily analytic, I have not shirked my duty to fill mysterious gaps with bold speculation. My theory of 'la Catalina,' for example, displays effrontery bordering on apocalypsis. On the other hand, I have taken pains to distinguish fact from inference and to identify (or frankly conceal) my sources. Castaneda did the best he could to show others exactly how he came by his knowledge, Paul Riesman said; I hope he will say the same of me.

To separate the seeds from the stems without throwing anything away, I will begin by drawing a line between Carlos and Castaneda.

TESTING THE TONAL

Q: *What do you think of Carlos Castaneda and the teachings of don Juan?*

A: Don Juan is the most important model for man since Jesus. If he is imaginary, then Carlos Castaneda is the principal psychological, spiritual, and literary genius of recent generations.

A: Castaneda's books accurately report the facts of his experience, which many people cannot accept because of their previous social conditioning. It's their problem, not his. The world is a much stranger place than most of us realize, or dare to admit.

A: Don Juan exists pretty much as he is portrayed in the first book, which was the scientific report that got Castaneda his Ph.D. The later books contain more and more allegory and symbolism, as Castaneda tries to reach a wider and wider audience.

A: Don Juan is a combination of various spiritual teachers Castaneda has met or read about. Many of the details in the books are factual, though disguised to protect people's privacy.

A: I don't know whether Castenyada's books are fact or fiction, and I couldn't care less. Either way, they're terrific.

A: Castaneda is obviously a science-fiction or metafiction writer, who makes a lot of good points he couldn't have gotten across to so many people if he had admitted he was writing fiction. It's a legitimate teaching maneuver, brilliantly executed.

A: Castaneda is a vulgar hoaxer and cheapjack con man, who writes blatant occultist trash and philosophic piffle, which is gobbled up by the ignorant and gullible but ignored by the informed and discriminating. I have nothing to say about what happened at UCLA.

A: Castaneda's only sorcery consisted of turning the University of California into an ass.

A: Carlos who?

2. CARLOS AND CASTANEDA

In those days Carlos was known as Carlos Aranha, which is sometimes spelled Aranja. He told me that his uncle, the ruler of the household, Oswaldo Aranha, ran for president of Brazil in 1960.

If Oswaldo Aranha ran for president of Brazil in 1960 it was a short campaign because he died on the 27th of January. Having been Minister of Justice, of Finance, and of Foreign Affairs, Ambassador to the United States, and President of the UN General Assembly, Oswaldo was the most famous member of a great Brazilian-Portuguese family and undoubtedly ruled the household, but he was definitely not Carlos Castaneda's uncle or any other relative. His mother was Luisa de Freitas-Valle, while Castaneda's grandmothers came from the families Burungaray and Novoa. They didn't live in Brazil either. They lived in Peru.

Carlos César Arana Castañeda was born on Christmas day 1925 in the historic Andean town of Cajamarca, where on 29 August 1533 night fell at noon as Pizarro's soldiers strangled Atau Huallpa. The unlucky 13th Royal Inca, whose name meant Turkey Fortunate in War, had consented at the last minute to be baptized Juan, in return for which the Spaniards had promised not to burn him at the stake. The bargain brought a double benefit, qualifying an Indian soul to enter a European heaven, and saving Atau Huallpa's body from destruction by earthly fire, which would have made him unacceptable after death to his divine father the sun.

25

Cajamarca is also known for its gold and silver industry. Baby Arana's father was a goldsmith and watchmaker named César Arana Burungaray, while his mother was Susana Castañeda Novoa. Arana and Castañeda are Spanish names, Burungaray is Basque, Novoa Portuguese. Though Indians and Mestizos make a majority in Peru, none of these names suggest any Indian or mixed heritage.

Young Arana went to high school in Cajamarca, but in 1948 the family moved to Lima, where some members still live and where the family jewelry store was doing business in 1973. After graduating from the Colegio Nacional de Nuestra Señora de Guadalupe, he studied at the National Fine Arts School of Peru. José Bracamonte, a fellow student and now a well known illustrator, remembered him as a resourceful blade who lived mainly off the horses, dice, and cards and harbored "like an obsession" the wish to move to the United States. "We all liked Carlos," Bracamonte told *Time's* Peruvian reporter Tomás Loayza. "He was witty, imaginative, cheerful—a big liar and a real friend."

In 1949, when his mother died, Carlos Arana declared he was going to leave home. He entered the United States at San Francisco in 1951. After a four year gap we find him enrolled as Carlos Castaneda at Los Angeles City College. Between 1955 and 1959, while following a pre-psychology curriculum, he took two courses in creative writing and one in journalism.

On 17 December 1955 he met Damon Runyon's very distant cousin Margaret, four years older than he, unattached, and deeply interested in popular metaphysics. Six months later they began to see a lot of each other, attending occasional metaphysical lectures, going to City College together, and spending hours talking about philosophy, mysticism, and spiritualism. According to Margaret he took his U.S. citizenship in 1959 as Carlos Castaneda. One day on the spur of the moment they went to Tijuana to get married; the certificate, dated 27 January 1960, shows his name as Carlos Aranha Castaneda. At home he did the cooking. Margaret thought his spaghetti was wonderful. Though they stayed together only six months as man and wife, they remained good friends after the separation and saw each other often. The marriage was not legally terminated until 17 December 1973. At UCLA Castaneda kept the marriage secret, but sometimes he showed up on campus mysteriously holding a towheaded youngster by the hand. The little boy, mentioned in Chapter 11 of *A Separate Reality,* is Margaret's child of another marriage.

Castaneda entered UCLA as an undergraduate in 1959 and received a B.A. in anthropology September 1962. He was enrolled on and off as a graduate student until 1971, receiving a Ph.D. in anthropology March 1973. His scholarly publications are limited to his dissertation and one paper read at an anthropological meeting in 1968.

Students at the Irvine campus of the University of California, empowered to select and hire two percent of the faculty, appointed Castaneda to lecture during the spring quarter of 1972. His graduate seminar, "The Phenomenology of Shamanism," drew over 50 persons, some of whom were faculty visitors curious to see the young anthropologist who had supposedly gotten inside the head of an authentic, pre-literate mesoamerican witch doctor. His undergraduate class in primitive religions was packed to the rafters and turned away hundreds. Occasionally he lectured at other institutions of learning or sat briefly in other professors' classrooms like a glowing mushroom stone.

Such engagements were prompted by his growing celebrity as a popular writer. His first book, *The Teachings of Don Juan: A Yaqui Way of Knowledge,* had been published by the University of California Press in 1968, then commercially marketed by Ballantine Books in 1969. *A Separate Reality* and *Journey to Ixtlan* followed from Simon and Schuster in 1971 and 1972. Sales were climbing rapidly, and media scribes were bestirring themselves to interview the new star shining so remotely in the documentary sky, hoping to bring him close enough for everybody to get a good look. The first thing they found out was that he didn't like to have his picture taken.

Castaneda stands a stocky five-foot-five, weighing 140 to 150 pounds. "From his waist to the top of his thick curly black hair," said Margaret, "his body is that of a man six feet tall. His legs . . . are disproportionately short." His hands, *Time* said, are stubby and calloused. Characteristically he wears unassuming sport shirts or business suits. Sometimes he wears or carries a hat. His hair is cut short. People have said he blends into the woodwork, or resembles a Cuban waiter. One of Margaret's snapshots shows a man surprisingly youthful for his 40 years, whose skin is dark but whose features are quite European—an impression worth mentioning since some people have said Castaneda looks like an Indian. Though his skin has been judged nut-brown, pale, and even gray, nobody has said it was red, copper, or bronze. I suspect Bruce Cook hit the right formula with his "sallow-swarthy," a paradoxical combination that brings to mind the olive skin of Spaniards, which is what I would call Castaneda: a basquish Peruvian Spaniard.

The foregoing sketch includes the major established and presumptive facts about Carlos Castaneda. It is a short sketch because convincing facts are few. Almost nothing credible is known about his childhood, family relations, early schooling, jobs, friends, women (beyond Margaret), or daily routines. "Neither Margaret nor I ever knew where Carlos was living," wrote Margaret's cousin Sue. "He came to us; we did not go to him." Though he wrote Margaret romantic letters, he didn't sign them. That erasure of personal history, identity, and character has been blamed on don Juan, but Margaret said: "Carlos was elusive before he learned this from Don Juan."

If we had only our few facts and nothing more to go on, Castaneda would be mysterious but not confusing. Fortunately for those who like complex, self-contradictory puzzles we have a never-ending supply of non-facts as well. In order to comb out this informational spaghetti I am going to split our central figure into several parts, to which cohesive sets of data can be assigned. The first split will separate Carlos from Castaneda.

From here on, established and presumptive facts will be assigned to "Castaneda," non-facts to "Carlos." Castaneda will be the writer of books, born Carlos Arana in Peru. Carlos will be an imaginary person appearing in the books Castaneda has written—and in countless rumors, misconceptions, unsubstantiated reports, errors, and fabrications promulgated by Castaneda or by others. It is not, of course, a revelation to say Castaneda contradicts himself. He admits it and the record shows it. My point is not to belabor the obvious but to bring order out of chaos. Naturally I have no control over what other people have said about him, so in quotations you will have to decide from the context whether "Carlos" means Castaneda or "Castaneda" means Carlos, if you see what I mean. Also, when I say "Carlos Castaneda" I mean Castaneda not Carlos.

Unlike Castaneda (though according to him) Carlos was born in São Paulo, Brazil, in 1935 (or as Margaret heard it, 1931— which made her seem only ten years older than he instead of 14). Grandfather Aranha had come from Italy (or in one version, Sicily) bringing his Portuguese name with him. Another grandfather (or maybe the same one) was a short-statured, red-haired, blue-eyed inventor, who married grandmother Margarita, nearly six feet tall (as Castaneda told Margaret, whom he sometimes called "Margarita"). Father César (Aranha, or as Gordon Wasson was told, Castaneda), who later became a professor of literature, was only 17 when Carlos was born, while mother Susana (Castaneda, or to Wasson, Aranha) was 15. Tragically, she died when Carlos was only six.

Because of his parents' extreme youth little Carlos was raised from the start by his grandparents on their chicken farm in the Brazilian back country (or as Margaret heard, by an aunt who lived in Peru), where he fought constantly during preschool years with 22 cousins until they finally left him alone, and where he inadvertently broke the collarbone of a firstgrader answering to the Spanish name Joaquín.

Having learned both Italian and Portuguese on the farm (languages no one has reported hearing Castaneda speak), Carlos acquired Spanish (and presumably his taste for the poetry of César Vallejo, born Peru 1892, died Paris 1938) at the "very proper" Nicolas Avellaneda boarding school in Buenos Aires, Argentina, where he stayed until he was 15. By 1951 he had grown so unruly that his uncle, the family patriarch, shipped him out to Los Angeles—California, that is—to live with a foster family. Besides Spanish he must have learned plenty of English at Nicolas Avellaneda, because he enrolled immediately at Hollywood High School, whence he graduated in two years. While there he met his friend Bill, who seven years later would introduce him to don Juan.

After high school Carlos journeyed to Italy, where he studied sculpting in Milan's Academy of Fine Arts, accomplishing little because he lacked "the sensitivity or openness to be a great artist." Despite this feeling of inadequacy, Margaret mentions beautiful sculptures and contest-winning poems created during the City College period. She and a friend were taken by Castaneda to see an architectural sculpture (of a goddess, the friend told me) which Carlos had done for the front of an office building on Wilshire Boulevard near Vermont Avenue. The building is gone now, and Margaret has no picture of the sculpture.

Sometimes, Margaret says, Castaneda told her things about Carlos that probably weren't true, like his marriage to a gypsy girl, which may have been trumped up to make her jealous, or his U.S. Army wartime service in Spain. Margaret wondered just which war that could have been.

Castaneda told Margaret about Carlos's sister Lucía, while

down in foggy Lima Castaneda's cousin Lucía, raised with him "like a sister," was saving his infrequent letters. One of them described a tour in the U.S. Army, from which Carlos was discharged after some trauma—mental or physical, Lucía was not sure. As befits one of the nation's great bureaucracies, the Defense Department can't find Carlos's service record anywhere.

Students at Irvine scribbled a primitive-religions note about Carlos's blond Scandinavian wife (the right sort of mom for a towheaded youngster whose dad is a sallow-swarthy Spaniard married to an anglo-French brunette). The furry gent with the micturated kilo heard about Carlos's wife and child languishing in Buenos Aires. Two women in a Sacramento bookstore sighed for a little Carlos who never had any real home because he was an "army brat," whose father continually dragged the family from one military post to another.

Until don Juan tricked him into it, Carlos knew little and cared less about metaphysics. "I'm no mystic," Lila Freilicher was told, "not a searcher of any sort. I'm an anthropologist, and this thing just happened to me without my looking for it."

"How often did you talk about mysticism and philosophy?" I asked Margaret.

"That's all we ever talked about," she said.

No one has imputed violence to Castaneda, but don Juan told Carlos he was "a violent fellow," and Gwyneth Cravens heard Carlos got so fed up being followed around by a nutty would-be disciple that he hurled him over a park bench. "The only way to deal with a psychotic is to be one yourself," Castaneda explained. Well, what would you expect from the 22-cousin-vanquisher and collarbone-smasher of the Brazilian (or Peruvian) backwoods?

Early in 1973 Carlos had "completed a book on the formation of perceptual glosses," which Castaneda has not yet published.

Of course, there are many similarities. Carlos and Castaneda are physically alike. Both enjoy running around in the countryside picking plants. One has a beach house, while the other lives at Malibu. And so on.

At the start of this project I invited Castaneda to lunch, but he didn't accept. I regret that, because I'm sure I could have learned significant things by sitting in a little Mexican restaurant or on a park bench with the source of all those different versions of Carlos's life. Without adding fuel to the fire by asking if he were related to Carlos E. Castañeda, the authority on Spanish-colonial administrators, or to Professor Enrique Arana, the Argentine historian, I would have tried to hear the man behind the stories.

At least six professional interviewers have reported what they learned by talking at length—some for days—with Castaneda. Most of what they learned was not true. Bruce Cook was so dismayed by Castaneda's credibility gap that he delayed publishing his interview for more than a year. "I wasn't sure he was completely on the level," Cook recalled. "I don't believe he is who he says he is." The name Castaneda, Cook observed, is not Italian though Carlos's grandfather came from Italy, nor is it Portuguese though Carlos was born in Brazil. It is Spanish.

I'm surprised more journalists didn't make the same comment early in the game. Suppose a certain Karlus Kastaniebaum, who is studying anthropology at the University of China, Fu Kien, publishes a best-seller called *The Teachings of Swami Goanananda: A Jhansi Way of Knowledge,* Jhansi being a district of India, right next door so to speak.

"Where were you born, Karlus?" asks reporter Broo Skuk of the *Foochow Observer.*

"Scotland," says Karlus with a mischievous twinkle in his big blue occidental eye, "where my grandfather Magnus Kastaniebaum immigrated in 1891 from Marseille, which is how I grew up speaking both Provençal and Gaelic."

"I notice," probes Skuk, "that Swami Goanananda always spoke to you in perfect German. Where did you learn that?"

"I learned perfect German," Karlus explains, "when my Scottish uncle, Ossian McFingal, the ruler of our clan, packed me off to the very proper Ferdinand Maximilian boarding school in Vienna. I learned plenty of Chinese there, too."

It shouldn't take a professor of linguistics at UCFK to find a flaw or two in that story.

and they brought us to the Queen of the people who place pots upon the heads of strangers, who is a magician having a knowledge of all things [and] she did take us, and lead us by terrible ways, by means of dark magic, to where the great pit is, in the mouth of which the old philosopher lay dead, and showed to us the rolling Pillar of Life that dies not, whereof the voice is as the voice of thunder; and she did stand in the flames, and come forth unharmed, and yet more beautiful. . . . I speak of those things, that though they be past belief, yet have I known, and lie not.

it scarcely seemed likely that such a story could have been invented by anybody. It was too original.

—H. Rider Haggard
She, A History of Adventure

The idea that I concocted a person like don Juan is inconceivable. . . . I didn't create anything. I am only a reporter.

—Carlos Castaneda to Sam Keen

3. FACT OR FICTION

It makes no difference whether the books are a record of an actual encounter or Castaneda is the author of a clever fiction.

When Joseph Margolis wrote that, he didn't mean it makes *no* difference. He meant (and said) it would not affect don Juan's potency as a fountain of philosophy or an instrument of our instruction. And there are other ways in which the factuality or fictiveness of Castaneda's books makes no difference. If we care solely for entertainment or inspiration, if we seek only an allegoric truth behind the fantasy, if we believe every story is true in its own way, then we may not care at all whether Castaneda actually interviewed anybody, or whether the person he interviewed was anything like the don Juan we have come to know. I am perfectly content to allow those who don't care about factuality to ignore the question. On the other hand, there are some good reasons for caring.

I don't think we can gauge the value of Castaneda's work if we have no definite opinion about whether his tale is true or false, in the ordinary sense of those terms. Never mind whether Carlos "really flew." What I want to know is, whom did Castaneda meet in the Nogales bus station? Where have the Spanish field notes been deposited? When can we listen to the tape recording of the conversation that took place in Lucio's house on the night of 4 September 1968?

Let me allay suspicion right now by saying that, however this inquiry comes out, I do believe Castaneda has contributed something of value to society by writing his books. At the least, he has widely popularized certain metaphysical propositions some people, including me, think are both important and defensible. Many people also credit him with being a scientific anthropologist, an original philosopher, a master teacher, a psychic visionary, a literary genius, or a practical sorcerer. To judge these additional qualifications, particularly his status as a scientific anthropologist, we need to know whether his books are fact or fiction.

A majority of the professional anthropologists who have rendered public judgments on Castaneda's works have either questioned or denied their factuality. Francis Hsu compared them to *Gulliver's Travels.* Jesús Ochoa thought they contained "a very high percentage of imagination." Marvin Harris doubted the existence of don Juan. Edmund Leach said *The Teachings* was "a work of art rather than of scholarship," while Weston La Barre called it "pseudo-ethnography," and ethnobotanist Gordon Wasson "smelled a hoax" on the first reading. Beyond Castaneda's solitary word there has been no evidence whatsoever don Juan existed or any field work was ever carried out. Scientifically, this is not an entirely satisfactory situation.

Even so, no one has presented a systematic proof that Castaneda's work is a hoax—only vague, intuitive dissatisfactions with his text, comments on isolated, incongruous details, or irrelevant objections like, "People can't turn into crows." It has been said such a proof would be impossible, don Juan's privacy must be protected, and so on. Joseph Margolis allows the four books seem to have been planned as a tetralogy from the beginning, which would certainly make them fiction, and he is quite sure the first book was dedicated (anonymously) to Pablito and don Genaro, whom the Carlos of the narrative hadn't even met yet, but these speculations are far from being proofs. With apparent relief, Daniel Noel declares he has not yet heard "any *conclusive* argument for the view that the books were an outright hoax." In this chapter I shall present the conclusive argument Professor Noel has not yet heard.

What is a hoax? My dictionary says it is a humorous or mischievous deception that imposes on the victim's credulity. Three main elements appear in that definition—deception, humor or mischief, and credulity. As I dwell on those elements, I perceive a logical structure joining them together. Deception is the core. A humorous deception will be a benignly playful deception, which most people will find amusing when the truth comes out. A mischievous deception will be a somewhat harmful deception, which may arise from malice; most people will not find it amusing, but some whose oxen escape ungored will think it a laugh riot at the expense of certain victims they do not love. Whether the deception will be judged playful or malicious will depend partly on the normal level of credulity. A hoax that deceives nearly everybody may be either playful or malicious, but a hoax that deceives only boobies will seem playful to anybody who is not both a booby and a victim. A second test will be the persistence of the deception. The sooner the hoaxer admits his trick, the fewer will judge it malicious. His admission need not be direct or explicit. He could, for instance, write a series of books making the hoax progressively more preposterous until everybody caught on. Hoaxes must be distinguished from frauds. Frauds are nearly always harmful, hardly ever amusing; hoaxes are often amusing, seldom harmful.

My dictionary defines hoaxing as deceiving by a fiction. In this chapter I shall prove to my satisfaction and perhaps to yours that Castaneda's books, though they may contain a fact here or there, are abundantly and essentially fictive and must be classified as fiction if we are going to classify them at all. Once persuaded by this proof, you can decide for yourself whether Castaneda's fiction constitutes a hoax.

Several writers have said it doesn't matter whether Castaneda wrote fact or fiction because all fact is fiction. That would have to be the extreme non-hoax position. Those of us who think we can tell the difference still have to pick a fair test. I would not call Castaneda a fiction writer just because he allowed don Juan to use a cover name, or condensed several conversations into one, or translated don Juan's Spanish into bouncy American slang. I wouldn't dismiss his factual reporting if I learned that *Tales of Power* alone was fiction. I certainly wouldn't say the books must be fiction because they describe fantastic visions.

Part of the apparent but I think illusory difficulty of deciding the question springs from Castaneda's terms, "ordinary and nonordinary reality." Anyone who says the books are not factual risks being told Carlos's adventures were real enough in the nonordinary reality. That may be true, but it also points a way out of the difficulty. While Castaneda's books *treat* a nonordinary reality, they *depend* on the ordinary reality for their acceptance as factual reports. The author implicitly agreed to that when he offered them as conventional reports of anthropology field work conducted on particular occasions dated by the ordinary calendar. "In the summer of 1960," he wrote, "while I was an anthropology student at the University of California, Los Angeles, I made several trips to the Southwest." He did not say, "Don Juan told me that in the summer of 1960 I made several trips," or "After smoking the mushroom mixture, I found I was a student at the University of California," or "When I crossed my eyes, I saw a white-haired old Indian sitting in the bus station." Castaneda the anthropologist may have had his left foot in the other world, but he had his right foot in this world. My task here is to pry up the sole of his this-world shoe to see whether there is a banana skin under it. My test of fact or fiction will be whether the *ordinary* events reported in his books would be possible in this ordinary world. If not, the books must be fiction.

In Chapter One I said we were not going to catch Castaneda in simple concrete errors. Since I wrote that, a friend has pointed out just such an error, which I relate here to show what we are not going to find any more of.

One day in October 1968, Carlos and don Juan drove deep into Mexico to visit don Genaro. Leaving the car somewhere, they walked for two days to reach Genaro's little shack perched on the side of a mountain. A few days later, Genaro proposed they should go to meet his apprentices Nestor and Pablito, who lived nearby. The next sentence is: "Both of them got into my car." A good trick, if the car had been left two days' walk from the shack.

That little slip is certainly incongruous, but it won't take us very far. Maybe Castaneda left something out. Maybe the car got stuck in the mud and a friend delivered it to the shack later. Maybe Genaro had two shacks, one on the mountainside, the other in the village. Who knows? A dozen ambiguities like that wouldn't prove the case. Almost anything can be explained by imagining special circumstances. To argue convincingly that Castaneda was writing fiction, I have to show that he deliberately violated the rules of the ordinary reality, that he covered up what he had done, and that he had a good reason for doing it. I have to produce the body, the weapon with his fingerprints on it, and the motive. Let's start with the body.

One night Carlos and don Juan were sitting in don Juan's room chatting in the dark, when don Juan asked Carlos what he used the darkness for when he was in Los Angeles. Carlos admitted he used it for sleeping. Don Juan said the darkness of the day was the best time to "see." "He stressed the word 'see,'" Castaneda wrote, "with a peculiar inflection. I wanted to know what he meant by that."

"What's it like to *see*, don Juan?" Carlos asked four days later. Don Juan said he couldn't tell him. Carlos would have to *see* for himself. "Is it a secret I shouldn't know?" Carlos persisted. No, don Juan reassured him, but he must do it to know it.

In the next book, we find don Juan and Carlos on a hilltop, when don Juan tells Carlos to run over and get some leaves from a certain bush. From where he stands Carlos can see a large green bush growing on the near slope of the next hill. He runs down one hill and up the other, but when he gets to the right spot the bush has disappeared. He returns and reports his mistake. Don Juan says there has been no mistake. He leads Carlos around to the far slope, out of the direct line of sight, where they find the bush, the only one of its kind within a mile. The bumbling apprentice doesn't grasp what has happened, of course, but don Juan is delighted and calls it an omen.

Later in the day, Carlos finds a place he will return to in his dreams, a place don Juan will give him as his own nonordinary domain, "not to use but to remember." "This spot," don Juan tells him, "is yours. This morning you *saw*, and that was the omen. You found this spot by *seeing*."

How gratifying that Carlos has finally achieved in this second episode the personal experience of *seeing* about which he could only wonder in the first. What would you say, though, if I told you I have given you these two episodes in the wrong order? Granted, they are in the right order for *seeing*. They are in the normal order for learning. They are in sequence as they were published, the first from *A Separate Reality*, the second from *Journey to Ixtlan*. But according to the author's meticulous chronology, the two men were chatting in the dark on 21 May 1968, while Carlos *saw* the bush on the wrong side of the hill and found his spot by *seeing* on 29 January 1962. Carlos first heard about *seeing* six years after he *saw*. That is not the way things work in the ordinary world.

Very odd, you say, but perhaps Castaneda got his notes mixed up. Why not? But I have to tell you this is only the victim's left ear. In "Carlos-One and Carlos-Two" I have laid the body out for your inspection. If you want the details of the autopsy, turn to that appendix. If cold surgery makes you faint, let me summarize my findings here.

All the evidence ever needed to prove a case of big-time fictioneering can be found in Castaneda's first three books. The secret is to make a chronological list of the events. After that, the case proves itself. Why hasn't it been done before? Book reviewers barely have time to read the books they review. Anthropologists who dismissed Castaneda's "pseudo-ethnography" didn't think any proofs were needed. Novelists saw him as a writer manipulating the market. Philosophers, mystics, or parapsychologists fastened on don Juan's wisdom, techniques, or powers, ignoring the question of his existence. Perhaps only a chronic puzzle addict would have traced that twisting time-like trail down past the ethnographic event horizon to discover the Einstein-Castaneda bridge from world to world buried under a pile of skillful flashbacks and plausible introductory remarks.

Though most readers thought they were getting a pretty straight story in *The Teachings of Don Juan*, many felt uneasy with *A Separate Reality*. Carlos's wonderful adventures were moving right along when suddenly he was seized by over-whelming recollections of 'la Catalina,' the only significant woman walking, hopping, or sailing through the books. As Carlos saw her, 'la Catalina' was an evil sorceress bent on killing him, or at least on sucking out his soul and leaving him exhausted and impotent. A frightening if fascinating prospect.

While the reader was delighted with 'la Catalina,' he couldn't help wondering just where she had gotten on the bus. In contrast with the author's careful dating of every bag of groceries and evacuation in the chaparral, the lady blackbird flew into the story on no particular day. A long time before the recollection surely, but even the year was hard to figure out. Too hard for anybody but a puzzle addict. Quite a few readers may have asked themselves why Castaneda found it necessary to treat 'la Catalina' in flashbacks when almost everything else was given in straight narration.

By the time we got to *Journey to Ixtlan*, however, we gave up trying to keep track of things. Castaneda had split that book into two parts, with a ten-year gap between them, and had started out by announcing that dull-witted Carlos had missed the whole point of his first two years in the desert, so now we had to go back and start the story over again. Many readers found that surprising, but I am sure few saw just how strange it really was.

My analysis shows beyond the shadow of a doubt that *Jour-*

ney to Ixtlan is logically incompatible with *The Teachings of Don Juan* and *A Separate Reality*. I don't mean there are some details that don't fit. I mean the entire structure, the integral time frame, the action and progression of the third book conflicts with that of the first two. There is no way to get from the pair to the single, or back. "Carlos-One and Carlos-Two" displays my finding that two different Carloses live in these books. The two are not even proper nagualian doubles. They don't share their experiences. They travel on parallel time tracks. They inhabit alternative universes. Since the factuality of the story depends on its conforming to the one ordinary universe in which Castaneda said he was logging his field work, the discovery of dual universes brings us willy-nilly to the conclusion not all of these books can be factual reports. To put it most plainly: Either *The Teachings of Don Juan* or *Journey to Ixtlan* is categorically a work of fiction. This bare finding will have important implications in Chapter Four, where we ask what the anthropologists at UCLA thought they were doing when they doctored Castaneda on the strength of field interviews that were either partly or wholly invented by the candidate, though they had all the evidence needed to prove any suspicions they may have felt about the legitimacy of his reports. A worthy puzzle in itself.

In the meantime, this investigation has uncovered the corpse of factuality slain. The autopsy has shown the victim died of systemic logical contortion, deliberately imposed by the author in his third book (and to a lesser degree in his second) but cleverly covered up with smooth talk and juggled chronology. Sufficient motives for this heinous deed (discussed in the appendix) were the author's presumed eagerness to produce a third book while the market was at its height and his wish to stop drug fiends from perverting don Juan's teachings. Either purpose would have required him to backdate *Journey to Ixtlan*, the first because he had run out of calendar time in which Carlos's further adventures could take place, the second because he wished to prove don Juan had acted impeccably from the beginning, while only the incompetent apprentice had been goofing.

While the charge of first-degree fictioneering has been amply proved, the case is far from over. The autopsy relied on strange twists in the victim's skeleton but ignored such bizarre features as the victim's eyelids, which were sewn shut, the victim's tongue, which was forked, and the victims lungs, which were stuffed with smoked mushrooms. To put it another way, I trust I have argued conclusively that some of Castaneda's work is fiction, but I believe all of it is fiction, and I have evidence to support that belief. This further evidence cannot compel us to a conclusion even against our will, as I think the previous evidence can, but it should convince almost anyone.

To simplify the argument, I am going to make one reasonable assumption, which is that given the conclusion that either *The Teachings* or *Journey to Ixtlan* is fiction, it would be ridiculous to assume *The Teachings* was fiction while *Ixtlan* was fact. If Castaneda had any facts to report, he would have reported them first. The fiction would have followed in an effort to extend a successful performance. Therefore I take the fictiveness of *Journey to Ixtlan* as proved and concentrate now on showing that *The Teachings* and *A Separate Reality* are also fiction.

The new evidence is of a different kind. Up to now I have used the strongest kind of evidence, comprising internal contradictions, errors of narrative construction, or logical incompatibilities that definitely rule out consistent factuality. Now I turn to a less strong but still persuasive kind of evidence, which falls into two categories. The first involves conflicts between *ordinary* events in the story and what common sense tells us is possible in the ordinary world. The second displays features of the author's style that contradict his premise that his interviews with don Juan were conducted in the Spanish language.

Before getting into all that, let me lay to rest a ghost that constantly pops up when we wander in this particular graveyard. Somebody is bound to say: "But Castaneda's books *do* contain a *lot* of *facts*!" Of course they do. Yuma, Tucson, Ciudad Obregón, Torim, Durango, Oaxaca, Ixtlán, Mexico City, even Los Angeles—those are real places. The Yaquis do live in Arizona and Sonora. Indians do have traditions of shamanism, curing, sorcery, eating peyote, saying unkind things about the Jimson weed, getting high on mushrooms, sending evil birds to make people sick or steal their souls. Philosophers, mystics, and parapsychologists recognize many of don Juan's teachings as eternal truths or empirical facts. But you can find those places on maps and those ideas in books. Castaneda could have found them there, too. The point of this chapter is not whether Castaneda's story *contains facts* but whether it is a *factual story*, not whether such things are true or could happen but whether they truly happened to Castaneda. I see no more evidence that any of them happened to Castaneda than that they happened to me. Well, they didn't happen to me, and I don't think they happened to him either.

A friend of mine asked, "Why are you writing a book about somebody you think is a liar?" That stopped me. Why was I? Shouldn't I simply dismiss Castaneda as Weston La Barre had dismissed him? My friend supplied the answer. Castaneda wasn't a common con man, he lied to bring us the truth. His stories are packed with truth, though they are not true stories, which he says they are. This is not your familiar literary allegorist painlessly instructing his readers in philosophy. Nor is it your fearless trustworthy ethnographer returned full of anecdotes from the forests of Ecuador. This is a sham-man bearing gifts, an ambiguous spellbinder dealing simultaneously in contrary commodities—wisdom and deception. That's unusual. It may be important. And it needs straightening out.

Anyone who struggled all the way through *The Magic Mountain* came down with tuberculosis at some point, and the reader who followed Carlos through his first ten psychotropic experiments was markedly disoriented by 20 December 1964, the day Carlos surrendered for the last time to that untamable horticultural shrew, the Devil's weed, whose leaves and stem cure Indian boils, whose root bestows the strength of twenty, whose seeds divine book thieves and vandals, whose flowers kill, enslave, or madden. Countless college instructors assigning Castaneda's books have exploited that same disorientation to destroy the earthbound complacency of their students, but I cite it here as a reason why no one has publicly questioned the prodigious feat Carlos achieved *before* he drank the Jimson potion, rubbed the paste on his temples twenty-five times, and quite against don Juan's advice smeared it all over his forehead. The thrill of that perilous mistake and the wonder of the resulting visions combine with the general psychedelic theme to dull the reader's critical faculty, but the episode contains a core of ordinary reality that can be drilled and assayed for factuality.

About six o'clock that Sunday morning Carlos returned to the place where for three years he had been privately cultivating a Jimson weed. Attending closely to instructions written into his field notes eighteen months earlier, he spent most of the day preparing the potion and the paste. Late in the afternoon he wasted an hour and a half, from five to six-thirty, trying to catch two lizards for his ritual. By the time he caught them, "it was almost dark."

In the failing dusk, directed only by don Juan's transcribed discourse on the subject, he accomplished a delicate task he had neither practiced before nor seen demonstrated. Having put each lizard into a separate bag, he drew one out, apologized for hurting her, then using the fiber of a century plant for thread and the thorn of a prickly pear as a needle sewed up her mouth, drawing the stitches tight. Taking the other lizard out, he apologized to her also, then sewed up her eyelids, so that deprived of sight she might be more inclined to talk to him about what the muted lizard was seeing.

Letting the muted lizard go, he tied the blinded lizard to his right shoulder with a string, so as not to "lose or injure her." It was important to keep both lizards alive. If the muted lizard had died, Carlos would have had to give up the Devil's weed for the next two years. (As things turned out, he gave it up forever, so perhaps that lizard did die.) If the blinded lizard had died also, Carlos might have gone mad. At least he would have had a very bad trip.

You who have passed a steel needle and a polished thread in a bright light through a piece of inert but paper-thin leather about as wide as a newborn baby's little fingernail without ripping it will, I am sure, appreciate Carlos's skill in passing a perforated cholla thorn trailing an agave fiber in the darkling twilight through the tiny fragile blinking membranes that shield a living lizard's eyes, without tearing them, never having tried it before, and never having seen anyone else do it. "The sewing of the mouth and eyes," Castaneda wrote, "was the most difficult task." No doubt. One would have to be a sorcerer to do such a trick. But this was no sorcery. It was not even hallucination, since Carlos had been without drugs for fifteen weeks. This was an ordinary exercise like collecting plants on a hillside or grinding seeds in a mortar. Ordinary, but incredible.

For a long time I couldn't figure out why a writer would gratuitously insult the confidence of an already indulgent reader when he could so easily modify the incident to make it more credible. Was he daring us (or his academic committee) to catch him? Could this be a message scrawled in cold lizard's blood on our mirror—"Stop me before I write again!" Why did he let such a frankly impossible *ordinary* event creep into *The Teachings*? Where did he get the idea? The answer came at last, up out of that bottomless well whence so many others will come in later chapters: *the library*. Though Castaneda has told students and friends alike that he reads very little, don Juan has somehow acquired an encyclopedic knowledge of anthropology. I quote from the *Handbook of South American Indians*:

"A [Peruvian] sorcerer who wished to bring sickness or death to an enemy might. . . . take a toad, sew up its eyes and mouth with thorns, tie its feet, bury it in a place where the enemy would be likely to sit down. The suffering of the toad was supposed to pass into the enemy."

The difference being that the Peruvian sorcerer (in the days of the Incas) was doing something anybody could do, sticking pins through the eyes and mouth of a toad that was not supposed to survive anyway. No threading crudely punched wooden needles with rough fibers and pulling stitches through flimsy minuscule moving targets in the dying gloam. Just simple skewering in broad daylight. Our Yaqui bookworm, however, did not notice the slight error of diction in the *Handbook*, where *sew* was used for *pin*. As he passed the quotation along to his collaborator (a contemporary Peruvian sorcerer) the idea assimilated to a modern culture, where sutures are made by fine steel needles drawing thin slick strands under brilliant lights through tough thick membranes, clamps and drugs immobilizing the patient. A subtle and understandable transformation, but an awkward slip for a supposed reporter of facts. The only one of its kind in the book.

Not that an actual factual reporter couldn't bring home a wonderful tale. Until 1957 most people who had heard of Robert Gordon Wasson thought he was only a Wall Street banker. That year *Life* magazine revealed his prowess as an ethno-botanic detective, co-discoverer of the hallucinogenic mushroom *Psilocybe mexicana* (and related fungi) and first among recorded white men to eat such mushrooms during an ancient shamanic ritual practiced in Mexico for thousands of years but carefully hidden from non-Indian eyes after the Spanish invasion. Wasson's adventure crowned a thirty-year quest for the mushrooms of vision.

Emerging from the center of the visual field, the mycogenic images would approach and expand, quickly or slowly as one willed, in colors beautiful and harmonious. At first they depicted graphic motifs, then palaces or mythical beasts. Next the seer's soul flew free, abandoning adobe walls, soaring into mid-space to view vast landscapes where camels plodded

across great slopes, mountains rose into the heavens, or pel-
lucid rivers flowed through endless expanses of reeds down to
measureless seas, while all was bathed in horizontal light from
a pastel sun. Once a beautiful enigmatic woman stood like a
breathing statue staring out across the water. Wasson felt no
hope of reaching her, for she belonged to a world apart, while he
hung poised in space, an incorporeal eye that saw but was not
seen.

The psilocybic visions neither blurred nor wavered but were
always vivid and sharp. They came to Wasson more real than
anything seen before, and he felt he was for the first time seeing
plain rather than with normal imperfection, face to face at last
with the archetypes themselves, with the very Ideas as Plato
had seen them in the Temple of Eleusis. Seized by the power of
the mushrooms he was privileged to glimpse that extraordinary world William Blake could visit as he wished, of which he
had said: "He who does not imagine in stronger and better
lineaments, and in stronger and better light than his perishing
eye can see, does not imagine at all."

Two years before tasting the acrid mushrooms Wasson asked
his bilingual muleteer to explain their Mazatec name, *'nti*[1]
shi[3]*tho*[3], the dear holy thing that springs forth. The muleteer
answered:

> *El honguillo viene por sí mismo, no se sabe de dónde,*
> *como el viento que viene sin saber de dónde ni porqué.*

As Wasson translated it:

> The little mushroom comes of itself, no one knows whence,
> like the wind that comes we know not whence or why.

Wasson was deeply impressed by the reverence his Indian
friends showed the mushroom (so different from their jocular
contempt for the alcohol they freely abused). He understood
the honor they did him by sharing a tradition so long kept from
Spanish-speaking oppressors and well-meaning missionaries
alike. He was touched by a generosity that asked only a few
dollars for the transitory and elusive mushrooms, gathered
perhaps by a virgin harvester in pre-dawn breezes from a mountainside at the time of the new moon. "We did not this for
money," he was told.

Twice in the remote mountain village of Huautla de Jiménez
he ate the mushrooms during night-long ceremonies conducted by the curing-shaman María Sabina, a lady without
blemish, one who had never dishonored her calling by using
her powers for evil. La Señora (sometimes addressed as Doña

María) was acknowledged by her people as *cho⁴to⁴chi⁴ne⁴, una mujer que sabe,* a woman who knows. The first ceremony was held on the night of 29-30 June 1955, in the house of deputy mayor Cayetano, whose brother Genaro also attended along with Wasson's friend photographer Allan Richardson and perhaps ten others of all ages from the immediate families. Though the Señora chanted for hours, the Americans did not learn for several years all that she was saying, for the mushrooms spoke only Mazatec. They also caused some vomiting, but that was taken in stride. Six weeks later and thousands of miles from the State of Oaxaca, Wasson ate the mushrooms dried in his New York apartment. Their potency was undiminished, but he recognized that to know their sacredness one had to eat them surrounded by reverent bemushroomed Indians as the vibrant voice and ubiquitous percussions of an impeccable woman of knowledge filled a darkness made luminous only by a private reality that was at once new and prehistoric.

In the twenty years that followed, as a research fellow of the Harvard University Botanical Museum, Wasson published numerous articles and three notable books on religious uses of visionary plants. From his mushrooms in 1958 came the psychotropic drug psilocybin, which in the early 1960s opened to many experimenters formal or informal a subjective world much like the one Carlos entered when he smoked don Juan's mixture in December 1963. It was only natural, then, for Wasson to review each of Castaneda's books as it came out.

The four reviews furnish the clearest example on record of the ambivalence serious critics have felt about Castaneda. Having been over the same ground himself, Wasson opened *The Teachings* hoping to find a kindred spirit and fellow scientist. If Castaneda had gratified or disappointed him on both counts, no difficulty would have arisen, but Wasson found himself simultaneously gratified *and* disappointed, as he saw the kindred spirit straying from the path of science. It was a paradigmatic exercise in weighing error against authenticity, or lies against truth. Almost everybody cares more about truth than about lies, which are perceived as mere bits of manure clinging to mushrooms of knowledge. Against them, any substantial truth will tip the scale. Lies do weigh something, however, and they continue to make trouble. Though human beings are notoriously inconsistent, we prefer to see them constant, wanting them purely good or bad, longing to accept or reject them without reservation. Our condemned should display no endearing habits, our master's feet should not be made of clay. Looking back on him across the centuries, we forgive Newton for perfecting his data, but we don't care to be conned by an upstart from UCLA. If Castaneda says something we like to hear, we give him the benefit of the doubt, but we keep our eyes peeled.

As Wasson proceeded through *The Teachings*, several things struck him as not quite right. Castaneda said the ally-bringing mushrooms were "possibly *Psilocybe mexicana*." Don Juan had told Carlos to tear the mushrooms into shreds so that they could pass through the narrow neck of a gourd, in which at the end of a year they would have dried to a fine dust. "All one needs to do is to mash the chunks," don Juan had said. Wasson's dried mushrooms, in contrast, had retained their shape for more than six years and could not be mashed into dust. He was sure don Juan's mushrooms could not be *Psilocybe*.

Though Don Juan taught Carlos to collect, sort, dry, grind, and mix many kinds of plants, Carlos never seemed to learn the names of any plants but peyote, Jimson weed, and mushrooms (*los honguitos*). Recalling centuries of botanical work in Mexico, Wasson wondered why Castaneda neglected to name any of the other plants Carlos could spot on sight, and why he offered no reason for the omission. At least he could have brought back some mushroom specimens for verification. Don Juan's special formula could still have been kept secret. "Until [Castaneda] submits his plants for identification," Wasson wrote, "the learned world will receive his books with a shrug of skepticism. Zoologists will yawn when they read [in *A Separate Reality* about] a puma that, quite unprovoked, 'charges' Don Juan."

Disconcerted as he was by such botanical and zoological omissions and anomalies, Wasson was bothered more by Castaneda's language. Why, he asked, did we get no flavor of Spanish discourse in *The Teachings*? Why, in *A Separate Reality*, did don Juan spout so much American slang, when he had spoken standard English before? Why, in *Journey to Ixtlan*, did Castaneda give us Spanish we didn't need but fail to tell us what Spanish phrases don Juan used for critical terms like *ally*, *not-doing*, and *stop the world*? "Any careful reader," he concluded, "would say the original language of the conversations with Don Juan was English."

Castaneda's inexplicably unhispanic translation of Carlos's

Spanish field notes had aroused suspicion from the start. In 1968 Wasson sent a letter expressing misgivings. Castaneda replied "fully and frankly," even sending xerox copies of 12 large ruled pages of worked-up field notes (not the kind Carlos had scribbled in the heat of the action, but a second generation, prepared in quieter moments). "They were in Spanish and carried questions, which Castaneda put to Don Juan, and replies, written in legible handwriting." Their substance appeared in *The Teachings* "satisfactorily rendered into English," for 8 and 15 April 1962, when Carlos and don Juan were talking about the four enemies of a man of knowledge. Within a year, Wasson met Castaneda twice and was favorably impressed. "He was obviously an honest and serious young man." Despite those assurances, Wasson's estimate of Castaneda as a factual reporter steadily declined, reaching its nadir in 1973, when he saw Castaneda vacillating between science and romance, "a poor pilgrim lost on his way to his own Ixtlan." The following year *Tales of Power* resolved the quandary and tipped the scale. Castaneda had abandoned science and was writing frank romance. "For me the best is the latest," Wasson said. The meaning of the tetralogy had at last come clear. The four books were an extended parable, an allegory revealing an alien, pre-literate world. Though some doubts lingered about where ancient traditions left off and idiosyncratic science-fiction began, Wasson felt Castaneda's artistic truth, whatever its details might prove to be, finally outweighed the fumbling pseudoscience of his first three books. Chapter Seven will take up Castaneda's truth; here we are still pursuing his pretensions.

Though Carlos itched to snap photos and spin tapes, don Juan wouldn't stand for anything more evidential than notebooks. Luckily Carlos was an outstanding note taker, a speedwriter "capable of writing down most of what [don Juan] said in the beginning . . . and everything that was said . . . later." "You really write everything?" Don Juan could hardly believe it. Later he complimented Carlos on the sorcery of writing without concentrating. Carlos admitted he paid no attention to the scribbling, which seemed to him a separate activity he had nothing to do with. To be sure, the conversations are so full and lively that only an automatic writer could have written them down while participating in them. Years of this writing produced volumes of notes, which had to be organized and edited, but Castaneda assured us his editing was only selecting, not rewriting. If, as I believe, no other anthropologist has used automatic writing to take notes in the field, Carlos's volumes of scribbled notes should without fail be deposited in some scholarly library, not merely to show that the interviews actually occurred, but also to illustrate a remarkable recording technique. If Castaneda could demonstrate the technique in person, that would be even better, methodologically.

Carlos's literal transcription of "everything that was said," and Castaneda's faithful reproduction of intact passages from Carlos's notes tempt us to believe only simple translation stands between us and don Juan's actual speech. How odd then to note as Wasson did that don Juan spoke standard English in *The Teachings* but slang in the later books. Granted, the don Juan of *The Teachings* did say, "Accident, my eye!" and repeated Carlos's judgment that a girl named H. was "off her rocker," but those were rare lapses. In *A Separate Reality* don Juan switched openly to slang—"yeah," "bull!" "big deal!" "piddle around," "clobbered"—and in *Ixtlan* he called the wind "sneaky," told Carlos he was "truly a pill," and said things like "Cut the guff," "Come on, beat your gums," "Some clown brought you to me," "Don't lose your marbles," and "Golly! We're in a fix." In *Tales of Power* don Juan told Carlos a warrior had to "prepare his *tonal* not to crap out," praised Carlos with a BBCdy "Good show," called him a "greenhorn," but acknowledged that "We all go through the same shenanigans." Don Genaro he dubbed "the real McCoy." Not only did don Juan speak standard English in 1965, slang in 1968; but throughout 1961 and 1962 he spoke standard English in *The Teachings*, slang in *Journey to Ixtlan*.

How can we explain such foreign and capricious speech in an aging Yaqui recluse? Wasson, a former English instructor and magazine editor, laid the blame on delinquent editors at Simon and Schuster. Having found but a single error in *The Teachings* (where "all right" was consistently spelled "alright"), he judged the later books to be editorial disasters, where one would meet such clumsy mistakes as: "the reason . . . is because," "I . . . recuperated my balance," or "I wanted to adapt [adopt in *The Teachings*] a fighting position." "What good," Wasson asked, "is an editor who . . . does not edit?" No good, surely— but I think we have to excuse Simon and Schuster's editors. A little blackbird has told me Castaneda refused to cooperate with editors from the moment he escaped the University of California Press, where his undisciplined, eclectic, anachronistic colloquialisms had been expunged for the sake of academic dignity and ethnographic plausibility. In other words, don Juan's habitual, authentic, uncensored speech is either American slang or some kind of Spanish that is more appropriately translated into American slang than into standard or hispanicized English. One wonders what kind of Spanish that could be.

Castaneda's favorite adjective is "weird," which he uses not as Macbeth did to connote destiny or supernatural influence but in the weak sense meaning odd, unusual, or strange. He is free to do so, of course, but he allows his Yaquis to do the same. Don Juan tells Carlos, "If you ever learn to *see*, I suppose you must do it in your own weird way." Don Juan's grandson Lucio (no doubt having picked the word up from his slangy old grandad) says, "If peyote is that weird, I'm glad I've never taken it." Castaneda's weak "weird" has no counterpart in Spanish and cannot be justified as a suitable translation of any word that could enter a Spanish context. Juan Tovar, who translated Castaneda's books into Spanish (or *back* into Spanish, if you are still a believer), had a hard time with it. He rendered don Juan's "weird" as *rarísimo,* very odd, but he gave up completely on Lucio's "weird," writing a phrase that has no connection with Castaneda's English.

Castaneda wrote that some of don Juan's hunting tactics were "based on what he called 'the quirks of quails.' " Here the author forgets he is supposed to be translating from Spanish and gives us a direct quote from don Juan in English. If don Juan had said *los caprichos de los codornices,* Castaneda could have told us so, as he told us don Juan said *cantidades de caminos, la yerba del diablo,* or *su nombre de leche,* but don Juan didn't say *los caprichos de los codornices,* he said "the quirks of quails."

Wasson was astonished to read that Carlos "was supposed to look up and see the sorceress ['la Catalina'] in all her 'magnificent evil splendor,' " and that "Don Juan actually used those words." Again the author forgets he is supposed to be translating. Don Juan could have said, *en todo su esplendor magnífico pero malévolo,* but he chose instead to express himself at that critical moment in English, which Castaneda let pass.

My second appendix, "Go to the Blackbird," analyses the Spanish phrases Castaneda sprinkled through *The Teachings* and finds two quite different reasons for sprinkling them. In 10 of 27 bilingual entries, the author was giving the reader useful information, revealing don Juan's names for unfamiliar plants or sorcerous entities, distinguishing Yaqui Spanish from Mexican Spanish, or explaining Spanish idioms don Juan could have used. Since the information in those 10 items could have arisen from don Juan's sorcery or speech but would not readily be found in a reference work, I called them Justifiable Entries. The other 17 I called Unjustifiable Entries, because they told the reader nothing he did not already know from the English and because they could easily be found in an abridged bilingual dictionary. I concluded the Unjustifiable Entries had been added at random to strengthen the reader's false impression that the conversations were based on notes in the Spanish language.

The foregoing observations convince me that, except for a handful of names and phrases, the conversations with don Juan never existed, spoken or written, on tape or in notebooks, in any language but English until Juan Tovar translated them into Spanish.

Just a minute, you are saying, what about the 12 pages of Spanish handwriting Castaneda sent to Gordon Wasson? Of course—the 12 pages. How silly of me. But they don't change anything. The passages Castaneda picked out to reassure Wasson were completely safe. Though they mimic conversation, they constitute a formal philosophic discourse, a metaphysical catechism quite incapable of betraying any misfit between Spanish and English repartee. A second-year student could translate them in either direction with the greatest of ease. Subject to refutation by long-awaited proofs from Castaneda, it is my solemn conviction that those 12 pages did not exist before Wasson wrote his letter, that they were manufactured for the occasion, and that they are the only pages of Spanish field notes to come out of Carlos's dozen years in the desert. I do admit I shall not be surprised if some fat volume of Spanish scribbling shows up somewhere purporting to haul Carlos's field work back into the ordinary reality. What would surprise me would be a careful examination of such a volume that did not find it to be just another linguistic leg-pull by those wonderful folks who brought you "Yaqui Shenanigans" and "Quirks of Quails," those incredible cactus conjurors, Carlos McCoy and His Sonora Spoofers.

Having substituted gringo fiction for Spanish fieldnotes on a big scale, Castaneda substituted Spanish for Indian names on a small scale. A major figure in the first two books is Mescalito, a berry-headed, green-warted, cricket-bodied, choral-voiced, cinema-handed supernatural personage, who appears when Carlos has been eating peyote and shows him a sparkling but enigmatic future. True to Indian tradition, don Juan does not distinguish the peyote cactus from the teacher and protector who comes when one eats it.

"You really are going to teach me about peyote?" Carlos exclaims.

"I prefer to call him Mescalito," says don Juan. "Do the same."

A month later, one of don Juan's Indian friends hands Carlos something called both peyote and mescal, which he must chew. But peyote is not mescal, and Indians know it is not, especially men of knowledge like don Juan. Weston La Barre lists plenty of Indian names for peyote—*hicuri, huatari, kamaba, pejori, beyo, kop, walena, ho, nesac, wokowi,* and so on. He does not list *mescal.* The original mescal was the Nahuatl *mexcalli,* the agave cactus, from which pre-Columbian Indians fermented beer. The hard-drinking Spaniards distilled the Indian beer into a liquor they called mescal, and prizing alcohol above all other mind-benders, they obtusely applied the same name to two unrelated vision-plants used by the Indians: the fairly poisonous red-bean plant, *Sophora secundiflora,* and the more benign peyote cactus. In 1896, as Bigwood and Ott record, a German scientist who isolated an alkaloid from peyote perpetuated the Spaniards' misnomer by naming his discovery "mezcalin."

Since Castaneda admits having read La Barre before Carlos's apprenticeship began, we can be pretty sure he knew peyote was not mescal. Why, then, did Castaneda's archetypal Indian call peyote "dear little mescal," a name provided by Spanish parochialism? For the same reason, I believe, that he called Jimson weed *la yerba del diablo* and mushrooms *honguitos* or *humito,* all Spanish names. If Indian names for such things had popped up in the story, don Juan's exclusively Spanish discourse would have come under question, and author Castaneda might have been held responsible for an extensive Indian vocabulary.

Reviewing *The Teachings of Don Juan,* Edward Spicer, author of the major ethnographic works on Yaqui Indians, pointed out that the subtitle *A Yaqui Way of Knowledge* could not be justified, since don Juan did not participate in any Yaqui community and since his use of hallucinogenic plants contradicted what was known of Yaqui culture. "No Yaqui words are mentioned," Spicer commented, "not even in connection with the most distinctive concepts in Don Juan's 'way of knowledge.'"

That does seem odd. Of course, very few readers have any conception of the Yaqui language. Before working on this book,

I certainly didn't. For all I knew, Yaqui could have been a dialect of Spanish. Well, it isn't. Yaqui is about as different from Spanish as Kickapoo is from Swedish. It is a language from a different continent, a different race, a different age.

If you happened to be spending the weekend in Yucatan—not the big peninsula that sticks out into the Gulf of Mexico, but the little Yaqui settlement just west of Guaymas, in Sonora, from where don Juan's Mexican daughter-in-law came over to tend him after he dislocated his ankle on that fateful occasion when the murderous lady blackbird flew all the way to his house and gave him a shove in his moment of weakness—and you complimented one of the local residents on having a handsome house, whereupon he acknowledged that he and his family were living fairly comfortably there, the exchange could go like this:

Es bonita su casa.

Sí señor. Como usted ve, tenemos aquí una casa bastante buena.

But if you were up on your Yaqui, it could go like this:

Tua emuhyoisi ho'ak.

Hewi achai. Itepo ala besa hiokut inilen inim ho'ak.

Don Juan grew up talking like that. Despite his "superb command" of Spanish and his Mazatec parleys with don Genaro, "he regarded himself as an Indian from Sonora," from Yaqui country that is, where we know his grandson Lucio lived in a typical Yaqui house. Don Juan spoke to Yaquis in their own language and even sang Yaqui songs when the occasion warranted. During "the great Yaqui wars" seven-year-old Juan had seen his mother murdered by Mexican soldiers. Two years later the central government had exiled the remnants of the family to another part of Mexico (which, though Castaneda calls it "central," was more plausibly the southerly State of Oaxaca, where Juan sold herbs in the market place as a youth). In the 1930s a relenting government allowed the Yaquis to come home, so that when Carlos met him in 1960 don Juan had been living for 20 years among or near Yaquis in Sonora and Arizona. If he had any cultural ties at all, he was, as he said he was, a Yaqui. If he spoke a native tongue, it was Yaqui. If he reverted to the language of his childhood when he got excited or could not find the right word in Spanish, he used Yaqui words. Nevertheless, Carlos learned not one word of Yaqui during his first five years with don Juan.

By the ninth year of the association, Carlos had learned two

Yaqui words: *yori*, white man, and *Torim*, the name of a Yaqui settlement—which means wood rats, though Castaneda didn't mention that. When don Juan sang to Eligio in Yaqui, Carlos wanted to know what had been said. Don Juan told him, "That was only for Yaquis." Carlos was sure he had missed something very important, but the rebuff did not spur him to learn the language of his cultural hosts, from whom he was hardly insulated even if he spent most of his time with don Juan. Bajea, Benigno, Esquere, Genaro (no relation to don Genaro), and Victor were Yaquis. Carlos talked with them for hours, as a recorder hidden in his briefcase taped the conversation (eyeing the briefcase, Benigno wondered if Carlos could be a tequila salesman); there must have been some Yaqui phrases on that tape. Touring Sonora on his own, Carlos inquired about diableros, questioning Indians named Choy, doña Luz, and Genaro (again no relation). He formed a friendship with a local man (possibly a Mexican) who gave him a shotgun on short notice to blast the lady blackbird with. Even when he was avoiding don Juan, he visited Sonora, for we know he first met Lucio in 1966. A dozen years frequenting the Land of the Talking Tree, surrounded by the spirit children of Yomumuli, and only *yori* and *Torim* to show for it.

Don Juan warned Carlos to shun the wrong kinds of mushrooms and taught him to pick the right ones from among the wrong ones. Are we to believe don Juan used no Indian names to distinguish those varieties, or to identify other kinds of plants Carlos came to know like the back of his hand? Perhaps an uncharacteristically taciturn *brujo* sketched the plants in Carlos's notebook, or recorded them with a polaroid camera. Or perhaps the story is fiction and the author didn't bother to do his homework on Indian names of plants, animals, artifacts, parts of the body, or social roles. That would explain why don Juan wouldn't help Carlos fill out his kinship charts. The author didn't want the Yaqui words for father (*achai*), mother (*maala*), or daughter-in-law (*haborai*) to come up. It would account for don Juan's never calling a rabbit *taabu*, a squirrel *teku*, a rat *chikul*, a bird *wiikit*, a lizard *wi'iku*, a fawn *malit*, a coyote *wo'i*, meat *tekua*, water *baa'a*, cactuses *nabu*, *siina*, *'ono'e*, or *aaki*, seeds *bauchi*, hands *mamam*, head *koba*, Indians *yoemem*, woman *hamut*, ramada *hekka*, hunter *'amureo*, or warrior *nassuawa*; never saying anything was *tu'i* (good), *uhyoi* (beautiful), or even *buita* (a "bunch of crap").

Not being an anthropologist I didn't miss those exotic Yaqui words the first time round, though I did hear a false note closer to home. On 5 September 1969, Carlos told don Juan he had been reading about people who had clinically died but then revived. "In all the cases I had read," Castaneda wrote, "the persons involved had made statements, upon reviving, that they could not recollect anything at all; that dying was simply a sensation of blacking out." That surprised me, because all the cases I had read reported just the opposite. Where could such cases have been published, I wondered. Then it occurred to me that writing up a series of negative cases would be a rather unlikely exercise in scholarly masochism. Perhaps Castaneda and I had read the same cases but he had turned them upside down so that he could throw the best lines to don Juan.

That would be a writer's trick to build up his main character. In the same vein, several critics have applauded or derided Carlos's invincible doubts and confusion, which for six calendar and 12 narrative years let skeptics side with the overcautious, easily-rattled apprentice, while believers rooted for his resolute teacher, all the while gluing everybody to the books until one view or the other should prevail. It was an effective way to perpetuate suspense, unless the reader knew how people normally react when they meet the supernatural.

Though anyone may catch an occasional, ambiguous glimpse of the metaworld—may witness, as don Juan would say, effects of the *nagual* or reflections of an indescribable unknown—few of us have met that fitful otherness face to face, in living color and quadraphonic sound. Conventional skepticism blots out nearly any second-hand report of flying saucers (or sorcerers), hurtling bric-a-brac, graceful levitations, demonic possessions, smiling apparitions, soul trysts, perspicuous mountains, or inexplicable foreknowledge, but naive complacency crumbles quickly when someone plunges without warning from the familiar Newtonian world into a universe of alternatives, a realm of what might be, an every where-when-what of which the here-now-this is only the most probable of possible realities. The following story, merely the most recent of its kind that I have read, illustrates how typically fragile is the defense of skepticism when the effects of don Juan's *nagual* are directly witnessed.

While his frantic fellows were trying to rescue him from waters off Key West, a Navy scuba diver trapped for hours below the surface suddenly found himself observing the interior of his New York apartment, where his wife had just come home from shopping. The phone rang, and the hapless woman heard a Navy official describe her husband's predicament, whereupon she made hasty arrangements to take the first flight to Florida.

Once rescued, the bemused diver declared what he thought his wife had said and done, who had called her, and when. The confirmed accuracy of his report startled and perplexed both him and his associates. Everyone said it was incredible, but no one could deny it. Despite his emphatic rejection of any spiritualist or idealist world view that would make sense of his discarnate travels, the traveler could neither explain them nor dismiss them but could only accept them as a genuine interruption of what he had believed was the only reality. His puzzled but frank acknowledgement of the anomaly typifies the reaction of most hard-headed skeptics to vivid, first-hand events they judge, correctly or incorrectly, to be impossible under the normal rules. Carlos's dogged refusal to accept his own experience belongs to quite a different order of behavior.

On 29 December 1961, the day after he saw a solid bridge joining a mountain to a bank of fog, then went to sleep in a cave that vanished by morning, Carlos appeased his conventional realism by indulging the suspicion don Juan had slipped him some drugged meat. Since that was only the sixth of 34 non-drug nonordinary events (listed in appendix Table 2), we may approve or at least defer to Carlos's caution. On 9 April 1962, having been frightfully menaced by entities of the night, Carlos supposed don Juan might have stationed some teaching assistants in the underbrush to make scary noises and cast sudden shadows—but that was only the ninth event. On 22 May 1971, nine years and 26 anomalies later, Carlos was still dragging his feet on the road to conviction. Having peered through solid rock; gasped at a magic show where he and four Indian apprentices simultaneously saw don Juan in five respective guises; beheld 'la Catalina' zipping like a shot across one country road, hopping as fast as he could run along another, and sailing silhouetted over his head like a ghastly female kite; heard his own dead mother laughing, calling him, and shuffling her slippers; seen her clearly standing beside him; observed don Genaro tumbling unsupported on a waterfall; struggled vainly to start his car after don Juan hexed its sparkplugs; recoiled from a moth as big as a man; viewed the rumble of a rolling mountain; watched the same leaf fall four times; heard, seen, and felt in his belly the ten-mile leap to the mountaintops—to say no-

thing of having his mind read over and over by don Juan—
having come through all that, Carlos still claimed to be from
Missouri.

"I always think I'm being tricked," he complained. After
summoning 47 luminous personal blobs, he called don Genaro
and was thunderstruck when the elfin benefactor stepped
lightly from a golden bubble, stood before him solid as a peyote
button, and swore he had just popped over from his house 1200
miles—as the eagle flew—away. Instead of welcoming the
master with awe and admiration, Carlos sulked in skeptical
confusion, suspecting the mighty leaper of lurking in the
bushes and sneaking into the room when he wasn't looking.
How many supernatural lessons does a hand-picked apprentice
need? Enough, apparently, to keep the reader guessing to the
very last page.

In the twelfth year of his magical studies, Carlos-Skeptic
noticed don Juan was always around when he dropped in. "It
had never occurred to me until then," Castaneda wrote, "to
think anything of it." *Buita.* Anyone so unreflective, so
rationalistic, so defensively skeptical would have dropped the
project on the first day right there in the bus station when don
Juan fixed the "chosen man" with a "stupendous look" that
numbed him so he could not speak or even think coherently.
Facing such a challenge to his emotional security, his conventional world view, and his personal independence, Carlos-
Skeptic would have beat a hasty retreat to the safety of the
campus, where he would have switched his undergraduate
major to creative writing. Rescued from waters off Key West, he
would have accused his chief petty officer of rigging an under-
water movie to dupe him. Carlos-Skeptic cannot share a personality with Carlos-Apprentice any more than Carlos-One
can keep a diary with Carlos-Two.

Don Juan is just as divided as Carlos. One minute he is don
Indian, speaking and acting (in Wasson's words) "as members
of any pre-literate community have always spoken and acted."
The next he becomes the Indian don, lecturing like an Oxford
fellow. "What impresses me in Castaneda's writings," said
Colombian anthropologist Gerardo Reichel-Dolmatoff, "is
that his Indians think and express themselves like the Indians I
have known." "The devil's weed," don Indian tells Carlos, "has
very few friends, and paloverde is the only tree in this area
which agrees with her." "Because the smoke is my ally," don
Indian says, "I don't need to smoke anymore. I can call him
anytime, anyplace."

Such pre-literate parables (just now personifying the Jimson weed and identifying the mushroom mixture with the spirit it calls) are the more extraordinary, Wasson comments, since in other respects don Juan is "a man of our times," confidently commanding literate Spanish while "most genuine shamans in Mexico are locked behind . . . linguistic barriers" that isolate them from European thought. The Indian don, Castaneda tells us, "was very careful to establish that the world was whatever we perceive." Bishop Berkeley would have liked to hear that. He "maintained that 'perceiving the world' entails a process of apprehending whatever presents itself to us. This particular 'perceiving' is done with our senses and our will." Such a Yaqui way of knowledge David Hume would gladly have endorsed.

How shall we reconcile the compact animism don Indian teaches his apprentice with the discursive phenomenology in which the Indian don tutors his pupil? Where did the Uto-Aztecan polymath acquire his modern conceptual repertory? Castaneda offers no hint of the intensive curriculum behind this erudition. The years don Juan must have spent in the library of the Universidad Autónoma are no less concealed from us than the reading lists assigned by Castaneda's UCLA professors. Don Juan admits to reading nothing, while Castaneda acknowledges six sources: the *Tibetan Book of the Dead*, some cases of returners who brought back no news, Weston La Barre on the peyote cult, Talcott Parsons on glosses, Ludwig Wittgenstein's linguistic philosophy, and Edmund Husserl's phenomenology. Hearing of Castaneda's interest, a former student of Husserl's (whom Castaneda neglects to name) gave Carlos a piece of ebony that had once sat on the philosopher's writing desk. After reading and discussing Husserl's *Ideas* (published in English) with the Indian don, Carlos gave the ebony to don Indian, who fondled it "as Husserl had done a generation before, and gave it an honored place in his treasury of power objects."

Not content with erasing the Indian don's academic history, Castaneda startles us with greater incongruities, as *Tales of Power* introduces don Parvenu, an urban sophisticate who keeps a wardrobe of natty business suits and boasts he is "a stockholder." The metamorphic Matus quickens and brightens Castaneda's allegory but nullifies his anthropology.

As *A Separate Reality* opened, we found Carlos and don Juan sitting on a park bench somewhere in the mountains (presumably of Oaxaca) about the middle of Tuesday afternoon, 2 April

1968, when Carlos pulled a copy of *The Teachings* from his briefcase.

"It's about you, don Juan," he said.

The unschooled sage appraised the proportions of the binding, felt the hard cloth cover with his palms, admired the green color of the dust jacket, riffled the pages like a deck of cards, and handed the book back.

"I want you to keep it," said Carlos.

"I better not." Don Juan smiled. "You know what we do with paper in Mexico." Carlos laughed. He thought don Juan's touch of irony was beautiful.

The two men were waiting to see don Genaro before driving back to Sonora. Genaro's house (*Tales of Power* would tell us) was a six- or seven-day drive from Los Angeles. This time the car had broken down, adding three days to the trip. Carlos could not have left Los Angeles later than 25 March.

The University of California Press published *The Teachings of Don Juan* on 27 June 1968. Carlos had received an advance copy "in April," but the Press did not send advance copies to reviewers until 3 June, though the normal schedule called for sending them three or four weeks earlier—in May, that is. Perhaps the books were delayed at the bindery. Unhampered by conventional time and sharing Castaneda's pride in the coming publication, the eager Carlos "felt compelled" to tuck a nonordinary copy of *The Teachings* into his briefcase on 25 March, a full ten weeks before the bindery plodding along the regular time track managed to deliver boxes of ordinary books to the Press. Castaneda's touch of irony is even more beautiful than don Juan's. You know what we do with facts in the separate reality.

Which brings me to a speculation that has been trying to break through ever since I read the following statement by Margaret Castaneda:

"One day in the summer of 1960 Carlos told me he had met a man he wanted to study with and it would mean being away for days or weeks at a time. He knew that would disturb me so he said maybe we should live in separate apartments."

"Did he mention the man's name?" I asked her on the phone.

"Don Juan," she said.

Having spent most of this chapter arguing that don Juan is imaginary, I now have to ask myself what it means when Castaneda's then wife says Carlos met don Juan just when Castaneda says he met him. Having shown how far narrative and calendar are out of phase in Castaneda's books, I must now explain this perfect synchrony. It could mean don Juan was as real as you or I, breathing ordinary air, treading silica sands, trapping the doomed *taabu* under clear Sonoran skies, making tiny stitches in the eyelids of the *wi'iku*—but I think the evidence has overwhelmed that hypothesis. It could mean Margaret Castaneda was trying to build up the myth of don Juan, but the rest of her article does not support that view. It could and I think it does mean narrative and calendar time were often the same for Castaneda, if for no one else. In other words, he was living in the story.

If Carlos gave *The Teachings* to don Juan the day after April Fool's Day 1968, that was when Castaneda wrote the scene. If Carlos met don Juan in the summer of 1960, that was when Castaneda conceived the idea, or made the first notes, or wrote the first version of the meeting. Though departing from the realities of commerce and family, science and academy, the separate reality was substantially true to itself. Much of the time, author and character lived, thought, and felt as one person.

In the fall of 1963 *The Psychedelic Review* carried a memorable article by four men who had eaten the mushrooms of vision in Huautla or had used psilocybin in the United States. Three of the four had seen eyes or faces glowing as don Juan's would later glow. One had felt himself submerged in water as Carlos would be submerged in the irrigation ditch. The same man had lost his body, all but the head, as Carlos would do before flying like a crow. The skull of a second man had expanded into a huge sphere, on whose inner walls his introspective eyes had skated freely about, observing rapidly changing scenes of the private world, as sorcerers would later observe the *tonal* within the bubble of perception. A third man had shot up into a standing position merely by willing it, as Carlos would "think" himself up during his first mushroom experiment— which would take place on 26 December 1963, shortly after the article appeared.

If Carlos's adventures were so closely linked in time and substance to Castaneda's clandestine reading, how did Carlos happen to meet don Juan in the summer of 1960? "By December of 1959," Margaret Castaneda recalled, "Carlos and I had read the Puharich book [*The Sacred Mushroom*] and somehow it changed us." Castaneda (she continued) "seemed withdrawn." He took trips "to Mexico," where he was "digging for bones." My theory places that particular "Mexico" in the UCLA library, where the rare "bones" Castaneda dug up were the bona fide fieldwork of Gordon and Valentina Wasson.

Puharich praised the Wassons' epochal *Mushrooms Russia and History*, a lavish two-volume edition, printed in Italy, priced at $125, limited to 512 copies, published in 1957 while Castaneda was still at Los Angeles City College studying psychology, journalism, and creative writing. Whether or not he had read Wasson's *Life* article in 1957, we can safely assume Castaneda would not have bothered with Puharich in 1959 if by then he had already held the Wassons' dazzling source-work in his hands. On Margaret's reckoning, he read Puharich during his first quarter as an undergraduate anthropology student at UCLA, where he had only to visit the University Research Library to join that elite group of scholars who knew the full, authentic details of Wasson's discoveries. My theory finds him there, early in 1960, sitting unobtrusively in a corner of the special-collections reading room, perusing Volume Two with unbending intent, taking copious notes (this time in English) on what the ethnomycologists had found in central and southern Mexico.

In the summer of 1953, while he was collecting information on the hallucinogenic plants used by the Indians of the area, Gordon Wasson met Don Aurelio, a resident of Huautla de Jiménez who spoke both Mazatec and Spanish. Though Don Aurelio possessed many of the secrets Wasson was searching for, he did not at first reveal himself as a curing-shaman. "For days," Wasson wrote, "we had been talking with a *curandero* all unawares." "I had known don Juan for a whole year," Castaneda would write, "before he took me into his confidence."

Like don Juan, Don Aurelio was "one who knows," seeing across time and distance, divining the thoughts and feelings of persons not present. Unlike don Juan he was only 45 years old, and his right eye was blind, whereas don Juan would tell Carlos, "The secret is in the left eye. . . . Usually the left eye of a warrior has a strange appearance." With the mushrooms, Don Aurelio said, "one sees everything, one sees where God is also." "The smoke. . . . will set you free to see anything you want to see," don Juan would say. "They carry you there where God is," several Indians told Wasson. "Mescalito takes you to another world," don Juan would say. "Is it heaven . . . where God is?" Carlos would ask.

The mushrooms, Wasson wrote, could be preserved in a dried state for as long as six months. Later he learned they could be kept for years. In my theory, Wasson's incomplete statement deceived don Juan into believing the mushrooms would crumble into dust before a year was out. Like María Sabina and her guests, Don Aurelio ate the mushrooms in their natural state. No one smoked them in a pipe. María Sabina, however, prepared the mushrooms for the ritual by passing them through the smoke of aromatic plants, as a photograph showed her doing. In my theory, the photo of Doña María aromatically "smoking" the mushrooms inspired don Juan to smoke mushroom dust in his pipe and to "sweeten the smoke mixture" with leaves and flowers he and Carlos would gather.

Aristeo, a Zapotec *mènjak* or man of knowledge, told Wasson three or four experiences of the mushrooms were necessary to get over the surprise of the visions. Don Juan would tell Carlos he must smoke the mushroom mixture as many times as he could to learn to handle its power.

Though Wasson thought María Sabina was in her fifties, her age was hard to guess. Like don Juan she combined youthful vigor with an aged visage; like his, her face was dark and deeply lined. Like him, she sat on a straw mat, was "seized" by the power of the plant, and did not want her photograph shown to outsiders. "It would be a betrayal," she said. For his part, Carlos would assure don Juan he had never betrayed his confidence by revealing his true name or whereabouts. In the 1957 *Life* article, Wasson called María Sabina "Eva Mendez," Cayetano "Filemón," Huautla "a remote village," the Mazatecs "Mixtecos." The real Mixtecos lived farther to the West, toward that "central Mexico" Carlos and don Juan would so often visit to see their Mazatec friend Genaro. Cayetano's brother Genaro was not mentioned in *Life*.

How does the crow fly from *Ixtlan* to Huautla? Backwards through Castaneda time, 60 miles NNW across Oaxaca, dropping from 6187 feet in the Sierra Madre del Sur to 5623, forsaking (in those days) 1075 people for 3314. A short hop in a big country. Shorter in imagination.

My theory holds Carlos's self-effacing friend Bill could introduce him to don Juan in the Nogales bus station in the summer of 1960 because earlier that year in the special-collections reading room at UCLA Gordon Wasson had introduced Castaneda to Don Aurelio, María Sabina, and Aristeo, three curing-shamans some of whose attributes found their way into the character of don Juan. Later chapters will reenter the library to seek further influences on don Juan's teachings, Carlos's exploits, and Castaneda's fiction, but first we inquire how one earns a Ph.D. in anthropology by reporting interviews with an imaginary *brujo*.

CARLITOS AND DON JUAN
(Karlosla into Achai Hoan)

A while back they say (*kaa haiki wasuktiam simsu-ka'apo'otea*) this white guy (*yooi*) drove down to Bataconsica in his VW bus (*'ili yoi-karopo*) to learn how the Yaquis fly (*Hiakim haisa nenne'epo ta'aabaekai*). He came all the way from the gringo University of California (*Kaliporniapo kateka, bwe'u 'ehkweela-betana weyekai*) but he didn't know nothing (*kaita ta'aak*).

Ha-ha! my boy (*heheeti in uusi*), said a funny old man (*musa'ala o'ola*) who was living by the irrigation ditch (*hakia bewit ho'akan*). Ha-ha-ha-ha-ha-ha-ha! (*heheheheheheeti!*) You sure don't know nothing. Looks like I got to be your teacher (*'enchi mah-mahtaneeme*).

Well (*pos*), as everybody finally found out, that comic old man was the famous unknown sorcerer don Juan (*yeesisibome achai hoan*), while the not-so-young anthropologist (*haibu kaa hu'ubwa-yo'otu tatta'abwi yoemraatat hu'uneebaeka 'au mahtame*) was Carlitos, the man with no past (*karlosla ka'etehoimta*).

Wow! (*heppa!*) You should have seen the two of them, charging around on the mountains like a pair of wild horses (*kaupo nau kum-kumti saka*), leaping from rock to rock (*tetammet chep-chepti-saka*) like a couple of jumping beans (*woi karpokaps asaltitans benasi*), talking to the plants (*mamyammak 'eteho*), spying on the birds (*wikitchimmet hiiu-sime*), singing sad Mexican songs (*hume'e siok-maisi yoi-bwikim 'am bwi-bwikan*), swapping tall stories (*eteteho*), and yelling at the wind (*hekaubicha chachaaen*). Carlitos learned to hunt (*aamu*), to set

62

traps (*wite'im*), to enjoy eating rattlesnake (*'aakame-hissobata 'ukkule*), to plaster leaves on his belly-button (*sawam sikupo yaaka*), to sew up the eyes of a lizard with a cactus thorn (*wikuim pusim, choa-wichammea 'am hi'ikak*), to sit under the ramada (*hekka betuku katek*), to chew peyote (*hikuri a'a chachamte*), to smoke the mushroom mixed with special bugs (*nanacata biichammak etemmak eelesukimmak untsoweiter buichia*), to turn his head into a crow (*'a'a kobawa 'a'a konitu-tuak*), to fly through the sky (*teekapo ne'e*), to see visions in the fog (*bahewapo hita bibicha*), and to stop the world (*'aniata kiiktetua*). During those years (*wasuktiampo*), he played with the electric pissing dog (*beokte sisi chuu'umake yeewesuk*), he took a shot at the pretty lady blackbird (*tutu'uli chana-hamutta muhuk*), he almost got run over by a giant gnat (*kaituuna weteepo'imea*), he said how-are-you to a Chicano coyote (*yoi-wo'ita tebotek*), and he played hide-and-seek with his invisible ally (*eusila a'a'aniareomake*).

Sometimes Carlitos got so scared in the night (*tukaariu awomtiwak*) that he cried (*abuanak*), he fell down (*ko'om wechek*), he threw up (*abisatak*), and he crapped in his pants (*ahaitauyak*), but he never stopped writing, writing, writing (*hihihi'ote*) about the life of the hunter (*'amureota haisa 'a'a hiapsa'u*), the death of the warrior (*nassuareota haisa 'a'a mukuka'u*), the man of knowledge (*susuakame*), and the path with heart (*boo'o hiapsita*). Since he never learned a single word of Yaqui (*napat senu yoemnoki ahikahak*), nobody (*kabe*) could tell him don Juan was just kidding him (*abaita'ak*) about all that fancy stuff (*uhyoi buita*). Well (*abwe*), they say he went back to California and wrote a book in English (*hi'osam inklenooka etea*) about the old Spanish-speaker (*epanookareo*) who taught him a Yaqui way of knowledge (*hiaki akad'emic puton*). He made a big pile of cash (*tomi*), and that's about it (*hunum chupe*).

4. WHAT HAPPENED AT UCLA?

Castaneda, as one professor put it, is 'a native genius,' for whom the usual red tape and bureaucratic rigmarole were waived; his truth as a witness is not in question.

After a wild-coyote chase across Italy, Argentina, and Brazil, where no trace was found of the quadrilingual, multinational Carlos, *Time* dug up a dusty immigration record for one Carlos Arana C. and read at last the facts of Castaneda's Peruvian origin. Seeing the case so deftly cracked we wondered if any secret could be kept from the global reach, the massed bushbeating, the skillful probing of *The Weekly News-magazine.* Indeed it could. Hot on the Westwood trail *Time's* Sandra Burton hit a stone wall of silence, whose pleasant ivy mantle was all that saved her a sore nose, as cordial professors chatted amiably with her but told her nothing that could explain Castaneda's unusual academic career. "A native genius," sighed one. "The type of student a teacher waits for," marveled another. "Power takes care of you and you don't know how," glossed the Separate Raconteur himself. Burton and her campus informants went round and round the subject, but nary a chink opened in the faculty façade through which an outsider might glimpse the forbidden Dance of the Dreaming Dissertator, in which for seven long years a tireless story-teller brings fairy tales to the learned elders, offering them as factual reports, until without warning the Men of Knowledge call him Earth Doctor and World Stopper, hoist him to their crumbling shoulders, bear him in stately procession out of the gloomy

Graduate Limbo, through the narrow Gate of Power, onto the limitless tundra of professional anthropology, where they hand him a scroll and bid him goodbye.

Why should this ritual from one isolated coastal village differ so markedly from what competent observers have seen almost everywhere else? Why has no ethnologist contrasted it normatively with more familiar rites? Why has no ethnographer tried to penetrate its indigenous meaning? Why, in short, has no scholar criticized what happened at UCLA or asked what the professors thought they were doing when they ratified Castaneda's fantasies?

Perhaps I assume too much. Who among us has seen the official document? *Time* said Castaneda received his Ph.D. "for" *Journey to Ixtlan,* but Castaneda told his Irvine students *Ixtlan* would have "an academic analysis appended to it for his dissertation." Perhaps the formal work he submitted contains both validating exhibits and scholarly apparatus going far beyond his popular writings.

While don Juan's privacy had to be protected, the legitimacy of the fieldwork could still have been fairly tested. Suppose Castaneda and his doctoral committee select a panel of disinterested experts, agreeing to take the word of any one of them about the existence and character of don Juan. Castaneda goes over the list with don Juan, who *sees* each member of the panel as a luminous mushroom, easily screening out any who cannot be trusted with the identity of a *brujo,* tolerated in a two-room shack, or taken on hikes to witness power in the mountains. One referee is chosen, sworn to secrecy, and charged to stay in Sonora long enough to satisfy himself either that the fieldwork happened as Castaneda said it did or that it was a swindle, a sham, a masquerade, a spoof, a hoax, or what you will. Though the visitor may lack the power to *see* magical events, he can certainly tell whether don Indian and the Indian don inhabit the same agile, wiry body and compose a single, transcultural personality.

"There is no way to escape the *doing* of our world," don Juan told Carlos. "Out there is your hunting ground." Clearly he would not despise the apprentice's need for the controlled folly of worldly recognition or balk at a modest request for one academic visitation. Perhaps, then, the validating testimony of some neutral observer like Pedro Carrasco or Peter Furst is recorded in the dissertation. And what a fine chapter that historic meeting will someday make in Castaneda's *Tales of Folly*!

"These friends of yours," don Juan said, "do they know more about Indians than Indians know?"

"Of course not," I protested. "It's just that some members of the committee don't think I am telling the truth."

Don Juan looked out across the desert. His eyelids were half-closed. "A warrior doesn't care whether a thing is true or untrue," he reminded me. "If a thing is said to be untrue, he can still act impeccably. He just doesn't believe in what he is doing. Did you tell them that?"

"They read it in the dissertation, don Juan, but that didn't make them warriors. They're just professors, a bunch of losers like my father."

Don Juan nodded. "If they are losers," he said softly, "then you're a losers' pimp." He took the list out of my hand and examined it intently. A tremendous apprehension seized me. My thoughts went back to a day many years before when, knowing nothing about don Juan, I had insisted on taking pictures of him and recording our conversations on tape. On that occasion don Juan had said that if I wanted to have anything more to do with him I should never mention such foolishness again. Now I was proposing to bring a total stranger to his house. I felt like an idiot. I wanted to grab the paper out of his hand and tell him to forget the whole thing, that I would drop anthropology and devote myself to sorcery, that I didn't give a fig for the world of the professors. An intense wave of sadness swept over me, but don Juan began to hum a Mexican tune, and I knew he was about to clobber me. I sat up straight, my body tense with expection.

"This Professor Furst," he said, pointing to the name at the top of the list. "What if we take him to a place of power, and the entities of the night crush him like a bug?"

Though Castaneda was "stubbornly indifferent to any similarities between his experience with Don Juan and Zen or any other discipline," though he affected to be unfamiliar with philosophic sources his Irvine students pointed out, though he routinely denied being a whizz in the stacks, perhaps that was all propaganda for his popular books while his dissertation cited scores of writers like Artaud, Atkinson, Beals, Bennett and Zingg, Harner, Kluckhohn, Klüver, Langer, Lévy-Bruhl, Nuñez, Rowe, Russell, Sapir, Swain, Thord-Gray, Weitlaner, Whorf, and of course the Wassons. He might be Carlos-Naïf on the platform but Castaneda-Scholar in Classifications B to GR.

Such speculations did not have to remain hypothetical. *Dis-*

sertation Abstracts International lists nearly every dissertation in the country. There I found 500 words by Castaneda
under the promising title, *Sorcery: A Description of the World.*
"The data that comprises the present work," Castaneda wrote,
"was gathered over a period of ten years of sporadic fieldwork in
northwestern Mexico, under the guidance and tutelage of a
Yaqui Indian sorcerer, don Juan Matus, who in 1961 took me as
his apprentice." Since *Journey to Ixtlan* covers only 1960-62
and a brief episode in 1971, the abstract implied the dissertation was a more inclusive study. Three times describing it as
"an emic account" (a term I had not seen before), the abstract
suggested the dissertation was a formal, theoretical work. Here
at last, I thought, might be the inner secrets of don Juan's
sorcery and ample justification of Castaneda's academic recognition. I was eager to examine the document.

Dissertations listed in the *Abstracts* can ordinarily be pur-
chased directly from Xerox University Microfilms, Ann Arbor,
unless the author has prohibited such distribution. Of 30-
thousand new works listed in one recent year, fewer than 50
were so restricted. The rare author (1 in 600) who does not want
us to order his dissertation typically plans to publish it in a
more profitable commercial form, or in an improved edition
that will instruct us more effectively. Whatever Castaneda's
reasons, he notified us we had to write to him in Westwood if
we wanted a copy. Seeing his notice was already two years old, I
ordered a copy from Ann Arbor anyway. Sorry, answered
Xerox's computer, input codes forbid me to bill out dissertation
73-13132. Please contact author for copies.

On 6 September 1975 I wrote to Castaneda, telling him I was
getting this book together, asking him to define *emic,* request-
ing permission to purchase *Sorcery* from Xerox, inquiring
about the topic of his next book, and inviting him to lunch. On
4 November, having received neither an answer nor my letter
back, I sent a reminder. Today, 2 April 1976, I am still waiting
for his reply.

While the author may control Xerox distribution, he has
nothing to say about the two copies of his dissertation that
must be deposited in the library. By early October I was holding
the mysterious volume in my hands, appraising the proportions of the binding, feeling the hard cloth cover with my
palms, admiring the dull red library color, turning the 368
leaves like pages of the *Visions of Hermas* (which, though they
were "not strictly canonical, the Fathers appointed to be read

for direction and confirmation in faith and piety") only to find that except for its title, five faculty signatures endorsing the fieldwork, a five-line vita, a four-item list of Castaneda's prior publications, the 500-word abstract, and a few minor editorial changes in the text, *Sorcery: A Description of the World* was indeed *Journey to Ixtlan* and nothing more. No appended academic analysis, no reference list, no archival deposits, no referee's testimony, not even a definition of *emic*. The circulation record indicated no scholar outside of UCLA had borrowed the dissertation.

Knowing these facts we can easily deduce some reasons for making *Sorcery* inaccessible, and rule out others. The fact that *Sorcery* and *Ixtlan* are virtually identical rules out the perfective motive. The fact that the bookstores were selling *Ixtlan* at $6.95 eight months before the *Abstracts* listed *Sorcery* at $11 rules out the commercial motive. Still unread, however, *Sorcery* could be thought to contain the solid scholarship, the supporting evidence, and the theoretical analysis normally expected and often found in scientific works. Unexamined, it would strengthen the myth of don Juan, attesting to his existence by its existence, protecting his privacy by its inaccessibility. Finally, if Xerox's computer refused to bill it out, no angry letters would come to the UCLA anthropology department protesting a four-dollar rip-off.

One of Castaneda's most favorable reviews and surely his biggest commercial boost came from anthropologist Paul Riesman, who praised his *science* in the strongest language anyone has used. Taken together, Riesman said, Castaneda's first three books "form a work which is among the best that the science of anthropology has produced. . . . [Castaneda] has done the best he could to show others exactly how he came by his knowledge." Believing Castaneda had done the best he could not to show but to hide that information, I wrote to Riesman expressing my views. In due course an answer came from 200-miles south of Timbuktu, where Riesman was doing palpable fieldwork. Though lacking the relevant materials, he answered forthrightly as follows:

"I am no longer convinced Castaneda has done the best he could to show others exactly how he came by his knowledge, for if he had, I do not think so many people would be suspicious of him. What he does do is with great artistic skill show the reader the experiences that led him to feel as real the world of the sorcerers, and if the reader is moved by the books he comes away from them feeling, at least with some part of his being, that that world is real. This is an important and valid anthropological enterprise, one that very few anthropologists can do well, but [not, of course] the only thing anthropologists should do. If I were writing my review today, I would omit the word 'science,' because while I feel Castaneda's work can be very useful to anthropology I do not think his goal in writing the books was to be scientific. I don't think I would criticize him for this, though I might want to [distinguish] between art and science in anthropology and [say] what I think their relationship is."

"What harm," I had asked Riesman, "has Castaneda done to anthropology?"

"I doubt that he has done any harm," he answered. "Even if it should be proven that his books are 'pure fiction,' that would make some anthropologists like me look foolish but I don't see [any harm to] anthropology."

How foolish was Riesman to take Castaneda at his word? How foolish was Edward Spicer, when he wrote that though *The Teachings* taught us nothing about Yaquis, it "should attain a solid place in the literature of both the hallucinogenic drugs and the field behavior of anthropologists"? That depends on whether scholars generally can trust their colleagues. If scholars usually lie, then nothing can be taken for granted, but if scholars usually tell the truth, then lacking contrary evidence the community of scholars does well to rely on a presumption of good faith. Spicer relied on that presumption, and he was right to do so, though the presumption was in the event mistaken. Even Riesman, writing as late as October 1972, but far from the village of the Dream Dance, defensibly relied on it. The burden of his review was that Carlos's progress from arrogance to humility, from ethnocentrism to empiricism, was a model for ethnographers. The point was well made whether don Juan existed or not.

"What," I had asked, "was going through the minds of the committee that gave Castaneda a Ph.D. for *Journey to Ixtlan*?"

"I wasn't aware," Riesman answered, "that he had gotten a Ph.D. for that book. I remember reading in a publication of the American Anthropological Association that Castaneda had written a thesis on the world of the sorcerers, or something like that, but the title was utterly different; I didn't realize it was the same book." Erasing academic history seems to work pretty well.

Responses from UCLA were less frank. When I asked one member of Castaneda's doctoral committee whether he had revised his estimate of how factual the fieldwork was, he replied: "I refer all questions about Carlos Castaneda to Carlos Castaneda. The validity of his work is not determined by second-hand information nor taking a vote on it." But the committee had voted affirmatively on the validity of the information that came to them second-hand from Castaneda. I was only asking if anyone had changed his vote in the meantime.

When I pressed a non-committee professor to confirm or deny his statement (told to me by a common friend) that he still did not know whether Castaneda had actually done the fieldwork, he complained about "intellectual blackmail."

When I admitted some of my questions were "quite probing," a second committee member said: "Frankly, I cannot even conceive of a purpose to your 'probing questions' [nor do I] see in what serious sense they can be called 'probing.'" One question my informant found neither purposive nor probing ran as follows:

"It has been said that even if Castaneda's fieldwork never really happened, and even if academics and the public were temporarily misled, the deception was justified by the result, which is that Castaneda has provided a valuable catalyst for re-examining ethnomethodology, particularly the fieldworker's attitudes toward his indigenous informant. My reaction to such a statement is:"

A second non-committee professor—let me call him Professor Blythe—reacted to that statement by saying, "I don't accept that there was any 'deception.'" Two prominent professors from other universities answered at greater length. One said: "The statement [fairly describes Castaneda's influence] but I cannot support any deception. If it was all deception, then no result can justify the procedure." The other said: "I don't think there is room in scholarly work for deception of any kind. As matters stand, our fieldwork is not always scientific even with the best of intentions." No professor said deception was justified.

In a letter to Professor Blythe, I remarked that Castaneda's philosophy was a real mess—an opinion I later moderated—but an interesting and important mess. "So far as I can see," he answered, "Carlos doesn't present any 'philosophy' of his own; he claims to be reporting Don Juan's words, and one wouldn't expect a Yaqui Indian to present a completely coherent philosophical system."

When Blythe acknowledged he was one of those who had advised the University Press to publish *The Teachings* and said he still approved the subtitle, *A Yaqui Way of Knowledge*, I asked how he could justify the subtitle after Spicer and others had rejected it as misleading. He answered: "The general outlines of Yaqui culture are fairly well known from the work of Spicer and others, so that Carlos could take that for granted." But the subtitle didn't take Yaqui culture for granted, it promised to bring new information about it, a promise the text broke and the author repudiated—in *The Teachings*, in *Ixtlan*, and in his dissertation abstract, where he wrote: "The conclusion I have arrived at after years of fieldwork is that sorcery does not have a cultural focus."

Asked to justify the doctoring of Castaneda, Blythe said: "One could argue his degree was awarded in recognition of the impact all his work (through *Journey to Ixtlan*) had made on anthropology and the reading public. Though the dissertation contained little conventional academic analysis, *The Teachings of Don Juan* had contained such an analysis, for which no academic recognition had been given." Blythe was referring to "A Structural Analysis," of which Weston La Barre had said: "This tedious attempt to play dutiful Lévi-Straussian games can have satisfied neither committee nor general reader." Now, we know La Barre could not stomach any of Castaneda's work, which he found "woefully inadequate. . . . pseudo-profound, sophomoric, and deeply vulgar. . . . tiresomely dull, posturing . . . and intellectually, kitsch," but even Castaneda's admirer Riesman deplored "A Structural Analysis," calling it "awful. . . . a pathetic denial of the reality of [Carlos's experiences, which] exemplifies the arrogance and fright of most of us Western anthropologists, who carry on as if we know the reality while 'other cultures' merely have approximate 'versions' of that reality." Of course, Riesman wrote that before he realized Castaneda was practicing art, not science. More attuned to literary artistry, novelist Joyce Carol Oates thought she recognized in "A Structural Analysis" a "parody that goes beyond what Vladimir Nabokov did in *Pale Fire* (his target being literary criticism)."

"It became obvious to me," wrote Castaneda (introducing *The Teachings*), "that don Juan's knowledge had to be examined in terms of how he himself understood it; only in such terms could it be made evident and convincing." Flatly ignoring don Juan's admittedly indispensable point of view, "A Structural Analysis" (Part Two of *The Teachings*) demonstrated for page after boring page, in soggy paragraphs sagging with deliberately redundant detail, nothing more illuminating than the obvious fact that don Juan's teachings were internally consistent and logically coherent, something every reader felt and no one had questioned, least of all don Juan. One might as well set out to clarify the theory of relativity by diagramming Einstein's sentence structure and reporting that he wrote no ungrammatical sentences. "A Structural Analysis" is an utterly empty exercise, and it was meant to be. As novelist Oates suspected, it is a merciless parody, whose sole and entire purpose was to fail pathetically, which it did triumphantly. If Castaneda's professors didn't see that, they were a lot dumber than I think they were. In his heart, Professor Blythe knows as well as you and I that "A Structural Analysis" is not a lecture appended to a story, but part of the story, the part that tells what happened when Carlos got back to UCLA and had to deal with his ethnocentric, frightened, but arrogant professors. As the years went by, the UCLA part of the story mushroomed into a surrealist play, Castaneda and his professors (including Professor Blythe) acting the roles of Carlos and *his* professors. Bravo for living theater! But no points for science, or good faith.

Laymen of different stripes have offered various explanations of what happened at UCLA: Professors are pointy-headed poltroons, UCLA is a ass, Anthropology is no science, Science is out and magic is in, or Something is missing. Judging Castaneda's career to have been a rare aberration, I find the last explanation most appealing. But what more can be missing? Based solidly on hunches and leaks, my theory may not stand as long as Ptolemy's, but at least it makes sense and fits all the data; no other I have heard can make that claim.

The minute I saw Castaneda's unfamiliar word *emic*, I knew something was up. The closest my portable decoder could get was *emicturate*, which I didn't think would help. Three times Castaneda said it: "This is an emic account of sorcery as it is practiced by the American Indians of modern Mexico. . . . The main premises of this thesis, being an emic account, were statements voiced by the sorcerer-teacher. . . . The present emic account, therefore, deals with the 'techniques' by virtue of which a new agreement about the nature of reality is attained with its concomitant, a new perceptual reality." In a

500-word abstract, that constitutes nagging repetition, giving the impression the dissertation not only *falls into* the emic category (whatever it may prove to be) but *treats* the category itself in theoretical discussion. As we all know by now, such an impression is false; *Sorcery* is only *Ixtlan*, and the word *emic* appears nowhere in the text. Nor could I find it in dictionaries of English, Latin, Greek, philosophy, social science, or anthropology. Evidently the author was at pains to signal the holders of some special code book, but who were they? I asked around. Nobody knew. *Emic*, one grad student recalled, formed a dichotomy with *etic*. Emmic-eetic I said, eemic-ettic she corrected, okay I said eemic-ettic but what do they mean? She couldn't remember—something about two different research strategies. At last a letter came from an impeccable ethnographic warrior I call Professor Volpe, who wrote as follows:

"In the early 1960s, a fad called 'ethnoscience' was born at Harvard, flourished briefly in many parts, then died almost everywhere outside of California. A lot of hot air was expended when the cognitive anthropologists, cultivating the fad of ethnoscience, accused the rest of us of not getting inside the native's head before interpreting his culture. The terms *emic* and *etic* (coined from *phonemic* and *phonetic* by linguist Kenneth Pike in the 1950s) were used respectively to distinguish ethnography that attempted to adopt the native's conception of reality from ethnography that relied on whatever personal or theoretical conception of reality the ethnographer might have brought with him into the field. At Columbia, Marvin Harris argued against doctrinaire emicism; Columbia and Michigan have been consistently pro-etic. Since they were mainly linguists (who are not as a class known for psychological insight) the emic anthropologists proceeded to get inside the native's head by collecting his names for things. After countless boring articles had been published on the native terms for firewood, plants, and roofing materials, Gerald Berreman started an interdepartmental row by telling a large gathering of emicists at Berkeley they had been practicing 'anemic anthropology.' I don't know how Castaneda got away with calling *Journey to Ixtlan* 'an emic account,' since it fails to meet the usual emic criteria of scientific rigor and narrow scope, but he certainly got farther into his native informant's head than most of us do. Of course, if don Juan was already in *his* head to begin with, he didn't have far to go to share the native reality, did he?"

Hunting up Harris's book in the library I found a chapter on

"Emics and Etics," which took Kenneth Pike to task for treating etics unjustly. To give the gist of Harris's argument, the fieldworker who starts out with no conceptual framework won't be able to find his way to the village; the one who can find the village takes his world view along with him and applies it when he arrives. "Despite brave talk . . . very few 'emicists' . . . trust the native's account of his inner life." Pike's procedure in particular cannot carry the anthropologist to "a valley of inner subjective truth," however much he may long for it.

First the emickers chastise the ettickers for beating about the native's head; then the ettickers retort that the emickers talk a lot about indigenocranial penetration but haven't the foggiest how to do it. If Castaneda wanted to join this argument on the side of the emickers, and show them how to live up to their ideals, he did a great job. Over and over Carlos-Etic caricatures the arrogant, ethnocentric fieldworker trying to wrestle an academic strait jacket onto nature's noble Indian. While Carlos-Emic crosses his eyes at gullies and bushes, watches his hands in dreams, luxuriates in the warmth of magic leaves, grinds up plants that have no names, and practices the gait of power, Carlos-Etic plagues don Juan with geneology and kinship charts, and is told, "Don't waste your time with that crap"; regrets the Indian's "coarse ways"; condescends to acknowledge his social equality and is called a professors' intellectual pimp; lectures him on the meteorology of wind and is told such opinions are "pure crap"; arrives in the land of saguaro and sage wearing a three-piece business suit, fears he will look ridiculous with a knapsack over his jacket, and is invited to wear his jacket over the knapsack, so as to seem only a hunchback; calls don Juan's chitchat with a magic deer "sort of dumb" and receives the answer: "What did you expect? I'm an Indian." When the allegoric Mazatecs offer food to the eternally homeward-bound Genaro, Carlos-Etic interrupts the story to ask whether Mazatecs customarily deny having food. Interviewed for *Harper's Magazine*, Castaneda-Emic accuses Carlos-Etic of asking: "What could a greasy old Indian teach *me*, a man of science?" On this view "A Structural Analysis" is Carlos-Etic-Procrustes cutting and fitting don Indian to a very short bed of mere logical coherence. Carlos-Total not only inhabits parallel universes and manifests incompatible personalities but takes both sides in methodological arguments.

As I perused "Emics and Etics," a feeling of *déjà vu* enveloped me. Harris quoted Edward Sapir, a giant in the history of linguistic anthropology: "It is impossible to say what an individual is doing unless we have tacitly accepted the essentially arbitrary modes of interpretation that social tradition is constantly suggesting to us from the very moment of our birth."

"From the very moment of our birth"? That had an oddly familiar ring. Going back through *Journey to Ixtlan* I found a passage I had underlined on the first reading: ". . . what I held in mind as the world at hand was merely a description of the world; a description that had been pounded into me from the moment I was born." The statement had struck me not (I assume) because I *saw* that I should later read its counterpart in Sapir's 50-year-old essay but because it marked an extreme position in the environmentalist-linguistic theory of child development, conjuring up visions of pedagogical parents leaning over the bassinet from either side, instructing the neonate in how to cognize his mothers face. *Oye, Carlitos! Mira la cara de tu Mamá. Aquí los ojos. Aquí la nariz. Aquí la boca. . . .*

Further reading persuaded me Sapir had rhetorically overshot and did not mean to impose the linguistic model so literally. "We must regretfully admit," he granted, "that the rebel who tampers with the truths of mathematics or physics or chemistry is not really the same kind of rebel as the one who plays ninepins with custom. . . ." (in which statement I assume the hard sciences stand for our non-social environment). For Sapir, the physical and social realms were not *equally* affected by language-mediated interpersonal agreement. The Indian don, in contrast, whose epistemology was strongly influenced by the concrete thinking of his alter ego, don Indian, cheerfully applied the same rule of social agreement, in the same degree, to perceptions of mountains or mothers' faces as to conceptions of impeccability or pimpishness.

"We are making this room," he told the befuddled Carlos. "Every one of us knows the *doing* of rooms. . . . We have all been taught to agree about *doing*. You don't have any idea of the power that that agreement brings with it." In the *social* world, Sapir had written, 'existence' is determined by consensus. Customs are what people say they are. Castaneda congealed Sapir's fluid customs into adobe walls much as he had materialized Sapir's hyperbole of infant pedagogy. By the flickering light of such abstruse transformations do we detect the sorcerer's silvery web shining across our path and learn what hoary spinner is helping him entangle us.

When Sapir talked about the social world, he put 'existence' in quotes, thus distinguishing a reality based on convention from a harder reality more broadly based on shared physical and physiological givens not so easily transformable by what people in one culture or another might say about them. Though don Juan usually scorns Sapir's physical-social distinction, he occasionally acknowledges an ordinary reality beyond a shaman's visionary control. Carlos flies through the sky "as a man who has taken the weed," not as the birds do, and his body remains prostrate "in the bushes." Though a sorcerer may go to the moon, he can't bring home a bag of rocks. Having made his own concession to rocks, Sapir asserted his *social* version of the separate reality. "Any individual," he said, "has cultural definitions which do not apply to all the members of his group, which even, in specific instances, apply to him alone." A certain Two Crows denied the existence of a custom well vouched for by other Omahas. His disagreement with his fellow Indians was not pathological or illusory but only personal and separate. "He had a special kind of rightness [and] if we think long enough about [it] we shall have to admit that in some sense Two Crows is never wrong." Don Juan told Carlos the world was whatever we perceive, however we choose to perceive it. For him, perception was an act of the will. The separate physical reality was as clear to the Sonoran One Crow as the separate social reality to the Omaha Two Crows.

So far we have found a methodological cause for Castaneda to take up and have seen Carlos-Emic skillfully promoting it while Carlos-Etic failed as devil's advocate. Paul Riesman said as much in his review, though he did not guess Carlos-Etic had failed deliberately. Our immediate question, however, is not what Castaneda was doing but what the professors were doing. How did a fabrication like The Teachings, with its Yaquiless Yaqui, its gratuitous Spanish, its anonymous actors, its vague setting, its parodic analysis, and its spurious subtitle, attract faculty sponsors who would urge the University Press to publish it. "When [the book] was originally submitted to us," a Press spokesman declared, "we realized the treatment was unorthodox, but all the eminent anthropologists we consulted recommended publication." Those eminent consultants must have been rather carefully selected. Stranger still, how did Journey to Ixtlan, easily shown to be logically incompatible with The Teachings, get by as a dissertation after so many critics had said Castaneda was writing fiction?

Did the genius dazzle his less gifted mentors? Did the Dreamer hypnotize the Learned Elders or cast a spell on them? Brilliant, magnetic, thaumaturgic though he is, I cannot believe Castaneda could outfox, mesmerize, or bewitch half-a-dozen tenured doctors of philosophy 13 years running. If he couldn't fool La Barre, Leach, Harris, Hsu, Ochoa, or Oates, who bore no grave responsibility for critically judging his work, it defies common sense to suppose he could bamboozle five dissertation signers and one or two other faculty members who did bear such responsibility. Confidently rejecting the rumor that Castaneda duped his professors, I do suspect he seduced them. Very likely they were not sure and preferred not to ask just whose hats he was pulling his metaphysical *taabum* out of, but they must have known they were dealing with an illusionist rather than a fieldworker. Why did they wish to foster the illusion?

"What was going through the academic mind?" I asked several professors. "After many years on campus," one replied, "I have come to the conclusion there is no academic mind." "I would rather not comment," said another, "since I am a firm believer in departmental autonomy." Well, so am I. Academic freedom is a cornerstone of the inquiring society—but what is academic freedom? Is it a right to carry on without answering to anyone? Certainly not. Academic freedom is a right of scholars to answer to their colleagues rather than to administrators, politicians, vigilantes, or gadflies like me, a right established to promote the growth of knowledge through the freest exercise of individual initiative consistent with standards upheld by the community of scholars, a right that carries a duty to communicate assumptions, procedures, and reasoning fully and clearly to that community. I would not for a minute challenge the right of Castaneda's committee to doctor him in anthropology for writing a fantasy, provided they said that was what they were doing and invited their colleagues to judge their action. As it turned out, the colleagues rendered judgment uninvited, and it was far from favorable, though it might have been favorable if the committee had come forth at some point—dare we still hope for that to happen?—with a frank, coherent explanation. "Waiving red tape" for a "native genius" is neither frank nor explanatory; it is artful dodging. If Castaneda's "truth as a witness" was "not in question," why wasn't it? Not, in 1973, because he was above suspicion but obviously because questioning his truth might have elicited some embarrassing answers. How do learned elders get themselves in such a pickle?

The theory I propose here can be tested against the special information insiders possess. Though I lack that information, I am sure the theory is worth testing, and I hope someone will test it. To wit: Certain schismatic culturologists at UCLA, feeling powerless to persuade their theoretical opponents by the tedious process of rational disputation, feeling shunted onto a sidetrack of scholastic history, feeling oppressed by the academic majority, feeling at the same time the surging rebellion of the 1960s, the boiling upheaval of dissent, greening, and expanding consciousness, suddenly finding themselves challenged by a uniquely talented and picaresque accomplice, could simply not resist the temptation to pull a fast one on their opponents. They sanctified *The Teachings*, spurious subtitle, parodic analysis, and all, not because they thought it was ethnography or even a factual memoir, but because they felt it would be a well-deserved kick in the pants for certain ethnocentric, arrogant, etic mossbacks. On this view, University publication of *The Teachings* as ethnography was a private joke on, about, among, and for culturologists. Laymen were not supposed to get in on it.

The University Press had bigger ideas. *Teachings* would appeal to youth, especially in the drug culture. Perhaps the book would persuade acid droppers and speed freaks more discipline was needed on the road to enlightenment, but disciplinary or not it would sell like penny uppers. Failing to recognize "A Structural Analysis" as part of the story, some directors of the Press wanted to delete it. Castaneda was not about to give up his devil's advocate; the unreadable parody stayed, a spokesman confided, "not at our insistence but the author's." The subtitle, too, was "the work of the author." It was needed to distinguish don Juan from the horny Spanish misogynist, a former editor assured me. What it did was expand the market. *A Yaqui Way of Knowledge* not only announced new wisdom from nature's nobleman but introduced a kind of red man no one had ever met—I mean, who in 1968 knew anything about Yaquis? A few dusty ethnographers in Arizona. It was a marketing masterstroke.

University Press editions generally run pretty small; *The Teachings* had an oversized first printing and was advertised as "nothing less than a revelation." The advance copy that hit the *New York Times Book Review* trailed a long fuse. The reviewer placed his charges well: young anthropologist, Indian sorcerer, peyote and other hallucinogenic plants, power over demons, science confronted by magic, spirituality stunted by rationalism, moving personal experience, turn-on, terror, danger, ecstasy, sinister *guru*, nervous breakdown. A Ballantine Books executive read the review, called the University Press, and the fuse was lit. April 1969 saw Ballantine's mass edition explode the private prank into a national fad. In three years *The Teachings* sold 300,000 copies, transforming an obscure graduate student into a pop-litt, quasi-scientific, neomystical cult figure, as he pressed on to publish his second, more novelesque adventure and to talk about his third.

Back at the village the elders realized they had let loose a monster. Though he had done nothing that would ordinarily merit such advancement, the Dreaming Dissertator made no secret of his aspiration to doctorhood. The pranksters had three choices. They could repudiate *The Teachings*, claiming Castaneda had deceived them, which would make them look like fools. They could boldly admit their prank, which would set off an endless professional wrangle, wherein they would suffer sorely, and which might provoke administrative reprisals. Or they could stonewall, thumbing a collective nose at critics, handing the prodigy his scroll, and closing the village gate behind him. Of three bad choices, the last was least.

It might be thought Castaneda's degree would secure his place in the world of the professors. The opposite is true. It transported him forever. "I can no longer be an integral part of that world," he said to Gwyneth Cravens. Between doctorhood and professorship yawns a chasm wide and deep. Prospective junior professors whose theses are known or suspected to be hoaxes will compete with difficulty against sober, earnest candidates whose work is conventional and whose appointment will invite no ridicule or censure. If the Dreamer made an ass of the University, the University got even by making him invisible, at least within the grove of Academe. The transparent doctor must have cried all the way to the bank; at 16-thousand copies a week, who needs students or committee assignments?

Could no one have held the ethnoscientific toboggan back from its perilous plunge? "What about committee members who felt misgivings?" I asked a learned elder of a neighboring tribe. "They may have used the whiteball system," he replied. Whiteballing, I learned, was the opposite of blackballing, where one negative vote excludes a candidate from a private club. In whiteballing, one positive vote outweighs all negative votes. Whiteballing professors live in a world of mutual backscratching; when you are scratching somebody's back, you are in no position to step on his toes. If a professor with status or prestige sponsors a dubious candidate, other professors do not voice their objections loud enough to prevent the candidate's advancement. "I have been quite embarrassed at some of the people who have gotten through this way," my informant said, "and I would guess one or two members of Castaneda's committee were pretty uncomfortable about what they were doing. I understand somebody asked him in his final oral, 'You don't really mean you became a crow do you, Carlos?' 'Oh yes,' he says, 'I was a crow. I flew.'"

Who whiteballed the man who had been a crow? Thus far I have not given actual names. One reason is that my theory of what happened at UCLA is only a theory, while names are facts. Another is that I am not sure how to assign individual responsibility for what was done. A third is that the responsible persons have been sufficiently embarrassed by now to satisfy anyone's Calvinistic cravings. If despite all this I now mention Professor Harold Garfinkel, UCLA sociologist and signer of Castaneda's dissertation, it is because he has already been identified by *Time* as Castaneda's thesis supervisor, nominated by UC San Diego psychiatry professor Arnold Mandell as Castaneda's putative sponsor, and described by MIT political scientist Christopher Schaefer as Castaneda's advisor and a member of "a very small group of social scientists who are working in an area called ethno-methodology which is an extension and elaboration of phenomenology," a description that echoes Professor Volpe's recollections of the "ethnoscientists."

Some years ago, Mandell endured an arduous post-doctoral apprenticeship under Garfinkel, whom he later recognized as his own don-Juan-in-the-mind, an academic rebel who held that social scientists found no truth in nature, but fabricated all. Mandell suspected that in making Castaneda rewrite an intended thesis three times Garfinkel had imposed his ethnographic nihilism so ruthlessly that the wily graduate student had determined to go him one better, to "outgarfinkel Garfinkel," to prepare a beautifully wrapped empty package, a bogus thesis, a fake ethnography, which would achieve continuity and a sense of reality, thereby demonstrating the student's capacity to manipulate ethnomethodologic tools, without contradicting the master's teaching that all reality in social science was manufactured by social scientists. "It has to be the only way to work with this scrambler of tenets," Mandell wrote.

In suggesting Garfinkel *forced* Castaneda to tell tall tales, I think Mandell went a step too far. If Carlos met don Juan in the summer of 1960, and Margaret Castaneda heard about it shortly thereafter, when Castaneda still had two years to go as an undergraduate, the tales must have begun to grow tall long before any thesis supervisor could have applied any pressure. Seeing the didactic relationship as symbiotic rather than exploitative, I suspect the two men found each other perfect partners, whose respective needs, interests, and talents were mutually sustaining. It may have been a beautiful collaboration.

Having piled nihilism on emicism, as the Navajos piled Pelion on Ossa to escape the flood Coyote heedlessly brought upon the Third World, we have climbed up finally out of the bog of speculation onto the firm ground of fact again. Walter Goldschmidt, then chairman of the UCLA anthropology department, conspicuously legitimized *The Teachings* in a laudatory Foreword whose first paragraph had only seven words: "This book is both ethnography and allegory." Let's take ethnography first.

Employing unmistakably concrete terms, Goldschmidt placed the fieldwork squarely in the ordinary reality. Castaneda's "interviews" with don Juan "were initiated" while he was a student of anthropology at UCLA. We are indebted to him for "reporting to us the details of his experiences," through which he was "guided" by don Juan's "subtle manipulations," with "the aid of . . . peyote, datura, and mushrooms." If, writing in 1967, Goldschmidt felt any doubts about whether Castaneda had actually done the fieldwork, he evidently gave Castaneda the benefit of those doubts.

Were the don Juan interviews ethnography? Spicer and others would say no, while Castaneda had already disclaimed any "intention . . . to determine his precise cultural milieu," but Goldschmidt said yes. What did he mean by that? Castaneda (he wrote) "demonstrates the essential skill of the good ethnographer—the capacity to enter into an alien world." Perhaps he meant to limit Castaneda's "ethnography" to his demonstration of a *skill*, which others could apply in cultural settings. "Ethnography" stretches to include the bare demonstration of an applicable technique, but we can still recognize it.

What about "allegory"? In Greek it means "speaking otherwise than one seems to speak." In English it means "describing
a subject under the guise of some other subject." If *The Teachings* is allegory, the common meaning of that word compels us
to suppose the book is not what it seems to be (a report of
fieldwork) but something else (an imitation of reporting, a fairy
tale about fieldwork). Goldschmidt's first paragraph should
then say: "This book seems to be ethnography (in a broad
sense), but actually it is an allegoric tale with important implications for ethnography." That would be both true and plain.
As it stands, the paragraph is misleading nonsense. Do eminent
professors write misleading nonsense? Hardly ever confined to
seven words.

Further study of Goldschmidt's graceful but ambiguous little essay persuaded me that when he said "allegory" he meant
"analogy." Now, of course, an allegory *is* a kind of analogy, but
to write "allegory" when you mean "analogy" is to be misun-
derstood by just about everybody. For one terrifying moment I
suspected Goldschmidt had been taking spoofing lessons from
McCoy and the Cactus Conjurors, but then it occurred to me
that social-science intellectuals live on the fringe of the English language indulging the hideous vice of jargon. Perhaps in
certain dingy academic corners "allegory" regularly stands in
the stead of "analogy." *Nagual* preserve me from such dens of
depravity!

Having broken Goldschmidt's code, let's see what he was
talking about. I believe he meant to say this: Any world we
continuously experience is only a cultural construct, a special
way of looking at things that is determined by our cultural
background. Any such culture-determined world is not the real
world but only an orderly and fairly stable representation of the
real world. It is an analogue of reality. An analogy to reality. An
"allegory" of reality, if you will. (I won't—but never mind.)
When we have known only one such analogue, we believe it is
the only one there is, but Castaneda and don Juan have helped
us to see there are many such analogic worlds, and by seeing
more than one, we can sometimes, if we are lucky, just for an
instant, catch a fleeting glimpse of the absolutely real world
that lies beyond our cultural constructs.

Joseph Chilton Pearce chided Goldschmidt for imagining
that one *really* real world stands behind some *imperfectly* real
worlds we (or sorcerers) habitually see (or *see*). While I quite
agree that Goldschmidt fell into a fallacy here (which I discuss

in Chapter Seven) I recognize it as don Juan's fallacy and appropriate for the Foreword. Though I think he was fair to don Juan, Goldschmidt's peculiar choice of words and failure to define the words he chose booby-trapped both him and the reading public. In two shakes of the Coyote's tall tale, the anthropological establishment in the august person of Edmund Leach dumped a heavy load of skeptical criticism on the Yaqui Way of Knowledge. Re-read today, after more and wilder versions of the story have appeared, after the ethnography has been called not skill but hoax, after the allegory has been labelled not phenomenal analogy but blatant fiction, Goldschmidt's first paragraph—"This book is both ethnography and allegory"—seems to say that anthropological reports based on fieldwork are not to be preferred to or even distinguished from those conceived in dreams—a message the writer can hardly have meant to convey.

Noting with relief that Goldschmidt five years later refrained from signing Castaneda's best-selling dissertation, I am inclined to count him, like don Juan's mother, a casualty in Castaneda's allegoric Yaqui Wars. Another and more obviously innocent victim was the Library of Congress, now approaching its second decade classifying the don Juan books as Yaqui history rather than fiction. Don Indian must have "roared, kicked, cried, coughed and choked with laughter" when the Indian don told him the cataloging data in *Tales of Power* gives no birthdate for Castaneda, who surely had one, but gives a birthdate for don Juan, who surely had none.

Why has no anthropologist complained in public about what happened at UCLA? I can see several reasons. Like other professionals, the anthropologists prefer to do their laundry in private. Again, should Castaneda enter the furious competition for junior faculty appointments, his anomalous career would handicap him severely. Third, since anthropologists generally do not recognize his books as ethnography, and since the main ethnographic claim was confined to one subtitle (the marketing misnomer, *A Yaqui Way of Knowledge*) which the author thrice repudiated, it doesn't strictly matter to anthropologists whether the books are fact or fiction. Fourth, fictive or not, the don Juan books uniquely illustrate an ideal of fieldwork many anthropologists want to teach. Last but not least, Castaneda's books have swelled the rolls of undergraduate anthropology at a time when the academic market is failing, and prudent instructors prefer to correct their students' enthusiastic misconceptions diplomatically, without biting the Coyote that feeds anthropologists.

Condemned for violating a rule (don Genaro told us) a warrior admits he has run out of ordinary time, thanks those who have taken care of him and helped him on his way, says goodbye to his friends atop the barren mesa, and walks away from them down the slope toward the woods to the west, as they raise their weapons and keep him in their sights. If he loses his head and starts to run, or if he cries out in his anguish, he will be cut down by an unknown sharpshooter, but if he walks slowly and steadily, eyes straight ahead, never stumbling or turning to look back, never questioning his condemnation or challenging his expulsion, his former associates recognizing his dignity, admiring his bravery, and appreciating his loyalty to the code, will hold their fire so that he can reach the woods alive. His only chance to escape execution lies in impeccable conduct. Once in the western woods he must remain there, waiting without hope of forgiveness or reward, alone but not lonely, completing certain unspecified, power-storing tasks. Someday perhaps he will be allowed to return and rejoin his comrades on the high ground.

Recently Walter Goldschmidt explained his characterization of *The Teachings* as an "allegory." "I meant that the book has a moral," he said. This explanation makes some sense, at last, of his calling the book "both ethnography and allegory"—though the statement is still misleading, since the book is not ethnography in any case. Ethnography is both cultural and factual, while don Juan's lore arises from no identified culture, certainly not from Yaqui culture, and the old man himself is by all reasonable tests not factual but imaginary. By finding a moral in *The Teachings*, Goldschmidt *rendered* the book an allegory, just as one might take the sinking of the *Titanic* to be an allegory of man's fate or of God's mysterious ways to man. This would be a *reader's allegory*, implying neither that the *Titanic* was an imaginary ship nor that reports of the sinking were written to convey a moral. Reports written to convey a moral would likely depart from accuracy, since intentional allegorizing conflicts with factual reporting in both purpose and technique. By using the bare term "allegory," which connotes writer's intent more strongly than reader's interpretation, Goldschmidt unwittingly but correctly told his readers *The Teachings* was a *writer's allegory*—which, when closely examined, is seen to offer a tract on methodology and metaphysics under the guise of a field report, thereby disqualifying itself as factual reporting. An inadvertently correct "allegory" contradicts a misleading "ethnography," making nonsense of "both ethnography and allegory."—RdeM 1978.

The *Disagi-ki* is an evil mythical bird, so small it is not visible to the eye. It is owned by sorcerers, men of ill repute, wizards, or witches. Only the owner or a shaman has the power to see a *Disagi-ki*. The Tarahumara believe such a bird can be sent by its master to any house to make someone sick. To do this, the bird is supposed to land on the food, take a bite, leave its excrement on the food, and return to its owner. If a shaman can catch one of these birds and throw it on the fire, the owner will become very sick. A shaman who can "see" the bird can drive it away by throwing powdered chile pepper into the air, as the bird does not like chile, which symbolizes fire. Further, the owner of a bird may sometimes be spotted, as he never touches chile.

When a person suffers from nose-bleeding and bilious dizziness, one of these birds has been at work. The man's soul has been stolen or eaten up while he was sleeping with his mouth open. To bring the soul back, the shaman boils four pieces of oak bark, three silver *pesos*, and three or four iron nails in a pot. A mouthful or two of this medicine will restore the soul. Another cure is to eat some chile and place some food outside the house for the bird.

—I. Thord-Gray
Tarahumara Dictionary

5. A MAN OF NOVELS

A warrior treats the world as an endless mystery. . . . stupendous, awesome . . . unfathomable. . . . The art of a warrior is to balance the terror of being a man with the wonder of being a man.

The quality which had enchanted me in his imaginative works turned out to be the quality of the real universe, the divine, magical, terrifying and ecstatic reality in which we all live.

The writer whose imagination enchanted Clive Staples Lewis was not Carlos Castaneda but the 19th-century allegorist whose dialogue between man and raven I quote at the end of Chapter Nine. As I trace the geneology and kinship charts, I find George MacDonald's *Phantastes* and *Lilith* to be direct literary ancestors of the don Juan books. MacDonald, Charles Williams, or C.S. Lewis would doubtless have been repelled by Castaneda's impersonal and loveless *nagual* but would instantly have felt at home among the actors in his tale—the naïve, persistent seeker, the well-meaning common folk blind to supernatural signs, the good and evil wizards and witches, the familiar spirits, and the benevolent talking animals. Those three great religious fantasists would have rejoiced in Carlos's longing for illumination and his tireless search for transcendental reality. They would, in Christian charity, have hailed him as a lost sheep bleating to be rescued from ancient and modern heresies and from self-imposed spiritual exile.

In 1956, during Castaneda's studies of creative writing at Los Angeles City College, Lewis published his last and most mysterious novel, a complex, obscure fantasy which like the don Juan books can be read as often as one likes without failing to yield new meaning. *Till We Have Faces* is the bitter polemical memoir of Orual, Queen of Glome, ruler of a dismal land where people worship the goddess Ungit, a powerful black stone without head or hands or face, a divine lump like a Peruvian *huaca*. Defiant at the end of her long and harrowing life, Orual dares to accuse Ungit and her son the mountain god of hateful injustice, writing she says in Greek so that when the next rare traveler from the Greeklands loses his way and wanders into Glome he will read her accusation and carry it back with him to where men speak openly of the gods and do not fear to judge their acts.

Sadly searching the mountains (she writes) for her younger sister Psyche, abandoned as a sacrificial bride for the mountain god, expecting to find only her bones, picked and bleached, Orual meets instead a laughing, smooth-limbed woman, with radiant face and eyes like stars. As the sisters sit together on the ground eating berries and drinking water from a spring, Psyche recalls how the temple girls at the bidding of her father gave her a drug to prepare her for the sacrifice, how she quickly entered a dream in which she was carried on a litter up into the mountains, where a bird-headed man bound her standing to a tree and left her alone, where she suffered thirst in the glaring sun and ached to lie down, where beasts gathered round her and a lynx sniffed at her feet, after which a shapeless change from within summoned a rainstorm, and wind that roared but softly all round her, seeming to lift her, but when she saw the wind he was a god, and she felt ashamed of being only a mortal before him, who took her in his beautiful arms which burned but gave no pain and pulled her painlessly up out of the iron girdle in which the priest had bound her and carried her into the air far above the ground and whirled her away.

"You must have been dreaming," Orual exclaims.

"And if it was a dream," counters Psyche, "how do you think I came here? More likely everything that happened to me before this was a dream."

Though Psyche saw the wind god only for an instant, as one sees in a lightning flash, she knew and trusted him from that moment forward and felt no fear of sailing with him through the sky. Presently he set her down in front of a great house like none before conceived, told her it was her own, and bade her enter as his bride. There unseen women welcomed her with wind-like voices, fed her and bathed her and put her to bed, where in the night her husband came to be with her.

Orual interrupts, saying she can bear no more, for if the story is true she has been mistaken about reality all her life and must begin anew. She begs Psyche to show her the wonderful palace. Psyche rises and invites her to go in, urging her not to be afraid at anything she may see or hear. Orual asks if it is far.

"Far to where?" says Psyche.

"To the palace, to this god's house."

"What do you mean?" Psyche begins to tremble.

"I mean," Orual is gripped by her own uncomprehending fear, "where is the palace? How far do we have to go to reach it?"

Psyche cries out sharply, stares white-faced into her sister's eyes, says, "But *this* is it, Orual! It is here! You are standing on the stairs of the great gate."

Then do the desperate women confront each other across the widening gulf that separates their two realities, Orual commanding Psyche to stop, to admit they are alone in a desolate mountain valley, Psyche turning to show Orual the shining palace walls, pleading with her to touch them, to beat her head against them if need be, Orual accusing Psyche of pretending, of making herself believe, but knowing she herself is lying to hold back the horror of that dread place, where even priests dare not go, so high in the mountains, so near to the gods, where a hundred things she cannot see may surround her, where the palace of the wind god may be standing before her, seen by Psyche but unseen by Orual. And with the horror of that thought (she writes) "came inconsolable grief. For the world had broken in pieces and Psyche and I were not in the same piece."

"We spun through the air with such speed and force that I couldn't see," said don Genaro. "Spinning with your ally," don Juan told Carlos, "will change your idea of the world. . . . and when that changes, the world itself changes." "After my encounter with the ally," Genaro said, "nothing was real any more."

Recognizing Castaneda's first two books as fiction, Joyce Carol Oates compared his story-telling unfavorably with that of Jorge Luis Borges and doubted (for the moment) she would read a third. *Time*, in contrast, found don Juan's world "as thoroughly articulated as . . . Faulkner's Yoknapatawpha County." Ridiculous! retorted novelist William Kennedy; when he gets down to concrete details, Castaneda is as clumsy as a brick mason touching up the gold leaf on the Taj Mahal; his fluid but gawky dialogue can be tolerated only if you don't think it is supposed to be realistic; his descriptions of ordinary activities are thin and repetitious; wading through his silly prose you grow to like him not for his literary skill but for his intense commitment and mountainous labor. Well, people have very different reactions to things. Thomas Wolfe's novels were called both the greatest American prose ever written and bombastic apocalyptic delirium. According to *Time's* Robert Hughes, Carlos's meeting with don Juan was "one of the most fortunate literary encounters since Boswell was introduced to Dr. Johnson," while according to William Kennedy many of Castaneda's passages would get him kicked out of any decent creative-writing class.

"If we define Literature as an art whose medium is words, then certainly [he] has no place in its first rank—perhaps not even in its second. [Occasionally his wisdom burns away] the baser elements in his style. . . . but he does not maintain this level for long. The texture of his writing as a whole is undistinguished, at times fumbling." I would call that a fair appraisal of Castaneda's writing, except for the fact that it was not written about him but about one of his allegorist forebears, George MacDonald, by another, C.S. Lewis. Badly as MacDonald often wrote, Lewis judged him a master of mythmaking, and myths, he said, have a life of their own, independent of their makers and of the words their makers use. Unless I am quite mistaken, don Juan will outlive not only his maker but the many critics who have rightly said his maker was not worth noticing as a literary stylist.

When the enthusiastic Joseph Pearce called Castaneda "the principal psychological, spiritual, and literary genius of recent generations," he said something triply absurd, but his absurdity carried a sound implication: don Juan the myth has come to stay. Pearce devoted many pages to comparing don Juan, an actual person, with Jesus, another actual person. Various earnest psychotherapists have hailed don Juan, an actual person, as a source of improved therapeutic concepts and techniques. Parodists have offered us burlesque *brujos*, thereby acknowl-

edging don Juan as a mythic figure who challenges the powers
of parodists to destroy him in the trial by guffaw. It is clear to
me that all such assaults must fail no matter how funny they
may be; don Juan is too big for burlesque, too strong for caricature; he brushes off parodists like hundred-micron gnats.

Though I am quite sure don Juan was invented by Castaneda,
I have not hesitated to write about him as though I knew him
personally, which of course I do, as anyone does who has
learned the Yaquiless Way of Knowledge. A few pages back, for
example, I said don Juan would not despise his apprentice's
need for the controlled folly of worldly recognition. While we
always risk error when speculating about the motives or
hypothetical acts of others, I feel at least as confident in saying
what don Juan would not despise as in saying what my editor or
publisher would not despise, because I know don Juan better
than I know them.

Don Juan lives! That is his inventor's prime achievement on
this earth. Though an undistinguished wordsmith, Castaneda
is an able, dedicated mythmaker and may well take his place
with MacDonald and Williams, whose language was an
adequate though not elegant vehicle for their allegories, but
not with Lewis, who was a literary artist as well as a master of
myths.

Beyond the looming of don Juan, when does Castaneda rise
above mediocrity? Notably, as several critics have remarked, in
his fable of Genaro's perpetual journey to Ixtlan, a retelling of
the universal folktale we might call "Sorcerers Can't Go
Home" but the Japanese called "Urashima Taro," Washington
Irving called *Rip Van Winkle*, and C.S. Lewis called *Till We
Have Faces*. Almost any literary version is better than Castaneda's, yet he does evoke the poignancy we look for in that
age-old story of the impetuous seeker or unlucky wanderer
irredeemably touched by the gods, of the sorcerer or innocent
suddenly privileged to look on hidden wonders but ever after
deprived of the joys men find in ordinary affairs.

Other high points in Castaneda's writing include some of his
comic episodes and many of his dignified or vulgar aphorisms:
The twilight is the crack between the worlds, There are no
survivors on this earth, Death is our eternal companion, To die
alone is not to die in loneliness, We are the prisoners of power,
Crap on the roof with your ass on the ground (perhaps a
mesoamerican or Hispano-Peruvian version of the old-world
Leap to the roof), Attacking a lion with your farts, When Ge-

naro shits the mountains tremble. These epigrammatic fungi are savored all the better if we brush off the occasional bits of stylistic manure that cling to them: A masterful caricature, A mountain of glass shreds, Don Juan placed each rock about a foot apart in two crevices, He sprung to his feet.

Understandably piqued, Kennedy called Castaneda a literary grand larcenist for peddling fantasies as facts in a market where fiction was hard to sell, then credited him with "the skills of a superb but flawed novelist" for artfully novelizing a series of philosophy lectures. Like Agatha Christie planting clues, Castaneda sows the seeds of our belief early in the season and waits patiently for them to bloom. Not many readers remember Carlos's first meeting with don Genaro, the unnamed Mazatec Indian who showed up three hours after don Juan threatened to use the nonordinary copy of *The Teachings* as ordinary toilet paper. That crucial off-stage meeting, in which don Juan recognized Genaro as Carlos's spiritual benefactor, was not mentioned again for 73 pages, was not explained for 755.

Unlike Agatha Christie, Castaneda does not hesitate to mislead us unfairly, as when he deftly palmed the dates on which 'la Catalina' scared the *buita* out of him. He mystifies us with doctrinal contradictions, purportedly don Juan's tricks to trap a reluctant pupil, but often obviously the result of the author's continuing education. As Elsa First remarked, his understanding grows from book to book (which growth helped us to confuse calendar with narrative time when the backdated *Ixtlan* came along).

Accomplished story-tellers pepper their tales with names and attributes. Castaneda's moonshine is watered down with anonymous and featureless plants, animals, places, and persons. Good old Nogales Bill for instance knew don Juan before Carlos did, but that didn't get him a last name or an occupation. (Outside the text but still inside the story he and Carlos went to Hollywood High together, or as further facts came out to Cajamarca High.) Carlos picked up some amusing mannerisms from a certain German Sinologist who lacked both name and institutional affiliation. (Outside the text he took some wild celery to be analyzed by a famous but nameless UCLA botanist. An unidentified student of Husserl's gave him the philosopher's very own paperweight.) "Oh, I am a bullshitter!" Castaneda "cackled" to Sandra Burton, "Oh, how I love to throw the bull around!" Those impulsive, careless conversational effluents seep often untreated into the bullslinger's prose. "With astounding speed and skill" but with no specific materials or operations, don Juan assembles a trap having no particular structure and catches three rodents described only as "chubby" and "squirrel-like." He sings an idiotic Mexican song so comically that Carlos has to laugh, but not a line of it can be recalled. He suggests "a series of hilarious rhetorical exclamations" which remain forever buried in Carlos's Spanish field notes. Castaneda strokes us with a broad brush but his paint is thin.

The prisoner of power stands convicted also of felonious self-plagiarism, as in "The Gait of Power," a chapter of *Ixtlan* that closely parallels in mood and action Section 16 of *A Separate Reality*, Carlos in both episodes menaced by things that go bump in the night, fleeing through the chaparral, cowering in terror, or galvanized by unseen popguns as directionless as María Sabina's midnight percussions in Cayetano's house. Castaneda's volume-bridging cliff-hangers belong in soap opera. After ten years of gruelling study, May 1971 saw Carlos's car re-appearing from under a hat, Carlos conversing with a glowing coyote, and the world sustained by internal dialogue finally collapsing. "On that occasion," Castaneda wrote, "my apprenticeship came to an end." It was a thrilling climax, "a bona fide termination," a last exit by Carlos-Apprentice promising a quick entrance by the long-awaited Carlos-Sorcerer. Three months later, in the next book, Carlos-Apprentice was back, sitting once more at the master's feet, learning his lessons in the same old way. One typical Saturday morning in the Apollo Theater on Hollywood Boulevard I saw with my own two eyes a run-away covered wagon plunge over a cliff carrying the heroine of our weekly serial to certain doom. Seven days (less 30 minutes) later *that same wagon* swerved at the last second to save the lady and the story but left an audience of prepubescent rubes feeling shamefully abused. In those days hardly anybody had heard of a separate reality.

Castaneda's narrative skill appears when we realize the events in don Juan's desert are nobody's bedrock experiences but parables, metaphors, theoretical models, concretized conceptions, solidified abstractions. *Tales of Power* is a play based on Wittgenstein's theory, a pretty sloppy play which needs cutting and rehearsal but better than no play at all. To those who didn't know Wittgenstein had a theory it's a revelation, and Carlos or don Juan is a world teacher. If Castaneda is not the Shakespeare of metaphysics, at least he is the Neil Simon.

Outstanding for a lecturer if not for a fantasy writer, his imagination caters to a pedestrian market. Seldom does he drop his dusty cloak of pedantry to carry us on wondrous wings beyond the boundary of what we can conceive. Characteristically he borrows conventional images—glowing varmints floating bubbles, falling leaves, personal auras, translucent mountains—or flatly says the experience is ineffable.

"It was something, something, something . . . like nothing I can tell," stutters Genaro (ellipsis in the original). "It is hard to see on the other side of the boundary," says don Juan. "Neither you nor I will ever know what really took place at those times." Saying the *tonal* and the *nagual* are both inexplicable, don Juan stands on solid metaphysical ground—if that does not sound like thin ice—but he is only postulating a transcendent quality, not making us feel it. His *nagual* taps us lightly and lets go of us quickly; rarely does it grip us. If Castaneda had the power to wrench us across the ultimate boundary and hold us there, not letting us return to the world we think we understand but losing us on the other side—in a world that is by definition only an amazing counterfeit projected by the writer from this side onto a faceless void—he might rise into the company of another imperfect wordsmith, the fabulous David Lindsay, a mythopoeic paragon who rushed into the pseudo-*nagual* too fast and too far for his contemporaries to follow—and died forgotten. Determined not to be forgotten before he was remembered, Castaneda obeyed the schoolteacher's rule and met his pupils where they were. Seeking ancient wisdom or doors to other worlds, they were not likely to have much background in science, philosophy, or literature. Uninstructed native wit might be their only educational resource. The low state of popular learning, the durability of native wit, and the ubiquity of metaphysical hunger have brought commercial success if not critical acclaim to the Malibu mythmaker.

As we have seen in previous chapters, one of Castaneda's prime talents is an ability to find, select, transform, marshall, and present other people's ideas without letting the sources show. I have uncovered so many of these sources by now that I am beginning to wonder if anything at all can be correctly attributed to Castaneda. What a terrific subject for a UCLA doctoral dissertation! Before saying goodbye to the man of novels, let's look at a few more instructive examples, all of which are possible Castaneda sources, some of which seem to me quite certain.

In his creative-writing days, Castaneda greatly admired Aldous Huxley, a literary pioneer in hallucinogens and mysticism. Huxley's good southern-California friend and fellow literary mystic Gerald Heard wrote a fantasy about a man transported by music, dance, and the very structure of a cathedral into a nonordinary state in which he "saw the whole choir—not outlined in light—rather the shafting, arcading, capitals, spandrels, the springers, ribs, vaulting, bosses . . . transparent and, like an immense phosphorescent billow, glowing with an inherent flush that shone through the translucent mass." There is luminous structure for you, as well as palpable detail. Having thus "seen" the cathedral, Sylvester Shelbourne "felt the awful spasm of a creature suddenly made to sustain the pressure of two universes, its frail twofold nature the sole link between two primal energies. . . . Temporal and Eternal, for a moment I knew both, and for an instant sustained the anguish of belonging to neither." Shortly afterwards the seer is found dead. "One becomes a man of knowledge for a very brief instant," don Juan said, "but that moment . . . is enough."

The human aura, wrote William Walker Atkinson, is shaped like an egg. "To the psychic vision it appears to be 'streaked' by numerous fine lines extending like stiff bristles from the body outward. In normal health and vitality these 'bristles' stand out stiffly, while in cases of impaired vitality or poor health they droop like the soft hair on an animal, and in some cases present the appearance of a ruffled coat of hair, the several 'hairs' standing out in all directions. . . ." "Fibers, like white cobwebs," don Juan said, "Very fine threads that circulate from the head to the navel. Thus a man looks like an egg of circulating fibers. And his arms and legs are like luminous bristles, bursting out in all directions." After taking peyote, Heinrich Klüver wrote, one may see the cobweb figure, "coloured threads running together in a revolving center, the whole similar to a cobweb."

Though Atkinson's popular occult books were published by the dozen in Chicago, he used the pseudonym "Yogi Ramacharaka." When Castaneda's students at Irvine pointed out the parallel between don Juan's luminous egg and "Ramacharaka's" oval aura, Castaneda "made the intriguing speculation that American Indian sorcery might have originated in Asia. He reasoned that since it is generally accepted that the Indians came from Asia across the Bering Strait when it was still a land bridge, it might very well be that they brought their religious views along with them"—all the way from Siberia's great frozen Lake Mishighan. I like an apprentice who thinks on his feet.

Directed by don Juan, Carlos called 47 persons who appeared as luminous blobs. Each had a characteristic shape and color, some yellowish, some whitish. Don Genaro came in a golden bubble. A golden aura, "Ramacharaka" told us, betokens great intellectual attainment. "Dr. B. named different persons," Heinrich Klüver wrote. "Soon, thereafter, they appeared to stand in perceived space." Before Klüver's own peyote-buttoned eyes, a drawing of a head changed into a mushroom, a man in greenish velvet jumped into a deep chasm (as a naked Carlos's perception would leap into the abyss), and a strange animal turned into a piece of wood in horizontal position (as Carlos's supine monstrous bird-beaked mammal would turn into a burnt branch).

Human beings, speculated Joseph Bogen, may have two distinct minds, a propositional, speaking mind typically lateralized in the left brain, and in the right brain an appositional mind whose functions we can barely guess. In don Juan's terms, the left brain would speak about the *tonal*, the right brain would intuit the *nagual*. Why, then, does death stand on the left? Because the nerves that carry sensations cross over to the opposite side of the brain before reaching the perceptual areas. For the same anatomical reason, well known to former City College psychology students but not to stone-age wizards, the naguallian Genaro whispered into Carlos's left ear, the tonallian don Juan into his right.

Even the bemushroomed ethnobotanist felt his mind split, "the rational side continuing to reason and to observe the sensations that the other side is enjoying," but the grandest revelation Wasson wrote for don Juan (quoted here on page 145) describes one dazzling moment when great gates towered before him at the edge of the comprehensible world, ready to open and admit him into the presence of the ultimate, whence he might not have returned, for he sensed a willingness to be extinguished in the divine radiance waiting beyond. "There is a crack between the two worlds," don Juan told Carlos. "It opens and closes like a door. . . . like a monumental door, a crack that goes up and down." Sorcerers, like botanists, could approach that door only after their limbs had shaken and they had vomited several times. "Journeying into the unknown is very much like dying," don Juan said. "Once you have entered the unknown . . . you must decide whether or not to return."

"Who will relinquish this willingly?" asked the psilocybin user whose skull expanded into a bubble of perception. His co-author, having eaten María Sabina's mushrooms, soared into the sky like Carlos, became a child like apprentice Nestor, and conversed with Mazatecs in English as Mescalito would let Carlos hear Arizona Indians talking Italian.

"Who are you really?" asked Carlos after several months.

"For you I am Juan Matus," came the opaque reply.

Where did magus Matus get his name? The two great heroes of Yaqui history were Juan Bandera and Juan "Rolling Stone" Maldonado. A third, lesser hero detained former president Álvaro Obregón at a Sonoran whistle stop for a friendly chat about Yaqui real estate, only to find himself in a shoot-out when the army came to rescue Obregón from what they thought was capture. That unsuccessful diplomat was General Luis Matus. The year was 1926. Coolidge was in the Casa Blanca, Carlos Arana C. was a baby in Perú, and (in a separate reality) don Juan was a 35-year-old herb seller in Oaxaca, where he was living under an unassumed name.

Yaquis, we now realize, do not speak to Mescalito, but some of their eastward neighbors (made famous in literary circles by Anaïs Nin's mad friend Antonin Artaud) both fear and venerate him. Digging him with a stick because he hates to have his roots broken when some fool pulls him up, the Tarahumaras call him *hikuri*, or "seize-whirling." Though a joyful *hikuri* protects impeccable Indians, an angry *hikuri* may throw peccable Indians off a cliff or drive them crazy. Only *hikuri* among the magic plants is strong enough to cure the wretch who has touched the Jimson weed without a shaman's supervision.

The Tarahumaran shaman who wants to see an invisible sorcerer eats ball cactus (*baka-nori*) to clear his sight. He knows the personal character of every kind of wind. The people of the whirlwind, who are born in river whirlpools, look like pigs. Their close relatives, the spirits of the waterholes, look like rattlesnakes. Crow is wise, but he eats up the corn. And don't forget that a *disagi-ki* can fly to your house any time to steal your soul. Better sleep with your mouth shut.

In the roar of an Air Force jet, in the crash of a falling rock, in the perking of his coffeepot, don Juan heard the world agreeing with him. In crows' flights, changes of wind, sunbeams, and set-up dreams he found omens of success or danger. *Ixtlan* abounds with these supernatural signs. While it was being written, the biography of a less famous Yaqui was published.

Rosalio Moisés (who lived until his tall candle burned down in heaven) was perpetually preoccupied by signs of good and bad luck. "Few events and happenings were left uninterpreted. . . . when snakes, frogs, and other animals climb trees, a bad flood is coming; buzzards circling a house calling a name means that that individual will die; black baby chicks are bad luck; a black baby chick that tries to crow like a rooster is double bad luck . . . if one casts one's shadow upon a wall at sunrise and the shadow has no head, death will follow."

Rosalio's most important omens "were visions and dreams that foretold the future. . . . On many occasions he went to bed with the intention of having a dream that would give him information about a particular subject." Often he dreamed that he was flying. "As he got older, he flew lower. When the flying dream first came to him, he saw tall buildings, big cities, and other things distant in time and space such as he had never seen at that time." In *Ixtlan* don Juan taught Carlos he could discover secrets or go to distant places by controlling his dreams. In *Tales of Power* a dreaming Carlos walked along a deserted street in an unknown foreign city.

Michael J. Harner, known for his studies of visionary plants, spent some of his childhood in South America, where he returned in 1956 to visit the Jívaro Indians, a tribe of headhunters inhabiting forests of Ecuador and Peru, about 300 condor miles from Castaneda's home town. Harner gives a vivid account of the Jívaro way of life before the encroachment of industrial civilization.

The traditional Jívaro viewed his neighbor with suspicion and hostility. One man in four was a sorcerer. Most deaths, illnesses, and accidental injuries were blamed on witchcraft and could be prevented or cured only by undoing spells. Without strong supernatural protection a man might be murdered any day of the week not only by strangers but by persons well known to him. Parties of Jívaros raided adjacent tribes partly for booty but mainly to take heads, whose soul power could be used to increase the yield of a vegetable plot or make animals more prolific.

The vision-soul, a specially powerful and protective kind of soul, could be found discarnate, playing like a breeze in the spray of a very high waterfall. Boys or men accompanied by their fathers or older men would journey to the sacred waterfall, where they would camp four or five days drinking tobacco water or the much stronger *Datura* water and waiting for visions. A lucky pilgrim would wake one night in what seemed to him a raging storm just in time to see something strange emerging from the forest. The vision, lasting less than a minute, might show him a pair of giant jaguars fighting, a huge human head floating toward him, or a ball of fire. A coward might flee in terror, but a brave man or boy would run forward and touch the vision, whereupon it would explode like dynamite, or silently vanish.

Telling no one about his success, the visionary would return to his home and sleep on the river bank, where in the night an old Jívaro man would come to him claiming to be his ancestor. The ancestor's soul would enter the sleeper's chest, filling him with confidence and forcefulness, endowing him with sharper wits and a more honorable character. To retain this vision-soul, he had to say nothing about it, but those around him would soon know what had happened because of the changes in his conduct.

It was a rare woman that could get a vision-soul, but some men got many and accumulated their power. Jívaro feuding was so intense that a boy would not be expected to survive puberty without at least one vision-soul to protect him. A sorcerer who wanted to kill a man by witchcraft would try to steal his last vision-soul. Family and friends would know it had been stolen if the victim fell ill or began to speak without his usual forcefulness.

When Carlos complained of constant anxiety, don Juan diagnosed the condition as "loss of soul." Whoever had trapped the soul, he said, must intend to kill Carlos or make him very sick. Like the stealing of souls, most of Harner's other Jívaro observations were first published in 1962 and 1963. Those two early publications share some two dozen sorcering ideas with Castaneda's books. To wit:

Young men are conducted by older men to a very high waterfall to seek visions that bring power. *Datura* (in Ecuador, *D. arborea*; in Sonora *D. inoxia*, or Jimson weed) brings not only visions but a surge of strength and confidence. Fatal danger lurks behind every bush, but magical power wards it off if the details of getting power are kept secret. Men can accumulate power and can give or sell it to others. Visionary plants bring spirit helpers, which may form a shield to protect the shaman. (Carlos's shield was psychological, formed by dwelling on heartening thoughts.) Stones, seeds, or insects can be collected, filled with power, and hurled at enemies to kill them. Shamans disdain non-magical herbal remedies. They rub their apprentices' bodies. An apprentice is likely to become the same kind of sorcerer his teacher was, curer or bewitcher, seeker of knowledge or *diablero*. On special occasions, men tell their visions to each other, the Jívaro before a raid, five apprentices after don Juan's magic show. Fearsome creatures come in visions—fighting jaguars, towering gnats, slavering coyotes, and colossal smothering felines. One's spirit helper may be a moth or a giant butterfly. The soul or perception of one person may enter the chest of another, as Carlos entered don Juan's chest. At death one's soul or personal life diffuses as a fog. A man attempts to kill a magical bird that has come to harm someone living in a house temporarily under his protection. And, as we have already seen, a shaman or sorceress may steal the soul of an intended victim, who can only guess why his strength is failing and who his assailant is.

A 1968 article by Harner contained the further idea that one's normal waking life is a lie. *"Doings* are lies," said don Juan in *Ixtlan*. Harner's 1972 book furnished three fresh bits of lore that were duplicated in *Ixtlan* though not in Castaneda's earlier books. Magic quartz crystals are especially deadly weapons. A father teaches his son by showing him a corpse and letting him shoot or touch it. A naughty boy's world should be temporarily replaced by something out the ordinary; the Jívaro father gives his son *Datura* to bring him visions; the American father, on don Juan's advice, would hire a bogeyman to frighten the little fellow out of his ordinary wits.

A thorough scholar keeps track of his sources, reading new contributions as they appear. Castaneda would have needed the manuscript of Harner's 1972 book some months before its publication, but that should have been no problem. According to Harner, the two specialists in visionary plants had been friends for at least nine years.

One day without warning young Joe Pearce slipped into a trance in which he knew nothing could hurt him. As dormitory fellows watched in amazement, he held glowing cigarettes steady against his palms, cheeks, and eyelids. He felt no pain, and he got no blisters. Years later, when his wife contracted cancer, he resisted the malignancy in a spontaneous, intuitive campaign of mental healing. Her symptoms disappeared for more than a year. From such experiences he acquired his mission, to search for better ways of creating reality.

Joseph Pearce cares more for truth than for the manner of its expression. He prizes the gift above the wrapping. He does not glance down at the giver's feet to see if they are clay. Taking *The Teachings* to be a factual account he hailed Carlos as a brave pioneer and "plainly loved" don Juan, but he found some flaws in the old man's Way and during two subsequent years of writing did his best to repair them.

Since *The Crack in the Cosmic Egg* was largely about don Juan, Castaneda could hardly have overlooked it. What would his reaction be, I wondered. Would he bask in Pearce's praise? Would he resent an attempt to improve the wisdom of don Juan? Would he simply shrug his shoulders? I don't consider myself naïve, but I wasn't ready for the answer.

Describing the Australian aborigine's Dream Time (a clairvoyant standing trance) Pearce wrote: "He knows when his own totem food animal is in the vicinity, though a hill intervenes. At the closest point of interception, he breaks his stance [and] intercepts his game." From where Carlos stood, Castaneda would write, he could see a large green bush, though a hill intervened. Walking around the crown of the hill, he came upon it.

The aborigine disdained houses, clothing, and other artifacts that interfered with Dream Time. The world where such things were valued was a world of "unreal men." "They were people," Genaro would say, "but they were no longer real."

A psychic young man guided by a spontaneous creative process became totally unpredictable. A hunter, don Juan would tell Carlos, "is not at all like the animals he is after, fixed by heavy routines . . . he is free, fluid, unpredictable."

To find the crack in the cosmos, Pearce wrote, one must surrender as if a child to a father-figure who assures the return of one's surrendered life. Genaro made Nestor a child again, Pablito would say. The benefactor opens the bubble of perception from the outside, don Juan would tell Carlos, allowing the one who has come under his protection to see his own totality.

The split between conscious and unconscious thinking, Pearce wrote, is necessary to achieve objectivity, but we must "develop a balance between the modes of thinking," and an "opening to the total process of mind." "What matters to a warrior," don Juan would say, "is arriving at the totality of oneself." The teacher arranges the apprentice's *tonal* (his reasoned view of the world) on one side of the bubble of perception, so that the *nagual* (his unaccountable will) can create nonordinary worlds on the other. Once the benefactor has opened the bubble, a warrior lives with the two sides in balance.

Pearce represented our actual and potential realities by the metaphor of a clearing in a forest. Don Juan would represent them as an island in a sea. "The *tonal* is an island," he would explain, running his hand over the table top. "The *nagual* is there," he would say with a sweep of his arm. "There, surrounding the island."

It is a mistake, Pearce said, to think the forest exists as the clearing exists. The trees we fell at the edge "need not always have *been*. Indeed, there may be no trees at all in the depths of that dark. Rather . . . the trees may grow according to the kind of light our reason throws," from the clearing into the darkness we mistake for a forest. "The *tonal*," don Juan would say, "is a creator that doesn't create [but it does make up] the rules by which it apprehends the world. So, in a manner of speaking, it creates the world."

"Our notions of what is real direct our perceptual apparatus [in] a reality-shaping procedure," said Pearce. "We *are* an open possibility." "How far one can go on the path of knowledge and power," don Juan would say, "is an issue which is open."

Pearce mentioned Susanne Langer's belief that we live in a world of verbal reality, where nature as we perceive it is a "language-made affair . . . prone to collapse into chaos if ideation fails." Carlos would grasp a Chicano coyote's thought because he had stopped his internal dialogue and let his ordinary world "collapse."

Far from resenting Pearce's extensions of don Juan's Way, Castaneda gave them a deft pseudo-Yaqui twist and folded them gently into his third and fourth books.

"Don't stare at the car. *Stop the world!*" shouted don Juan one narrative day in May 1971. One calendar night in October 1962 a creech of critics crowded into Broadway's Shubert Theatre to see Anthony Newley's cockney Mr. Littlechap escape poverty, marry the boss's daughter, and rise to empty glory as M.P., peer of the realm, and member of the Snobs club. Buying success with conformity Littlechap like Carlos had trapped himself in a sterile, boring world. As Carlos indulged in self-pity, so Littlechap loudly complained. Reported *Time*: "Littlechap periodically shouts 'Stop the World!'" Said *Saturday Review*: " A number of comeuppances . . . cause him to shout, 'Stop the World!' But he always swallows the rest of the sentence [as if] rejecting drastic commitment." Don Juan we know welcomed drastic commitment, and his creator had long since abandoned family, home, and native land to seek fame, fortune, and life's deeper meaning, but Carlos needed nine more years before he could believe himself when he said: *Stop the World—I Want to Get Off.*

"I *dream* my books," Castaneda told Gwyneth Cravens. "In the afternoon I go through the notebooks with all my field notes in them and translate them into English. Then I sleep in the early evening and dream what I want to write. When I wake up, I can work all night. Everything has arranged itself smoothly in my head, and I don't need to rewrite. My regular writing is actually very dry and labored."

"The dream world is becoming my specialty," Anaïs Nin had written in her diary 39 years before. "Most dreamwriting is false and intellectually composed . . . the real dream has an authenticity and can be recognized. The intellectually composed or fabricated dream does not arouse the dream sensation in others. . . . There is no dialogue in the dream, and very few words. The words are condensed like the phrases of poems. The language must be a kind of non-language. The dream happens without language, beyond language."

"It is Nin more than any other writer I can think of who has over the years insisted on the continuity of dream and reality, as Don Juan does, and whose theories about fiction as controlled dreaming provide such a precise counterpart to don Juan's ideas about learning to control one's dreams."

Ronald Sukenick's "precise counterpart" seems pretty imprecise to me. Nin and Castaneda are obviously talking about radically different uses of dreams, one authentically dreamlike, the other featuring an ordinary nap between ordinary preparation and composition. Whatever pointers Castaneda picked up during his few visits to Nin's house in the 1960s, dreamwriting did not grow out of them. Sukenick may be the wrong man to contrast these dreamings, since he decries our culture's "false separation . . . of imagination from reality" and apparently believes Castaneda's conventional descriptions and expository dialogue actually rolled out of evening dreams about translated Spanish field notes into a midnight typewriter, like Clifford Irving's Howard Hughes hoax rolling out of the tape-reader into the high-speed printer after-hours at the computer center. Maybe *Carlos* dreams *his* books, but a bag of fresh-roasted wild *hikuri* nuts says Castaneda writes like everybody else. If the first draft never gets re-written (which I doubt), it's not because Castaneda is Samuel Taylor Coleridge but because he is editorially self-indulgent.

Margaret Castaneda's cousin Wanda Sue Parrott knew the napwriter well, before he met don Juan. "In those days," she wrote, "my impression was that he was an author in search of a publisher." Like Oates and Kennedy, Parrott recognized Castaneda as a fellow writer.

Clement Benedict (I call him here) worked on the manuscript of *The Teachings*. "I had already seen auras," Benedict told me. "*The Teachings* freed me to accept them. Carlos has used some of my experiences in his books."

"Writing to get my Ph.D. was . . . my sorcery," Castaneda told Sandra Burton.

"Your notebook is the only sorcery you have," don Juan said to Carlos. "You started on the path of knowledge writing, and you will finish the same way."

I'll go along with dJ on that. More than anything else, Castaneda is a writer—one who cares little for style but much for content, a story-teller who tricks us into learning, a fantasist on a pedagogical mission, a mythmaker who has made himself a myth. In the next chapter we take up the myth of Carlos Coyote, Trickster Teacher.

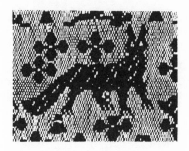

Coyote, over the whole western half of North America, is
the most important figure of myth . . . trickster and dupe
by turns . . . aiding, willy-nilly, the First People to the discovery of their final and appropriate shapes. He is . . . a
great transformer . . . and in parts, at least, of California,
his deeds are represented as almost invariably beneficent
in their outcomes; he is a true, if often unintentional,
culture hero.

—Hartley Burr Alexander
North American Mythology

Every generation occupies itself with interpreting Trickster anew. No generation understands him fully but no
generation can do without him.

—Paul Radin
The Trickster

6. TRICKSTER TEACHER

Coyotes are not reliable. They are tricksters. . . . I would never trust a coyote. But you are different and you may even become a coyote sorcerer.

And so he became and remained everything to every man. . . .

One day as Trickster was wandering aimlessly around the oval island of the world, he came upon a lodge. Inside two raccoon women were tending their children. When Trickster tossed some ripe plums through the hole at the top, the women came out.

"Where did you pick these, Older Brother?" they asked him.

Trickster described a place a good way off where the ripening of plums was reddening the sky, but the women said they could not leave their disobedient children, so Trickster offered to take care of them.

"You are very kind to us," said the women, setting off to find the plums.

The minute they were out of sight Trickster killed the children, singed the hair off them, and boiled them in a pot.

"Now is the time I will eat some fat," he said.

When his belly was full he cut one child's head off, stuck it on a stick, and set the stick at the door of the lodge as though a naughty child were peeping out. Then he went on his way well pleased with himself.

Having found no plums where Trickster had said they would,

the angry women were returning to the lodge when they spied a disobedient child peeping mischievously out at the door.

"What kind of joke is this?" said the child's mother, slapping the naughty face. The head flew through the air and rolled over and over on the ground.

"Oh my children!" shrieked the women. "He has killed them! It must have been Trickster!"

As often as Trickster duped others, he fell dupe. Once he ate many laxative bulbs to show they could not affect him against his will. Soon he was up in a tree climbing higher and higher to escape his own excrement. When it reached the top of the tree, he fell in.

Another time Trickster caught sight of someone in a black shirt pointing at him across a lake.

"What are you pointing at, Younger Brother?" he called, but the person said nothing. After calling three times without getting an answer, Trickster put on his own black shirt and stood there still as a stick pointing his finger at the offensive stranger. Some hours later Trickster tried to talk the challenger out of the contest, even offering to kill a fine animal for him to eat, but the fellow ignored his remarks. Finally Trickster gave up in disgust and resumed his stroll along the edge of the lake. Glancing back once more at his stubborn opponent, he was astonished to see a burnt tree stump from which a branch was protruding.

"It is because of things like this," he said, "that people call me foolish."

Indeed, Trickster was not only foolish but divided against himself. While his right arm was busy skinning a buffalo, his left arm took hold of it.

"Let go," said the right arm, "or I will cut you with my knife."

The left arm would not stop interfering, and soon the two arms were in a vicious fight. When it ended, the left arm was bleeding badly.

"Why have I done this?" cried Trickster when he saw what had happened. "Why do I make myself suffer this way?"

Seeing his predicament, the birds began to make fun of him, calling his name again and again, but Trickster pretended not to know what they were saying.

In spite of such pranks and foolishness, Trickster sometimes did good things for the people and brought them useful knowledge. One day he heard a noise like many people having a party.

Drawing closer he found an elk's skull filled with flies. The flies were making the party noise by rushing in and out. Envying their good time, Trickster asked how he could join them.

"Enter as we do, through the neck," they said.

When Trickster picked the skull up and jammed it down over his head, the flies all fled through various holes, leaving him alone again. Wearing his great bone face and wide branching antlers, he walked slowly up river till he met some people. Before they could recover from their astonishment, he said to them:

"Bless you, good people. I am an Elk Spirit. This river is my home. Strike off the top of my head with your ax, and you will find good medicine." The people obeyed, but when they split the skull open they found Trickster grinning at them.

"See how you have spoiled my fine headdress!" he jibed.

"It is Trickster!" they said in dismay, but he told them:

"Now that you have helped me, I will give you the pieces of this skull. Use them for any purpose you wish, and you will be successful."

Then the people made bone instruments and used them to cure sickness.

Another time he made the mistake of probing a hollow log with his penis and got only a short stump of it back out of the hole. Smashing the log, he found Chipmunk chewing his penis to bits. After flattening Chipmunk, he distributed the useless pieces around the world as potatoes, turnips, artichokes, rice, beans, and water lillies for the people to use.

As he got older Trickster thought less about playing tricks and more about helping people. Toward the end he walked the length of the Mississippi River preparing it for Indian habitation, removing obstacles, shoving the waterspirits' holes below the surface so that boats would not fall into them, and eating any creatures that might molest the people. Finding a most inconvenient waterfall, he commanded it to be gone. When the waterfall refused to move, he shoved it onto the land, out of the people's way. Journeying westward he became Coyote, and there he stole fire from the Fire People and left it among the trees where men could find it.

Returning to the fork of the Mississippi and Missouri Rivers, Trickster prepared his last meal on earth before ascending into the heavens. The big rock where he sat down to eat it still bears the imprint of his buttocks and testicles.

Though Trickster walks in every land, his North American

Indian guises are the most archaic. Here he is Coyote, there he is Old Man, elsewhere he is Raven, Hare, or Spider, but essentially he has no fixed form, coming to men as a formless presence foreshadowing their possible futures. In the Winnebago Trickster cycle, which we have been sampling, he hauls his intestines and pre-Chipmunk penis wrapped around his body, not yet having discovered proper places in himself for his constant hunger, his unruly gut reactions, and his irrepressible sexual urges.

Once Trickster saw a chief's daughter and her young friends swimming at the other side of a lake. Unwinding his penis, he spoke as follows:

"Younger Brother, you are now going after the chief's daughter. Pass her friends by, but see that you lodge in her squarely."

When the women saw Trickster's penis gliding toward them, they rushed to get out of the water, but the chief's daughter was last and could not get away. Coming to her aid, the others tried to pull the penis out, but it was stuck fast and would not budge. The strongest men in the village were sent for but did no better. Finally the wise woman arrived. Recognizing the intruder right away, she took out her awl, straddled the penis, and chanted, "Pull it out, Trickster! Pull it out if it is you!"—meanwhile jabbing away with the awl. Suddenly the penis jerked free, throwing the old woman a great distance, while everyone could hear Trickster howling and laughing on the far shore.

Having no form of his own Trickster is all things to all men—giver, taker, creator, destroyer, duper, duped, liar, and bringer of truth. Willing nothing consciously he brings everything about. Lacking morals he elicits moral standards from men who contemplate his insupportable acts. Easy going he does harm. Careless he does good. Whether annoying, frightening, or admirable, his acts are permeated with laughter, his own and other people's.

Symbolically we may take Trickster for man struggling to master himself, man trying to cope with a world he did not ask to enter and cannot control, man pulling himself together, man doing great things as much by accident as on purpose, man pretending he knows what he is doing, man in the making, man changing from one character to another with little stability or selfhood. Psychologically we may recognize him as the unconscious source of human acts, unpredictably creative, absurd, or destructive. Educationally we may take him to be a teacher of man's imagination, one who violates all rules of man or nature, who makes water run uphill, who irreverently stamps his warbundle into the ground, who offers fairy tales to the learned elders as factual reports. "See here," says Trickster, "this world is not fully or finally formed. I can make my part of it any way I want to. So can you. There are many realities, and we need not agree on this particular one." Socially we may recognize him as a big liar and a nonordinary friend.

Though one of the first to suspect Castaneda as Trickster for the Seventies, Vincent Crapanzano did not develop the theme beyond saying Castaneda might be falling dupe to his own tricks. A cursory study of the myth persuades me Oswaldo's false nephew is Trickster's true incarnation—so many traits do they share.

Trickster is metamorphic, appearing in countless guises. Castaneda comes on as Carlos-Ethnographer, Carlos-One, Carlos-Two, Carlos-Apprentice, Carlos-Skeptic, Carlos-Emic, Carlos-Etic, don Indian, the Indian don, Pablito, Nestor, Nogales Bill, don Genaro, the Dreaming Dissertator, Earth Doctor, World Stopper, Castaneda-Anthropologist, Carlos-Psychic, Carlos-Sorcerer, Carlos-Philosopher, Carlos-Naïf, Castaneda-Scholar, and Trickster Teacher—to mention a few. Trickster is ageless, a boyish or childish Old Man. Castaneda is notably youthful for his years and enjoys a movable birthdate.

Both talk to, kill, eat, and may become, animals. Both have fragmented selves. Trickster's penis swims off to molest the chief's daughter, while Carlos's double visits Castaneda's publisher or pops down to Mexico for the afternoon. Trickster confronts his shadowy antagonist across a lake, Carlos worries about wrestling with his ally, a projection of his naguallian self. Trickster's left hand fights with his right, Carlos's subselves stumble all over each other.

Both are shaped by public opinion. Indians make Trickster a fool by calling him one. Carlos and Castaneda erase personal history so that other people's expectations will not form their characters or direct their acts.

Trickster wanders the world alone, partying with flies, dancing with the wind. Carlos spends 13 years in the company of imaginary companions. Both marry but do not remain at home.

Trickster is a spirit of disorder, an enemy of boundaries. Castaneda disrupts academic protocol and rubs out the line between real and unreal. Trickster was a bad boy. Carlos baffled the school principal with his pranks. The early Trickster made a mess of things. The early Apprentice bemoaned the fruitlessness of his life and the inadequacy of his character.

Trickster is not guided by conventional morality. Don Juan taught Carlos the folly of truth. Trickster symbolizes rebellion. Carlos is "a horse that doesn't like to be saddled," a son who rejects his father's conventional world. Castaneda rose to fame by breaking rules of scholarship.

Trickster has little control over his impulses. Castaneda cannot resist making up stories during interviews even if they will trip him up later. Trickster is always hungry for food, Carlos for love. Trickster, like don Juan's warrior, takes what he wants but expects to be used by others when it is their turn.

Trickster wreaks havoc wherever he goes, destroying lives and making the innocent suffer. Castaneda has been a painful embarrassment to colleagues, some of whom suffer so sorely they cannot speak about it. All the same Trickster does not go on the warpath and no one has called Castaneda violent.

Never malicious, Trickster, Carlos, and Castaneda are good natured, entertaining fellows whose tricks are only jokes, bladders filled with irony hurled from heights of glee. You know what we do with facts in the separate reality. When Trickster returns to the village, the people build him a long lodge right next to the chief's, and the young men spend hours in his company. "We all liked Carlos," said José. When the young men go courting, Trickster goes along with them just for the fun of it.

Both temporarily switch sex roles. Trickster transexualizes himself with elk's-liver vulva and elk's-kidney breasts into "a very pretty woman indeed," so he can marry a big-meal-ticket chief's son and bear him three boys, the first illegitimately sired by Fox, Jaybird, and Nit. Margaret's Carlos did the cooking (in 1960, when cooking was women's work).

Both play tricks on men and women. Trickster slipped Mink a laxative that made him soil the chief's daughter during an illicit conjunction, then ran all round the camp shouting Mink's disgrace. Funny Falcon Coyote persuaded a furry friend to steep his stems and get a superheadache. Castaneda warned Margaret's cousin Sue not to open the door of his archeology closet next to her guest bed. "Eef you do," he said, "the bones, they weel get up and walk around all night."

Both pretend ignorance of what they know—and people know they know. Trickster has no idea what the birds are saying about him. Carlos-Naïf has never heard of Yogi Ramacharaka.

Both are notably preoccupied with fecal matters. Trickster is forever putting his foot in it, while Carlos has to take his clothes off so as not to ruin them during naguallian leaps. Little Genaro's evacuations make the mountains tremble. Trickster blasts trees, rocks, and hills to smithereens by firing borrowed skunk charges out of his anus and vainly hopes to kill deer the same way. Don Juan warns Carlos not to attack the lion with his farts.

When circumstances beyond his control reduce the incremental cost to zero, Trickster gives of himself for the good of others. After Chipmunk chewed his root to bits, Trickster founded agriculture. Cut off by his own character from intimate exchanges with his fellow men, Castaneda turned inexpressible yearning into philosophy, as don Juan turned loneliness into art, to be packaged in books and distributed among the people. Toward the end of his life Trickster acknowledged his mission to help the people. Castaneda rejected a life of fruitless self-indulgence in Peru to become mankind's teacher.

Both hold what is eating them inside. Trickster subdued Hawk by closing his rectum tightly around Hawk's head but then had to endure Hawk's fitful gnawing and flapping. Carlos's trite, superficial whinings are mere cosmetics for Castaneda's unspoken suffering. Rebuffed again and again, Trickster finally gets what he wants. Castaneda, *Time* said, had to rewrite his thesis three times.

A man in one of Ray Bradbury's stories wore a Rorschach shirt in which passers-by saw their inner worlds animated. Castaneda is a whole Rorschach man, writing Rorschach books. In him and in them people find what they are looking for. Occultists find a practical sorcerer. Theodore Roszak found an improver on Timothy Leary. Paul Riesman momentarily found a scientific anthropologist. Joseph Margolis found an original philosopher or a master teacher. Elmer and Alyce Green found an open-minded observer. Joseph Pearce found a literary genius. Bruce Cook found a new James Macpherson (whose don Juan was Ossian). Charles Tart found an altered-states-of-consciousness technician. Gordon Globus found an outstanding hypnotic subject. Weston La Barre found a mercenary charlatan. Nancy Wood found another ruthless exploiter of Lo, the poor Indian. Marvin Harris found a counter-revolutionist. Richard Gott found an infuriator of Ronald Reagan. James Sire found a breaker of the First Commandment. Hal Lindsey found a worshipper of demons. Patricia Garfield found a chronicler of dream technique, while professional helpers have found in don Juan (an actual person) a model for counselors or a successor to Frederick Perls.

Some who have known Castaneda face to face cherish in him a valued colleague, a spiritual leader, or an appealing rebel, for whom they feel warm regard, deep loyalty, or fierce partisanship. Others believe they have faced an impenetrable, discomforting con man, whom they dismiss with a shrug, a sneer, or a shudder. Seeing so many different reactions to Castaneda, I can only join the Winnebago birds in saying:

"Look, look! There is Trickster! There he is walking about!"

In the summer of 1966 Ramón Medina showed Barbara Myerhoff and Peter Furst what it meant to have balance. Knowing his anthropologist friends lacked the power to *see* the narrow bridge a Huichol shaman must walk to cross the great chasm separating the ordinary world from the otherworld beyond, the *curandero* determined to give them a concrete demonstration of physical balance in this world standing for spiritual balance in that world.

Ramón led his party to a spectacular waterfall, from whose edge the water dropped hundreds of feet to the valley below. As his Huichol companions sat in a semicircle to watch, Ramón took his sandals off, gestured to the world directions, then leapt—or flew—from one rock to another with arms stretched wide, often landing but a few inches from the slippery edge. Now he vanished behind a boulder, now he stood motionless on the brink of destruction, but never did he or his Huichol observers show the slightest concern that he might fall, though the visitors from California were terrified.

On narrative 17 October 1968 don Genaro led his party to the bottom of a roaring waterfall, where don Juan, Carlos, Nestor, and Pablito sat down in a straight line to watch. Genaro took his sandals off, then climbed the hazardous 150 feet, several times seeming to lose his footing and hang in the air by his fingertips. Reaching the top, he leapt out upon the edge of the fall, where he seemed to be standing on the water. There he perched for a long time, occasionally leaning out into space with no visible support, but mostly standing unaccountably still, resisting the rushing current. Though his performance struck terror to Carlos's heart, the watching Indians evinced no concern for his safety. At the end Genaro turned a lateral somersault to vanish behind a boulder.

In the spring of 1970, having been Associate Director of the

UCLA Latin American Center since 1967, Peter Furst organized a series of lectures on the ritual use of hallucinogens, during which he and Carlos Castaneda presented their respective accounts of shamans manifesting agility or magic atop lofty Mexican waterfalls. Though Castaneda's version had the observers sitting in a straight line at the bottom rather than a semicircle at the top, though it added levitation and Bolivian somersaulting, and though the rocks Ramón landed on were easier to make out than Genaro's (possibly because of the observers' different location), Furst recognized Castaneda's account as "strikingly similar" to his own. In *Flesh of the Gods* he reproduced it as a footnote, with no further comment.

Other specialists in hallucinogens and shamanism have saluted Castaneda's contribution to their science. Janet Siskind acknowledged the fieldworker's need to relearn his worldview under the shaman's guidance as Carlos had done. An expert on psychedelic healing told me Castaneda had published certain facts of shamanism before anyone else knew of them. When I asked for an example, none came forth.

Gullibility aside, what would blind such scholars to Castaneda's fictioneering? A powerful reason would be that they admire his literary illustration of getting inside the native's head. A second, and I think crucial, reason would be that he broke the psychedelic-fieldworker barrier with a bigger bang than any predecessor. Before Castaneda, prudent candidates did not declare to their dissertation committees that they planned to eat peyote or drink *Banisteriopsis* as a preparation for scientific observation. When Douglas Sharon set off in the summer of 1970 to eat the San Pedro cactus under a *curandero's* guidance 50 miles from Castaneda's birthplace, he was inspired by two pioneers—James Slotkin who had gained full membership some 15 years before in the peyote-eating Native American Church, and Carlos Castaneda, a UCLA graduate student whose catalytic first book was just at the height of its academic popularity. Without Castaneda's literary intervention, such a project might have been guided into safer channels by a cautious graduate-school committee.

"When I first undertook research among the Jívaro in 1956-57," confessed Michael Harner, "I did not fully appreciate the psychological impact of the *Banisteriopsis* drink upon the native view of reality, but in 1961 I had occasion to drink the hallucinogen [and to find] myself, though wide awake, in a world literally beyond my wildest dreams [where] I met bird-headed people, as well as dragon-like creatures who explained that they were the true gods of this world. . . . I realized that anthropologists, including myself, had profoundly underestimated the importance of the drug in affecting native ideology."

That statement was published in 1968. What did Harner's 1962 article and 1963 dissertation have to say about anthropologists drinking *Banisteriopsis* in 1961? Not a word. Harner waited seven years to tell the academic world about his conversation with the true gods. On a parallel track in a separate reality, Carlos began his psychotropic experiments in 1961 and Castaneda told the world about them in 1968.

It is easy to see how legitimate fieldworkers would feel grateful to Castaneda for making frankness safer and funds for the research of their choice easier to get. Some have expressed their gratitude by citing Castaneda in the scholarly literature as though he were just another scholar. Others have gone further to build the myth of Carlos-Ethnographer.

"Some years ago," wrote Harner, "I ran across a reference to the use of a *Datura* ointment by the Yaqui Indians of northern Mexico, reportedly rubbed on the stomach 'to see visions.' I called this to the attention of my colleague and friend Carlos Castaneda, who was studying under a Yaqui shaman, and asked him to find out if the Yaqui used the ointment for flying and to determine its effects."

Observing the narrative chronology, Harner's request must have come before 4 July 1963, when Carlos did fly with the aid of *Datura* (Jimson weed) and the supervision of the Yaquiless Yaqui. Harner quoted Castaneda's subsequent description of the flight, saying it furnished impressive evidence for the impact of *Datura*. While there was already some evidence that *Datura* would make people fly, Harner's request constitutes our only evidence, however circumstantial, of legitimacy in Castaneda's enterprise. Unfortunately for Carlos-Ethnographer, the evidence is suspect.

If Harner queried Castaneda in or before 1963, why did an eager, repetitious questioner like Carlos-Apprentice not once link *Datura* to Yaquis, *Datura* to flying, or Yaquis to flying before he flew, though don Juan himself had dropped a few hints about flying? My guess is neither Carlos nor Castaneda had heard the *Datura* query because it didn't exist until Harner mythopoetically "remembered" it around 1968 or later.

Harner's article lists 37 references to the literature but not one reference to Yaquis using *Datura* for any purpose what-

soever. Why not? I would guess, because the lost reference did
not exist before Harner needed it to flesh out his account of a
request supposedly made some years earlier. "I know of no
information or reference concerning Yaquis using *datura*,"
writes Edward Spicer. On such stuff are dreams and Tricksters
made.

When a coyote sees the shadow of a roosting chicken by
moonlight he pounces on the shadow and brings down the bird.
When a Coyote-Ethnographer sees the shadow of a sorcering
Crow by the light of his silvery mind he pounces on it and
brings down the Temple of Learning. Out of the rubble will rise
a new construction of the relation between art and science in
anthropology. Amid the groans of dying illusion we hear a
Yaquity-Iberian laugh. Through the dust of collapsing confidence we spy an impish stocky man wearing a naughty wolfish
head, and we know at once it is he, Trickster-Academe, the
Rogue who Teaches. Well pleased with himself, Coyote Ph.D.
is going on his way now, leaving us to pick up the pieces.

Under the world where Earthmaker lives there is another
world just like it and of this world he, Trickster, is in charge.

I thought my hint that Michael Harner had invented the
Yaqui-*Datura* reference to build up the myth of Carlos-
Ethnographer might provoke some clarification, but Harner
has buoyantly rebuffed every request from friend or stranger to
reconsider Castaneda. David Christie, a Canadian anthropology student, hounded Harner by phone and letter for the best
part of a year, and at one point Harner promised to send him the
missing reference if he could find it. Now a timely note from
Hans Peter Duerr, University of Zurich, turns up what could
well be a reference Harner read and then lost track of: José
Pérez de Barradas, *Plantas Mágicas Americanas*, Instituto
Sahagún (Madrid) 1957: 239, 310-312. Apparently depending
on V. A. Reko's unreliable *La Flora Diabólica de México*, Pérez
asserts—erroneously by most accounts—that the Yaqui Indians use both peyote and *Datura*. I translate the pertinent
passage: "The most curious thing is that the women make a
salve, mixing various greases with seeds of *Datura* [es-
tramonio, or thorn apple] and belladonna and rub themselves
with it, just like European witches in the middle ages, on chest
and belly" (312). This plausible identification of the missing
reference puts the matter in a new light, suggesting Harner was
convinced of Castaneda's legitimacy all along and did ask him
to query don Juan about *Datura*. —RdeM 1978.

But what if man had eyes to see beauty itself, the true beauty, whole, pure, and unalloyed? Beholding that beauty with the eye of the mind, he would conceive not images of beauty but realities.

—Diotima to Socrates
Symposium of Plato

Η ΑΛΗΘΩΣ ΓΗ

We who live in hollows of the earth imagine that we dwell on the surface above—as if a creature at the bottom of the sea were to fancy itself living on the surface of the water. But if any man could take wings and fly upward, he would—like a fish putting its head out of the water and seeing this world—see a world above this world, where common stones are transparent gems, where unknown colors shine, where gods really walk in the sacred groves and speak to men in the temples. And if man's nature could bear such a seeing, he would acknowledge that there, not here, is the true earth.

—Socrates to Simmias
Phaedo of Plato

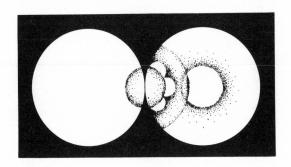

7. THE TEACHINGS OF
DON JUAN

The world is. . . . also as you picture it, but that's not all there is to the world.

Don Juan teaches what is, how to know what is, and how to live so as to know what is—ontology, epistemology, ethics. Other writers have traced bits of his eclectic wisdom back to well known sources and no doubt more will do the same but I want only to point out the chief signs along don Juan's Way and say how I read them. My readings will hardly meet with universal approval but they may foment some worthwhile discussion.

Carlos met don Juan at the beginning of the road to knowledge and walked with him to the chasm that separates what is from what might be. Because this is an essay, not a story, you and I can walk from the chasm back to the beginning, which will make the signs easier to read.

The central proposition in the teachings of don Juan is the distinction between *tonal* and *nagual*—Aztec words George Foster defined authoritatively in 1944. The new meanings Castaneda gave them have little or nothing to do with their Aztec meanings. Don Juan's *nagual* is the metaphysical void of potentiality out of which all actualities come. Though it is empty of actuality, it is filled with potentiality. What does potentiality look like? Nobody knows. Nobody can know. As it was in the beginning, is now, and ever shall be, the *nagual* is indescribable, unspeakable. "Of what cannot be said," Carlos no doubt read to don Juan out of the *Tractatus*, "thereof one must be silent." Not only silent but blind and deaf. The *nagual* is void as well as unspeakable. There is nothing in it though all things come out of it.

To me, the most interesting metaphysical question is: Where did all this come from? Or: Why is there something and not nothing? Don Juan's *nagual* idea is a way of asking that question. It is a gratifying way because it sounds a lot like an answer, but when you say the world comes out of an unspeakable void filled with potentiality you have not exactly told anybody how to get to the men's room. An answer like that is an ultimate question in disguise. When Castaneda made that question live in the minds of a million readers he earned our consideration as a Culture Hero despite all his tricks.

The *tonal* is what happens when the *nagual* gives birth. The *tonal* is what exists. More properly, it is people's perception or imagination of things. The idea of the *nagual* is part of the tonal, but the *nagual* itself is not part of the *tonal*. Everybody has a *tonal* but the *nagual* has everybody. When something ceases to exist—like an ocean wave, a life, or a *tonal*—it returns to its potential state in the *nagual*, perhaps to emerge again. Everything on don Juan's dinner table—thoughtful spoon, graceful napkin, divine tablecloth—was tonallian because it existed, it was there, and don Juan and Carlos were looking at it. Surrounding the table was a naguallian formlessness out of which tablecloths, napkins, and spoons might come to rest on the table (the waiter who brought them was not part of the metaphor). Though it is more familiar, don Juan said, the *tonal* is just as mysterious as the *nagual* from which it comes. Potentiality and actuality are coordinately inexplicable.

Our *tonal* experience (the only experience we have) can be divided into several kinds of reality, the most obvious being ordinary reality, or ordinary experience. This book, Castaneda's books, Castaneda himself, and Carlos understood as a character in a book are part of today's ordinary reality, but when don Juan appears in your dreams or talks to you after you have gone 72 hours without sleep, he is not part of the ordinary reality.

The ordinary reality is not the same thing as the physical world, but it contains our ordinary view of the physical world, whether that view is correct or incorrect. Some years ago the ordinary reality contained a flat world; today it usually contains a spherical world.

Ordinary reality tends to be fairly stable. One thing that keeps it stable is social convention, the sort of thing Edward Sapir was talking about. When most people admire the emperor's new clothes, few see him naked. A more powerful stabilizing factor is the physical system in which our sensing bodies are immersed. Under a four-billion-year-old physico-biological contract we structurally and instinctually "agree" to distinguish night from day, air from water, heat from cold, and peyote from chicken salad. Though the ordinary reality is not more real than an LSD trip, it is more constant, accessible, and communicable than LSD trips are. In this life it is the boss reality. Don Juan generally admits its bossness, but he likes to keep Carlos guessing about it. Where was my body when I flew, queries Carlos. In the bushes, says don Juan. What if I chained myself to a heavy rock before flying? Then you would have to fly holding the rock. Carlos is plenty confused, and no wonder, because don Juan is playing with a crooked cue. *Myself* is not *my body*: body stays in the bushes while self goes flying. The kind of rock I can chain my *self* to can be taken along on the flight. Semantic sleight of hand. Later don Juan talks a little straighter. Can a sorcerer go to the moon? Yes, but he can't bring back a bag of rocks. Did my body leap into the gorge? No, it was your perception. (The incorrigible magus Matus can't leave it at that. He has to fuzz up the "No." Perhaps Carlos's "reason" will "admit all of him jumped." Castaneda-Cliffhanger forever keeping his occult options open for the next book. Potboiler *perennis*. Trickster *sempervirens*.)

A second kind of reality is the sorcerer's reality, which Carlos enjoyed during his 22 drug experiments and 34 non-drug nonordinary events. Others might call it psychedelic reality or altered states of consciousness, but Carlos's guide kept talking about sorcering, so we have to acknowledge that special emphasis. More important than the emphasis on sorcering is the separateness of the reality. It is not much like the ordinary reality, often containing such things as giant gnats, slavering coyotes, transparent mountains, little guys running up and down trees defying gravity. It is unstable. And it is only partially or fitfully communicable to other people. Peyoteros may share the same visions, merely believe they share them, or know their visions are different. (Anthropologists usually attribute shared visions to shared expectations about visions, but some now contemplate the possibility ESP is a factor.) Visionaries have a hard time telling non-visionaries what they have experienced. Their experience is ineffable, unspeakable. Such ineffability may be nothing more than lack of common experience and vocabulary. If enough people had the same visions, and if some visionaries were verbally competent, there might be no more ineffability of visionary experience. As things stand, certain explorers visit otherworlds and come back to say they defy description, or that it takes another visionary to understand the description. People say the same thing about the Grand Canyon: If you haven't been there, you don't know how deep it is. Even CBS has not sent crews into otherworlds with camera, tape, and tendentious list of questions to put to giant gnats.

Though few of us are sorcerers, mystics, or conscious psychics, all of us have separate realities. We all dream, we all imagine, we all misperceive things. The excursions (or self-incursions) of sorcerers, mystics, and psychics are not more separate than our dreams, only less usual. They are not less real than waking experience. Reality is a subjective quality. If something feels real, it is real. That doesn't mean you can eat it, copulate with it, or cash it at the bank. Those operations require participation in the boss reality, which is massively coordinated with the physical system we seem to be immersed in. It is therefore a good idea to be able to tell the ordinary, boss reality from other, nonordinary realities. People who get them mixed up come to grief. Don Juan makes that clear on occasion but like the good Trickster he is, he mixes the realities up whenever he wants to—like substituting *self* for *body* when Carlos isn't paying attention, like saying the Little Smoke took Carlos's body away, that for a while he did not have an ordinary body, that don Juan didn't know where his body had gone, and so on. Undoubtedly one could find a point of view from which those statements would be true, but neither Carlos nor the reader is warned that don Juan is not at that moment sitting in the boss chair, speaking from the ordinary point of view. Perhaps don Juan is doing the right thing to shake up the reader's complacency by keeping him off balance this way, but he plants a seed of nondiscrimination that must grow into a devil's weed of confusion for some readers. Trickster is not the kind of teacher vulnerable people should seek out.

Most of the time don Juan puts boss and nonboss in their proper places. A warrior can tell things apart; he can tell "what is real and what is not" (don Juan slipping here into the common parlance, equating *real* with *boss, not* with *nonboss*). "A

Structural Analysis" says a sorcerer shifts back and forth between realities at will, distinguishing them by their different
uses. If he doesn't distinguish them (don Juan would surely add)
he will soon be a dead sorcerer. The luminous coyote, don Juan
insisted, "was not talking the way you and I talk." Genaro
didn't remove Carlos's car from the boss reality; he merely
forced Carlos to look at the sorcerer's reality, where no car was.
The separate reality is definitely separate, and it should be kept
that way.

Unhappily for neatness and complacency, even sane, grown
up people can't separate the realities categorically. The field of
parapsychology (psychical research, paraphysics, implicit
communication, or whatever it may be called next year) recognizes apparent invasions of the boss reality by what ought to be
imaginary events. Non-fradulent mind reading, knowledge of
objects or events not present to anyone's senses, non-muscular
mental control over physical forces, validly foreseeing events
that cannot be inferred—such anomalies look very much like
dreams come true or the impossible made actual. Though
Carlos looks into the past to discover a book thief, sees a bush
through a hill, finds his notebook by not-doing, and visits
Sunday's Lagunilla market on Wednesday, Castaneda does not
direct the reader explicitly or by implication to the serious
literature treating such transordinary feats. Specialists and informed readers know magical events abound, puny ones in
laboratories, monstrous ones in convents, annoying ones in
kitchens and warehouses. Fraud, insanity, and credulity aside,
the impossible does stick up out of the probable like a sore
thaum defying us to understand it—and we don't understand
it. Some of it is demonic, some of it is angelic, and some of it is
merely puzzling, but we don't need a Yaquiless Yaqui or a
Coyote Ph.D. to tell us about it. A lot of solid citizens have
plenty to say on the subject, and their truth is stranger than
Castaneda's fiction. When I asked philosopher-
parapsychologist Bob Brier whether Castaneda had done any
harm by linking psi manifestations to a suspected hoax, he said
he didn't know anyone who thought so, but I can't help wondering how many prospective readers of serious psi literature
may have been shunted off in another direction by Trickster-
Psychic.

A third kind of reality is true reality, the sort of ideal reality
Plato had in mind after consuming fly agaric in the Temple of
Eleusis. The true reality is a world above this world, where

common stones are transparent gems, where unknown colors shine, where gods really walk in the sacred groves, and so on. Castaneda and don Juan don't endorse the true reality, but sometimes a fleeting wish to trade this evil world for a better one speaks out in ways not consistent with the gospel according to don Juan. Though he knows the true reality is just a gold-plated private world no truer than a sorcerer's reality, don Juan flirts with a perfectable *tonal* when he says *seeing* will show things the way they really are, or that only by pitting two views against each other can one weasel between them to arrive at the real world, or that Carlos's power-plant trips were true excursions into the *nagual*—as though the *nagual* were some transcendental Disneyland rather than a void filled with potentialities. A more donnic Juan might have said the *nagual* had produced new visions in Carlos's *tonal*, the only place for them.

Carlos's path to knowledge begins with the sorcerer's reality and ends at the source of realities. It begins with shamanic ritual and concrete imagery and ends with European metaphysical abstractions. Though Joseph Margolis thought Castaneda had planned the tetralogy, I believe this progression reflects continuous learning as much as initial planning. The author would hardly have planned so many inconsistencies and contradictions. Much of don Juan's tedious, occasionally sophistical academic recapitulation in *Tales of Power* serves to disguise Castaneda's intellectual growth as tortuous didactics devised by the devious master.

So far we have been talking about don Juan's theory of what is. Now we come to his method of knowing what is. One of his major epistemologic tools is the bubble of perception, a quasi-spherical private world encompassing the *tonal*. Within the bubble, the teacher helps the apprentice divide the *tonal* into two sectors. Everything he is used to perceiving and understanding, the ordinary objects and events of daily life, the memories, the concepts, the familiar fantasies, the habitual roles and routines are to be herded into one sector, on the right side, leaving the other side empty. To prevent crowding or resurgence the apprentice should junk as much of his mental content as possible.

The empty side of his mind will now be dedicated to the *nagual*. This does not mean it will *be* the *nagual*, which cannot be mentalized, but that it will offer little or no resistance to new manifestations of the *nagual*. The apprentice will not have to sit around wondering what the new manifestations will be, because the benefactor, acting as agent and personification of the *nagual*, will catalyze one or more startling naguallian irruptions into the bubble. In the process he will open the bubble from the outside, maybe even sticking his head in to say hello. These wondrous events will leave the apprentice a changed man. Thenceforth he will live with the conservative and innovative sides of his *tonal* in balance, alert for signals from the unknown.

Twice don Juan draws a diagram showing Carlos the eight points of his totality. My figure reproduces don Juan's topography (the exact arrangement didn't matter he said). On the right we have the tonallian *tonal*, containing everything ordinarily associated with mental life and social communication. On the left we have the naguallian *tonal*, a mental receptacle yearning to be filled. The yearning is shown by the overlap of will into the left sector. Don Juan's *will* signifies not stubbornness or even conscious intent but unconscious, intuitive desire. "The *tonal*," he said, "doesn't know that decisions are in the realm of the *nagual*."

Often don Juan equates will and non-reflective awareness with *body*. Carlos's body learns, knows, decides, accumulates power, practices not-doing, or detects the presence of the ally. The usage strikes me as rather odd, since it vaguely and incongruously suggests identity of mind and brain. Perhaps Castaneda chose the term as a way of separating ideas, which he handles constantly and expertly, from feelings, which he handles seldom and awkwardly. Between his exaggerated emotive clichés—chills, suffocation, paralysis, spasms, whining, shrieking—and don Juan's curt dismissals of Carlos's "indulging," we get very little emotion naturally expressed or plausibly interpreted. Let the unmanageable feelings stay in the body, where they will not disrupt the smooth flow of ideas.

Don Juan's discourse on the totality of the self is not as clear as his diagram, a difference that may betray the Man of Novels getting ready for a fifth, clarifying book, or Castaneda-Learner not quite having mastered the concepts he is working with. I suspect it is the latter. In spite of some fuzziness, however, the bubble of perception is a vivid metaphor persuading the reader to open his mind to what may be, whatever it may be.

Often don Juan tells Carlos to stop his internal dialogue, so that the ordinary world will stop and another reality can present itself. This formula combines yoga and linguistics.

Meditators cultivate inner silence as a step toward illumination. The Sapir-Whorf hypothesis suggests "that all one's life one has been tricked, all unaware, by the structure of language into a certain way of perceiving reality, with the implication that awareness of this trickery will enable one to see the world with fresh insight." Susanne Langer said the experiential world would collapse if language failed. Don Juan puts more emphasis on this technique than I think it deserves, since meditative inner silence is only the first of many steps, and since the Sapir-Whorf hypothesis unduly stresses the influence of language on perception.

Don Juan's *seeing* is of several kinds. Ideally it illuminates the world, showing the hidden power that maintains it, showing people as luminous eggs, but often don Juan sees through people as character readers do or sees remote events as psychics see them. "I believe you," he says. "I've smoked you." "How did you know about the white falcon?" Carlos asks. "I saw it," says don Juan. Some seeing mimics the ordinary reality, like seeing the bridge to the other world. Other seeing mixes the senses, as when Carlos saw the sound of Genaro's great boulder.

A nagging ambiguity in don Juan's teaching is the uncertain relation between knowledge and power. Weston La Barre judges the accumulation of supernatural power to be the core of New World shamanism, as it came across the Siberian land bridge in Paleolithic times. Whether found in lightning-struck wood, in strangers' severed heads, or in visionary plants, power controlled such things as weather and animal fertility, making man's environment more friendly. Don Juan urges Carlos to accumulate power as a means to knowledge, but he never quite subordinates the instrument (power) to the goal (knowledge), never fully persuades us a man of knowledge despises shamanic manipulations of the environment and cares only for the essential naguallian character of all worlds.

Power doesn't matter any more, he says. Who cares about frightening Indians these days? It's better to smoke the mushroom and *see* than to get power from the devil's weed and kill men. A sorcerer is a sad fellow who uses power that doesn't really belong to him for unworthy ends. My benefactor was a man of great power but not a man of knowledge. He didn't know his own totality until he died. Power is the strongest enemy a man of knowledge has.

On the other hand don Juan "conveyed the impression that

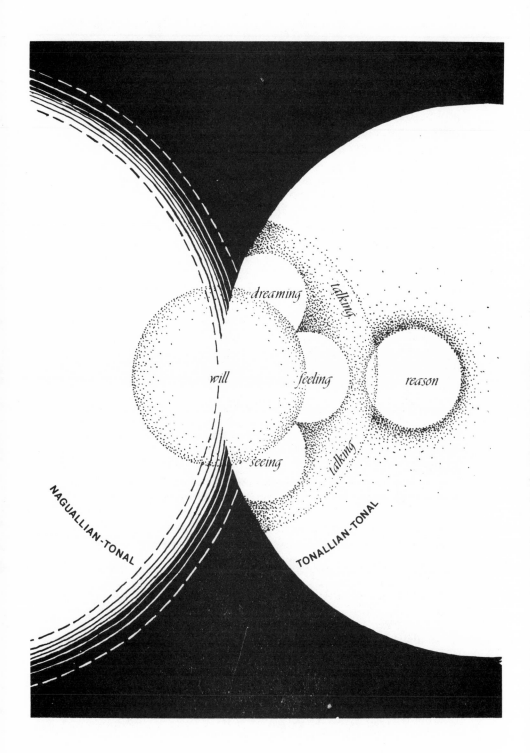

other parts of his teaching were incidental to the acquisition of power." Mescalito, he said, teaches us how to live, the Little Smoke brings power to see and know, the devil's weed gives sorcering power. Coming with feelings of buoyancy or anger, power makes a sorcerer invincible—a master of his fellows or a terror to his enemies. Even warriors have the great fortune to be prisoners of power, awaiting unknown fulfillments of its promise. With all this loose talk don Juan never cleanses his teaching of the taint of sorcery. Cynics can still suspect Carlos or Castaneda if not Genaro or don Juan of taking perverse pleasure in performing unworthy tricks.

James Boyd shows connections between Buddhism and don Juan's not-doing or stopping the world. He finds the warrior's controlled folly similar to a Buddhist's detachment. Stan Wilk recognizes controlled folly from the teachings of Lao Tzu.

Twilight may be the crack between the ordinary and nonordinary worlds because it is a time of uncertain perception, when imagination plays a greater part in what we see. A warrior's climactic leap into the unknown, whence he may return to live differently, could symbolize the mystical experience of oneness and the changed life many believe will follow it. The gait of power—charging down steep banks on moonless nights amid gullies, boulders, and spiney cactuses—could be a practical test of bat-like clairvoyance or of bone fragility, but I interpret it more confidently as a writer's fantasy of abandoning himself to racing, plunging creative dreams.

Before don Juan's power-hunting and knowledge-seeking techniques can be practiced, the apprentice must begin to live like a warrior. A warrior never goes to war but he faces up to his impending death. Knowing his time on earth is short, he lives impeccably to maximize his accomplishments. Feeling him always nearby, glimpsing him occasionally an arm's length to the left, a warrior frequently consults death, his only wise advisor.

To become a man of knowledge if only for an instant, a warrior knows he must conquer four enemies. Fear can make him run away from knowledge. Clarity can make him believe he is already a man of knowledge when he is not. Power can seduce him into unworthy preoccupations. Old age can weaken his resolve, so that he will not stand ready for the test.

A warrior chooses a path with heart, which is any way of living that brings him peace and gives him pleasure while leading him to knowledge. On that path he does not suffer the anxieties that plague non-warriors. His passions are focused and do not stray to distracting objects. He journeys eagerly from wonder to wonder, detached from ordinary concerns. Though he may mingle with men or even women, he knows their activities are folly. Their great goals and gripping crises he finds no more important than their idle pleasures and trivial routines. If he joins or imitates them, his only obligation is to control his folly so as to preserve his impeccability.

A warrior erases personal history. He does not tell his name, his origin, or his previous occupation. Sometimes he forgets those things himself. Having no idea what to expect of him, other people cannot pin him down with their thoughts.

Since he cares nothing for the follies of his fellows, a warrior does not submit to the tests they constantly make to determine what is happening and who can be trusted. Valuing truth no more than untruth, he acts on truth believing in what he is doing, on untruth disbelieving. Either way, he acts impeccably—which is to say he acts without awkwardness or miscalculation.

"What is a truthful life?" asks Carlos.

"A life lived with deliberateness," says don Juan, "a good, strong life." To thine own self be true, Polonius might have added. Thou needst not then be true to other men.

A warrior assumes responsibility for the consequences of his acts, making "his decisions so carefully that nothing that may happen as a result of them can surprise him, much less drain his power." Steadfastly unsurprised and unaffected, he loses control neither of his life nor of his emotions. You will not find him indulging in remorse or self-pity. Having jettisoned his past, he is not beset by feelings arising from earlier times. No flickering strangers with familiar faces confront him unless he is ready for them, no ambassadors come uncalled from unknown regions of his mind. He never meets his double face to face, for that would kill him. His life has its own spontaneous order, but nobody can predict his movements. He does not wait around to be clobbered, and no one catches up with him. He is never idle and never in a hurry.

A warrior, then, has some notable virtues. I go along with him on contemplating death, watching out for the four enemies, and taking responsibility for consequences, but I cannot believe a warrior is never surprised, and my heart does not choose such a solitary path. However wise cold death may be, one likes to have some advisor more congenial. A warrior

who could not steer his own course if anyone expected anything of him must have been remarkably docile. A warrior who
banishes the man or child he used to be is asking to meet
himself coming back from exile just when he is least ready to
face himself. A warrior who shares neither his past nor his
feelings nor any ordinary standard or commitment may be fit
to hunt power or pursue knowledge but he is in no condition to
live with people. Isolation is don Juan's flaw, said Joseph
Pearce. Not so, answered Genaro, three books later.

   A warrior's life cannot possibly be lonely or lack feeling,
Genaro told Carlos, because it is dedicated to his beloved. Who
is a warrior's beloved? Genaro began to roll or glide along the
ground like an eel in water or an infant wriggling joyfully on its
mother's belly. Little Genaro loves the world, don Juan explained. He swims on it to express the only love that can
release his great sadness, to adore the one beloved that can turn
his loneliness to solitude. This enormous earth, this lovely
being alive to its last recesses gives a warrior shelter, accepts
his love, understands his feelings, soothes his distress, cures
his pain, and teaches him to be free. Only if he loves the earth
with unbending passion and receives its wondrous gifts as a
sign that it cares for him can a warrior be complete.

   Castaneda filled 1000 pages before he told us about love in
the separate reality. Like most of us, a warrior loves the biosphere. Unlike most of us, he loves only the biosphere. That is
his choice, and his secret.

When Pizarro obtained possession of Cuzco, he found a country well advanced in the arts of civilization; institutions under which the people lived in tranquillity and personal safety; the mountains and the uplands whitened with flocks; the valleys teeming with the fruits of a scientific husbandry; the graneries and warehouses filled to overflowing; the whole land rejoicing in its abundance; and the character of the nation, softened under the influence of the mildest and most innocent form of superstition, well prepared for the reception of a higher and a Christian civilization. But, far from introducing this, Pizarro delivered up the conquered races to his brutal soldiery; the sacred cloisters were abandoned to their lust; the towns and villages were given up to pillage; the wretched natives were parcelled out like slaves, to toil for their conquerors in the mines; the flocks were scattered and wantonly destroyed; the graneries were dissipated; the beautiful contrivances for the more perfect culture of the soil were suffered to fall into decay; the paradise was converted into a desert. Instead of profiting by the ancient forms of civilization, Pizarro preferred to efface every vestige of them from the land, and on their ruin to erect the institutions of his own country. Yet these institutions did little for the poor Indian, held in iron bondage. It was little to him that the shores of the Pacific were studded with rising communities and cities, the marts of a flourishing commerce. He had no share in the goodly heritage. He was an alien in the land of his fathers.

—William Hickling Prescott
The Conquest of Peru

129

8. THE POWER AND THE ALLEGORY

Trust your personal power. That's all one has in this whole mysterious world.

At the time I met don Juan I had very little personal power. . . . my back was against the wall.

When Carlos Arana was a little boy 15-thousand people lived in Cajamarca but the railroad didn't go there. From the end of the line one had to ride three days on a mule. An unpaved road that eventually came winding through the mountains from the rest of the world washed out regularly during the six-month rainy season. The obscure youth who would later win fame in the United States as Carlos Castaneda spent most of his Peruvian life in those Andean sticks, walled in by formidable peaks, rusticated at 9000 feet, cut off from coastal commerce much of the time, and perpetually out of touch with Lima 300 miles away, where the big decisions were made and where those who counted lived. It was not a promising start on the road to the cover of *Time*.

Some 500 years earlier people in that skyward valley had owed their allegiance to the Chimu kings, who reigned in the great coastal city of Chanchan. The Cajamarca Indians raised crops, pastured animals, and spoke a language of their own, until a royal Inca came north to conquer them anew. His name *Yupanqui* meant that he counted for something, as those he conquered did not.

Conquest brought the sierra dwellers a new capital city, Cuzco, a new language, Quechua, and a new status as "worthless people." Since they would thenceforth do the work of the empire, their worthlessness was not economic but hereditary, consisting in their failure to have descended from the sun. Though the Incas may have numbered no more than 20-thousand at any time, their brief empire was one of the great power trips of the world. By sheer will and novel mythmaking they constituted themselves supermen of the Andes. Learning to fight better than any other tribe and to hold their gains with ostentatious arrogance and bureaucratic cunning, they conquered millions of their fellows and organized Peru as a wheel of wealth and power whose hub was not only a capital city but a resplendent shrine.

The mythopoeic Incas superimposed recently discovered heavenly gods on ancient Peruvian shamanism. Conquered sorcerers read the future in the veins of inflated llama lungs under the scrutiny of Inca priests. Those who divined wrongly were killed or mutilated. No word for priest was needed, since every Inca was a priest of Inti, the sun. As archpriest, the Royal Inca brought together and personified priesthood and caste, church and state, divine and political power.

At first the Incas were impeccable warriors, vigilant against attack, never caught without a plan, eager for battle, swift in pursuit. A most popular name for an Inca man was Hawk. The word for fighting meant also to enjoy playing games with the enemy. As their conquests succeeded, the Incas became ritualists of power.

The region around Cuzco was laid out as a model of the empire. Serfs from every nation lived at distances from the shrine theoretically corresponding to the remoteness of their homelands from the capital. No one could leave his assigned hamlet, where native custom was kept and native garb was worn. Weaving cloth in an unaccustomed pattern or wearing the headgear of another nation was discouraged by fatal blows from stone hammers. Within the city, adulterous harem girls and their lovers would be hanged naked by the hair until frost and birds had dealt with them sufficiently. Their relatives would be hunted down and dispatched. Lesser offenders might have heavy stones dropped on their backs from a height of three feet. Noble criminals were cast into a famous pit of poisonous snakes. Captured enemy captains were routinely deprived of their skins, which were stuffed with grass to serve as man-drums, objects of merry contempt in victory parades. Toasts would be drunk from their skulls.

That good Christian gentleman William Hickling Prescott was right about the land rejoicing in its abundance. Inca engineers knew how to build roads and channel water. Effective military administrators made sure the transport and water systems did not fall into disrepair. The tranquility and personal safety Prescott praised were generally available to both Incas and worthless people who did exactly as they were told, but Prescott's "mildest and most innocent form of superstition" needs further examining.

Peru is a land of power spots—of mountains, stones, streams, and winds charged with supernatural power. These ubiquitous, multiform *huaca* required propitiation in their own right and, under the Inca regime, as intermediaries to the gods on high. When a sickly Inca lord wished to beg for better health, he might choose his most beautiful daughter to intercede for him, since only the purest and most pleasing messenger was fit to address the gods. The Royal Inca, needing many divine favors, needed also many messengers, some on short notice. Good administration meant keeping such messengers always in readiness. Down the long mountain roads that carried tributes of gold, grain, cloth, and leather came also the most beautiful children of the empire, dutifully though presumably not always gladly surrendered by their parents to serve as the emperor's spokeslings. These boys and girls, five to twelve years old, were kept in huts near the sacred llama corrals, where priests came to inspect them three times a year for soundness and purity of body. Speaking many different languages, the children no doubt had little to say to each other about their predicament. Now and then certain of them would be chosen and taken away for messenger duty.

On the ceremonial day a reverent party gathered round some massive outcropping, the visible form or delegate of a god such as the creator Viracocha. While the party blew solemn kisses to the *huaca*, the emperor descended from his litter and approached the stone to pray. Up the trail came the messenger children, dressed for the first time in elegant clothing, adorned with gold and silver bangles. Having been plied below with many cups of sacred beer, they were staggering drunk and had to be led by the hand. At the proper moment each was led around the rock by a strangler-priest and deftly strangled, to the crowd's approving murmurs. Still undefiled by sickness or carnal passion, each small body tumbled into its sacrificial grave, along with gold and silver figurines to further please the god. Then trembling workmen used their sacred digging sticks to cover all. At the coronation of Huascar, whose name meant humming bird, 200 children carried royal greetings to the gods. Not all were strangled. Some were decapitated, while others had their hearts torn out and their blood smeared across the face of the *huaca*. By such mild and innocent superstition was the character of the nation softened, preparing it for the higher, Christian civilization that Pizarro did not promptly bring.

The conquistadors were brutal men seeking wealth and fame among heathens. The capable, persuasive, illiterate Pizarro had started his career as a swineherd. Some say he was nursed by a sow. We have rightly been told the cruel Spaniards betrayed and murdered Atauhuallpa, but few have read how Atauhuallpa's captains prepared to celebrate his coronation. Hanging trussed on poles in Cuzco's Recreation Square, Atauhuallpa's half-brother, the deposed emperor Huascar, saw a hundred women of his harem who were or might be pregnant torn open and his progeny removed. The bodies were spitted on heavy posts set along the road whereon the victor would approach the city, the unborn children pinned into the mother's folded arms. Women with born children were treated the same way, and hundreds of additional posts were set for loyal half-brothers, servants, and friends. Atauhuallpa never saw those triumphal decorations because the Spaniards had already captured him in bloody battle at Cajamarca.

Pizarro's men were few but hard. They had the great luck to land on the Peruvian shore at the very moment when the Inca regime corrupted by royal sacrilege, torn by fratricidal strife was spontaneously disintegrating. In the turmoil many Incas took the Spaniards to be the legendary army of Viracocha, who would stop time, overturn the world, and institute a new creation. Unable to choose between sullied rival emperors and legendary renewers, the warriors were caught without a plan. Hating them in turn, many of the worthless people sided with the hairy invaders. Had the Spaniards landed 50 years earlier, they would surely have been struck down with stone hammers and paraded as man-drums through the streets of Cuzco. As things stood, they proved just enough bolder, harder, crueler, and more determined to prevail against the faltering supermen. Thirty years after the landing the Inca caste and nation was no more. The most sacred statue of Inti had been rooted out of its

mountain hiding place and melted down to pay the debts of the
Spanish king. The Indians were starving in the ruins of their
economy, dying from European diseases, slaving for masters
who took their women but gave them no viaducts in return.

Facing a vast crowd assembled to see him executed for rebellion, the last legitimate Inca heir is said to have told his followers the oracles of Inti had been a royal lie and trick. The truth,
he said, was in the law of Christ, to which he had just been
converted and under which he was ready to die. Thus in cities
and towns did supernatural power pass from Inti to Jesus,
secular power from Royal Inca to royal Philip, while deep in the
mountains the Indians turned for solace to their *huacas*, as
they do today.

The Peruvian colony was so loyal to Spain that its fight for
independence was led by outsiders. As a nation it continued
divided, Europeans and Mestizos dominating the coast and
lower sierra, Indians populating the high plateaus. Those who
counted ran the nation's business, politics, and military affairs
from Lima. Great families owned the land, while peasants
tilled the soil and tended the animals. Between these major
classes an industrial-merchant-professional class was making
its influence felt about the time Carlos Arana came on the
scene. The little we know about his family suggests they were
establishing themselves as merchants during his youth. Growing wealth and rising status would have been prime family
concerns. Castaneda's false portrait of his father as an
academic snob who wouldn't talk to anybody that hadn't read
Plato combines a fantasy of descent from intellectuals with
rejection of rural conservatism and middle class conformity.
Though Carlos's father became a mediocre professor, Carlos
was raised on a farm in the backwoods.

In a land that reeked of power, ancient and modern, sacred
and secular, young Arana had little of his own. The fountain of
supernatural power for a person of his class would have been
the Church, and the Castaneda we know today might have
made an outstanding monseigneur had not young Arana rejected everything Catholic save the untypical San Juan de la
Cruz, who died imprisoned and accused of heresy. As for don
Juan de Sonora, Tom Torquemada would gladly have inciner-
ated him for teachings that transformed God Almighty into a
tablecloth and went downhill from there. Carlos, don Juan
jibes, hasn't been to confession in all the years they have been
running around together and has lost his last medallion. In a

horrendous scene of mountain witchcraft, superhuman Juan and Genaro boom out demonic laughter at a terrified comical Trinity of Carlos the Father, Pablito the Son, and Nestor the Holy Ghost. Standing cold sober in Mexico City's main square, Carlos notices the cathedral more slanted than before. He ventures a few feet inside, when a "cynical thought" crosses his mind. The reader, risking his own salvation not Carlos's, is to imagine the cathedral toppling over or crashing down. Juan and Genaro can indulge in blatant heresy, but Carlos and Castaneda can only hint subtly at the collapse of the One Holy Church. Could this be the fearful resentment of the apostate? The chapter is titled, "Having to Believe." A few minutes after escaping the falling stonework, Carlos is tapped on the shoulder in the marketplace. A shiver shakes his body from head to toe.

"My God, don Juan!" he exclaims. "What are you doing here?"

"What are you doing here?" echoes Juan divine.

Apostate Arana belonged to no powerful secular class. His family were not aristocrats or landholders, and he felt no inclination toward the military, a possible road to power in Peru. Though Margaret's Carlos "was always talking about starting a revolution" to help the underdogs of Latin America, José's Carlos busied himself taking money from less adept gamblers and displayed no revolutionary ardor or activism on behalf of oppressed Indians. Repelled by industry and commerce, scorning the managerial or professional career that might have brought him modest influence, he was alive to poetry and sculpture. Like the Indian, he lived outside the economic and political life of his country. Like the Indian, he was not content but longed for power of another order.

Castaneda recalled Carlos's childhood as an eternity of helplessness, a desert of loneliness, a jungle of fear, a trial of pain. Summers without the busyness of school were hot and suffocating. Boredom occasionally erupted into anger. Carlos was a violent fellow, don Juan would say, capable of frothing at the mouth, but we may imagine Carlitos dared not show his temper in father Arana's house any more than in the house of his Heavenly Father. Kicking or hurling stones in a remote corner of the garden, he would feel ashamed if an adult noticed his display of feeling.

At school he couldn't help picking on pesty little Joaquín and eventually broke his collarbone. Feelings of guilt were so

strong that Carlos swore "not ever to win again." We don't have
to take the incident at face value to find in it the paradigm of
anger turned inward. Castaneda has been described as a pas-
sive, gentle person but also as an annoying jokester. Deprived
of its original family targets, his submerged anger bursts out in
little pranks easily forgiven, or in subtle insults seldom recognized by friendly or adoring victims.

Before he met don Juan, Carlos could almost always get his
way by wheedling, arguing, whining, complaining, or showing
false anger. Oddly, don Juan admitted having used the same
tactics when he was still a member of society. "It's funny the
way you sometimes remind me of myself," he said.

"What injures the spirit," he told Carlos, "is having someone
always on your back, beating you, telling you what to do and
what not to do." Eight-year-old Carlos evened the score by
playing real or imaginary tricks on the principal. Teenage Carlos chose the typical tactic of humoring people, saying yes and
meaning no. Graduate student Castaneda humored his professors by reporting imaginary fieldwork.

Devious dealing has its costs. "I confessed," wrote Castaneda "that I had never respected or liked anybody, not even
myself, and that I had always felt I was inherently evil."

"True," said don Juan, "you don't like yourself at all." He
then distracted Carlos from the history of his self-
condemnation, the sources of his misery, and the roots of his
rebellion by saying social conduct was folly unworthy of a
warrior's regret. The truth that Carlos was ugly and rotten
could be dispelled by realizing all truths were lies, all perceptions illusions. Such comforting sophistry, such intellectual
shields against the cruel barbs of self-reproach were presumably not available in the parish of Cajamarca. Besides devious
dealing, what sins made one feel rotten and ugly there? Oppres-
sing Indians, Defacing schoolbooks, Maiming first-graders,
Cursing parents under one's breath, Ducking mass, Performing
unauthorized hedonic exercises? Embraces are permissible
only between men and women, Genaro said, or between a man
and his burro. Don Juan gave Carlos a piercing look.

"What are you doing in your pocket?" he asked frowning.
"Are you playing with your whanger?" Pretty familiar for the
second interview, but fathers don't always stand on ceremony.
Carlos said he was writing notes in his pocket. Father Matus
laughed heartily, but maybe father Arana didn't swallow ex-
cuses like that. In any case, as don Juan said, Carlos's father had

him all figured out, knew his habits and his character. Carlos felt pinned down by the old man's opinion of him, which no power on earth could change. One solution was to put thousands of miles between himself and that opinion. Another was to alter and then abandon his father's name. A third was to banish an imaginary father to a life of futility in Brazil, as "a literary man who has never written a thing." A fourth was to deplete the paternal power by making the father only seven years older than the son. A fifth was to find an Indian foster father. A sixth was to be the father himself. An exorcist does well to employ a variety of spells.

The Brazilian fatherling's efforts to become a writer were "a farce of indecision," Castaneda told Sandra Burton, but added: "I am my father. Before I met don Juan I would spend years sharpening my pencils and then get a headache every time I sat down to write." The blocked paternal author portrays the filial Man of Novels struggling in quicksands of inherent evil. Writers who don't like themselves tear up their manuscripts in advance.

"There is no longer a war within you," don Juan said. How was it fought or settled? Who won or who surrendered? The evidence does not support the idea that Castaneda ever found anyone to open his heart to. Many wished to be his friend and would have listened gladly to whatever he needed to tell, but he couldn't reveal anything important about himself except in his books, allegorically. Margaret knew him for years and never really knew him. If he wouldn't tell her, whom would he tell? Don Juan?

Suffering is only a thought, said Doctor Matus. A warrior does not indulge in self pity. Look directly at the funny things but through the sad things. Laughing feels a lot better than crying. If someone you love dies, don't look at her body in the coffin, see her life expanding into a fog of crystals. That way you will not hear the cry inside you.

Though earnest psychotherapists have hailed don Juan as a contributor to their art, he never permits his client to welcome or express painful emotion—a crucial error that is to be expected when therapist and client are the same person, shrinking from the same anguish, fleeing the same distress. In his years of roaming, Carlos had grown callous to pain and sadness. Occasionally they caught him off guard, but most of the time he played the buoyant clown turning sadness into jokes, or the wise man turning loneliness into philosophy.

Carlitos is really cool.

He's got a bit of a poet, a nut, and a fool.

Genaro's doggerel must have been more elegant in the original Spanish, but he's on to something. Carlos thought he might be "a bit crazy" wanting to spend his time with don Juan, who called him in turn "a very strange plugged up fool" because he couldn't *see*. More plugged up than *seeing* is feeling. Carlos can't open his gap and let his passion flow into another person. He can't commit himself to anything but the separate reality, first in his mind, then on paper, rarely in an interview or on the podium. Telling stories excites him but only displays his power to fill up the social world with cobwebs. He does not embrace people, causes, or even his burro. Socially, he is really cool.

Carlos did not know where to go or what to do. He was chronically bored. Most of his lies were told to stir up a little excitement. Often he sank into a depression, which robbed him of his buoyancy or wisdom and incapacitated him for dealing with people. "I can like my fellow men only when I am at the peak of my vigor and not depressed," Castaneda told Sam Keen. "At one point in my apprenticeship I became profoundly depressed. I was overwhelmed with terror and gloom and thoughts of suicide."

We don't have to credit the apprenticeship or the terror to take note of the depression, gloom, and thoughts of suicide. Helpless, desolate self condemnation may be the worst thing anyone can feel. Terror could be an improvement. Imaginary terror could be positively delightful. Living a fantasy of mysterious danger, the perfect companion always by one's side—there is a cure for boredom and depression. If no one else can be trusted, it may be the only cure. Not everyone can do it. The apprenticeship starts early.

Mama, I saw a falcon sitting in the fig tree.

Show me.

It's gone now. It was all white.

Margarita, I met a man I want to study with.

Who is he?

His name is don Juan.

The fantasies of childhood usually give way to the conventions of adulthood, but not always. When they act as shields to cover naked feelings and keep out the world that stirs up those feelings, taking them off is an agony too severe to be borne in solitude. However lonely, the separate reality can be secure and comforting. Like don Juan, Carlos quit his apprenticeship because it was too hard. Like don Juan, he came back to it because there was "no other way to live."

The labor in Castaneda's academic put-on was obviously so much greater than in legitimate research that *Time* could not believe the don Juan books were a hoax. Where was the motive for a superior student with a good record to choose such a hard, slow, dangerous, unpromising path to professional membership? I can see two motives. Castaneda wanted to test his personal power—to solidify his private world, to harden his shields against inner pain and outer pressure, to realize his career as a writer, to impose his separate reality on the world outside and see it taken for the boss reality. He couldn't do those things as a novelist. His writing skill was not great enough to impress fiction editors, but what was more important, he would have conceded that he was making a myth. That concession would have destroyed most of his power. Students do not run around the British Isles searching for hobbits.

Second, he was apparently seeking social passage from childhood to adulthood, symbolic passage from human to superhuman status. His ceremonial egress through the Westwood Gate of Power stood for the shaman's perilous walk across the bridge to the otherworld or the paradoxical visionary passage through the eye of the needle or the strait gate. Transition from the degradation of candidacy to the glory of doctorhood would make Castaneda "a sorcerer for sure." "You are like an infant that can't get out of the crib," don Juan would say. Climbing out of the crib at last, Castaneda would leave behind the stains of childhood. There is a place of power (he told John Wallace a year before receiving his degree) where you can go to get rid of the undesirable things that attach themselves to a sorcerer. As you squeeze between two sheer cliff walls, the evil things are rubbed off and remain forever in the place of power. Like any other shamanistic candidate, Castaneda prepared himself by arcane rituals, which included creating illusions of transcendence and where necessary playing sorcerer's tricks.

British neurologist Sir Henry Head (1861-1940) was famous for studies of brain function. I suppose for every brain specialist named Head there may be another named Foote, and so no correlation between name and occupation or name and trait, but in case names do affect lives, you will want to know the translation of Castaneda's true family name. History tells us Diego de Arana helped Columbus discover America, Jesuit Antonio Arana wrote Latin biographies, Cesáreo Arana politicked in San Salvador, and Vicente Arana translated Tennyson. None was accused of trickery, so far as I know, except maybe Cesáreo, but *arana* (Latin *aranea*, spiderweb) means: trap, snare, fib, lie, deceit, fraud, swindle, or trick. In his native land, Carlitos Arana was Charlie Trick.

"It was believed," wrote a sixteenth-century historian, "that he who had no *nagual* could never be rich." A young man possessing the latent power to transform the *nagual* from a jaguar-witch into a formless void containing everything was wasting his time in a conservative pre-industrial country run by land barons and political soldiers. Vallejo had gone to Paris to die, Arana would go to the United States and begin to live. Fortune smiling upon him, he might pave the path of heart with blocks of gold and become a stockholder like the future don Juan. In the United States, Castaneda did what Arana had done in Peru. He made up fantastic stories. The market was much better in the United States, and so were the stories.

Carlos met don Juan as a UCLA undergraduate, when his back was against the wall. A doctoral aspirant in a big university feels excruciatingly powerless. He has to propitiate an Olympian crew by ingesting the Augean contents of the library. He knows he can't do it, but he thinks they mean him to. The most important thing he learns while acquiring membership is that the Olympians haven't done it either. They just talk as if they had. Though he pretended to have seen only six sources, Castaneda mastered more literature than most. Retrieving his thrice-conquered Cajamarca Indians from the mental file, he transformed them into Yaquis and Mazatecs, mixed a new *brujo* from old ingredients, and synthesized the integrated mesoamerican-European wise man. He never cracked a smile that wasn't in the script.

Success was largely due to his personal presence. Campusmate Sam Bunsen described him as follows:

"I had expected an intellectual or a magician but he looked like a farm worker. I thought a sorcerer would be fierce but he was mild and gentle. Though he knew so much, when students asked questions, he suggested answers very humbly. I bumped into him on campus a couple of times and we talked about sorcery. He was friendly but not what you call outgoing. He listened respectfully to anything I said, but I felt he either already knew what I was going to say or he wasn't interested in my ideas. Maybe he is limited to a master-disciple relationship. He was always serious. I never heard him make any jokes.

Sometimes I would see him walking across the campus, not looking at anybody. He seemed alone in the crowd, the kind of person who would prefer to avoid people."

"How did you feel after you had been with him?" I asked.

"Excited," Sam said. "Filled with a sense of wonder. Not so much by him as by what he had to say. I knew it was authentic."

"He certainly does not resemble the inert undergraduate sophist he claims he once was," wrote Gwyneth Cravens several years after Sam had known Castaneda. "He is alert, inquisitive, convivial."

Sandra Burton found him a ceaseless, self-mocking, mesmerizing talker. Men and women who have known him more privately have seen him playful and even boisterous.

Castaneda's public conduct grew more assertive and ironic as he gained confidence, but like magus Matus he consistently wielded a baton of mystery, evoking wonder from his listeners. The power of his hidden agenda was always felt. Leaders of secret causes fascinate their followers in the same way. They do not tell the whole plan, but everyone knows where the plan will come from when the moment of truth is at hand. Castaneda had not only a plan but a separate world.

Most people are painfully aware of the evils of this world and of their powerlessness to correct them, but they dream of having unlimited power or of finding a better world. When a well recommended, sober looking fellow stands up barefaced in front of them and says he has come back from another world where he has been accumulating personal power from nature and supernature, the dream bursts open inside of them. "There was a curious air of suspended disbelief in the seminar room," John Wallace wrote. "The students *wanted* to believe these . . . incredible accounts . . . but they seemed embarrassed in their believing. There was a lot of tense laughter." The ambassador from another world who can elicit tense laughter from a respectful audience commands power in this world.

Wallace told a remarkable story of Castaneda-Puppetmaster manipulating casual friends and colleagues. Castaneda suggested he come to Wallace's campus office, whence they would go to lunch. Wallace waited through the appointed time, but Castaneda didn't show up. Wallace went to Castaneda's office. The door was locked and nobody answered his pounding. Castaneda's teaching assistant said he had gone to Mexico on the spur of the moment. He needed a couple of fast answers from don Juan. Anyway, she said, don't worry about it. He never shows up when he says he is going to. About one o'clock Ronald Sukenick arrived for *his* lunch date with Castaneda. The two stood-ups went to lunch together. On the way back Wallace met Castaneda in the elevator. "I thought you were in Mexico," he said. "I waited in my office from eleven till one with the door open," said Castaneda. Wallace stared at him aghast. "But we *must* talk, John," Castaneda continued. "We have so much to talk about."

The best way to meet Castaneda was by accident, Sukenick wrote, like the time they noticed each other in a Los Angeles coffee shop after a lecture by Anaïs Nin. Not only was it a poor place for conversation but Castaneda looked Sukenick straight in the eye and said: "I'm in Mexico. I go back and forth very fast. Why don't you get in touch next time you're in Los Angeles. We should talk."

A high-pressure executive I once knew used to get rid of people he didn't want to talk to by making them promise to look him up for a talk. It's a wizard technique. On one occasion when she knew where he was living, Margaret had a phone installed in Carlos's apartment so she could call him. He never picked up the receiver. The next time she visited him she found the phone wrapped in towels in the closet.

When Sukenick read *A Separate Reality* the possibility that don Juan was a Yaqui Ossian occurred to him right away, but after he had met the author four times (the last time in the coffee shop) he no longer believed Castaneda could write a sustained work of fiction—his mind was just too literal. The don Juan story must therefore be true.

Bruce Cook doubted Castaneda had written the books by himself. His English was so laden with social-science jargon and his syntax was so pedantic that Cook could not see him spinning absorbing tales. Some experienced novelist must have taken the field notes in hand. Cook suggested Clifford Irving.

Playing various roles in life as well as in books, Castaneda adapted to the needs of time and place. His performance as colorless pedant qualified him as a sober, trustworthy student at the University. More important, if he had little or no imagination, he could hardly have invented don Juan.

His power over his reader proceeds from allegory. Describing one thing under the guise of another, philosophy as anthropology, separate as boss reality, daydreams as facts, he appeals to the reader's hunger for myth, magic, ancient wisdom, noble savages, true reality, self-improvement, other worlds, or imaginary playmates. The allegory protects him and teaches us. For him it is the only way to live. For us it is the only way to know him. He speaks to us in the only way he can.

"Thus we see him," wrote Claude Lévi-Strauss of the Zuñi apprentice accused of witchcraft, "with a mixture of cunning and good faith, progressively construct the impersonation which is thrust upon him . . . drawing on his knowledge and his memories, improvising somewhat, but above all living his role. . . . At the end of his adventure, what remains of his earlier hoaxes? To what extent has the hero become the dupe of his own impersonation? What is more, has he not truly become a sorcerer? We are told that. . . . At times his face became radiant with satisfaction at his power over his listeners."

Michael Harner describes the Jívaro shaman curing the patient by sucking a magical dart out of his body. The dart merges with an object the shaman is already holding in his mouth, and the combination of essence and object is shown to the patient as proof of the cure. Though Lévi-Strauss would say the shaman is practicing fakery (in which he may believe), Harner says the shaman is not lying because the object serves as a visible sign that the invisible magic dart has been removed. Without such a sign, the patient might not believe, and the cure might fail.

An important (though not the sole) criterion for choosing between these subtly different views is the fact that the patient gets well. Who is to say that his recovery is an illusion? More to the point, who is to say that his recovery has not been effected by magic rather than mere belief? If it comes down to that, what is mere belief? Sometimes belief or intention makes things happen in the ordinary world without psychosomatic or other mechanical mediation. The separate reality merges with the boss reality.

Castaneda's literary magic can be viewed in the same way. The words that come out of his mouth or typewriter are charged with an essence that makes things happen in both separate and boss realities. Some of these things may be beneficial. He is not lying, we can say, because the meaning we get from his allegory is more important than his secret preparations. As the shaman's patient recovers, so we grasp a new meaning of reality and recognize the existence of alternative realities. He is not lying because he is careless of being found out, making his tales progressively more preposterous, leaving clues that betray their synthetic eclecticism. Finally he is not lying because the story is more real to him than the paper on which it is printed. Don Juan's irony cuts both ways.

Joseph Pearce chided Hugh Schonfield for supposing Jesus took a drug to simulate death. Jesus-Trickster cannot be Jesus-Benefactor Pearce protested. No good fruit from a bad tree. No feet of clay. I am not sure about that. Any allegory is a bit of a trick. Mustard or Jimson seed can fall on good ground. Castaneda has sorely tested our capacity to tell one kind of reality from another, and many readers have failed the test, but those of us who do not believe don Juan walks Sonoran sands still feel he somehow lives. Whatever disrespect I may have shown the old metamorph in these pages, I have paid him the compliment of meeting him frequently on his own turf, and if he walks through the door tomorrow we can have it around the room and see what comes out.

When eventually recognized as other-saying, Castaneda's allegory still retains its power. Our commitment to his reality charges it with life. Sorcery turns out to have a social context after all.

On both nights RGW stood up for a long time in Cayetano's room, at the foot of the stairway, holding on to the rail transfixed in ecstasy by the visions that he was seeing in the darkness with his open eyes. For the first time that word 'ecstasy' took on a subjective meaning for him. 'Ecstasy' was not someone else's state of mind. It was no longer a trite superlative cheapened by overuse. It signified something different and superior in kind, about which RGW could now testify as a competent witness. There came one moment when it seemed as though the visions themselves were about to be transcended, and dark gates reaching upward beyond sight were about to part, and we were to find ourselves in the presence of the Ultimate. We seemed to be flying at the dark gates as a swallow at a dazzling lighthouse, and the gates were to part and admit us. But they did not open, and with a thud we fell back gasping. We felt disappointed, but also frightened and half relieved, that we had not entered into the presence of the Ineffable, whence, it seemed to us at the time, we might not have returned, for we had sensed that a willing extinction in the divine radiance had been awaiting us.

—R. Gordon Wasson & Valentina P. Wasson
Mushrooms Russia & History

145

9. JOURNEY TO CAXAMALCA

Lest flesh and blood quicken with natural love, which is ever alive among kinsfolk. . . . Hold them all as strangers to thee. . . . Think not of them at all . . . flee from them in so far as thou humanly canst. . . . for in no other way canst thou free thyself from the imperfections and evils which the soul obtains from creatures.

We are all alone, Carlitos. That's our condition.

Yet they keep trying to go home fully aware that they can't. It's very tragic; their control over their loneliness is superb.

On 24 June 1542 at Fontíveros near Ávila in old Castile was born to Gonzalo and Catalina de Yepes their third son, whom they named Juan. Gonzalo died soon after, leaving the beautiful Catalina in poverty, to raise the boy without a father. From infancy she taught the future saint to look to the Blessed Virgin for solace and salvation. At 12 he boarded at the poor-school. At 15, feeling no inclination toward carpentry, tailoring, wood-carving, or painting, he found employment nursing the sick when not pursuing his studies. At 21 he went to learn theology at Salamanca, where he voluntarily practiced extreme austerities and mortifications, sleeping in a bare, coffin-like trough, scourging his body till the blood ran, wearing rough sackcloth over the sores. Seeking only solitary contemplation, Juan humbly asked to continue as a lay brother, but he had proved such an able scholar that he was made a priest at 25, and a year later Teresa de Jesús (Saint Teresa of Ávila) appointed

him the first member of the first monastery of barefoot Carme-
lite friars. There he took the name Juan de la Cruz (John of the
Cross). The monastery was a dilapidated shack which young
Padre Juan adorned with many skulls and crosses, one of which
bore a paper Christ. Walking barefoot through rural snows he
gained a great reputation among the good people whom he
inspired with the love of God.

Love was the core of Juan's teaching—not love of man for
woman, of mother for child, or of neighbor for neighbor, but of
the soul for God. The soul, he wrote, was the bride of God.
Describing that mystical marriage he dismayed many who
believed holiness and passionate pleasure made strange bedfel-
lows. Judge for yourself from these typical verses:

Upon my flowery breast
Kept wholly for himself alone,
There he stayed sleeping and I caressed him. . . .

There he gave me his breast,
There he taught me a science most delectable,
And I gave myself to him reserving nothing.
There I promised to be his bride.

When the mystical union failed to occur for a long time, Juan
wrote of the soul's desolation:

Where hast thou gone hiding,
Beloved, and left me moaning?
Thou didst flee like the hart,
Having wounded me.

Such language required volumes of Juan's clarifying com-
mentaries to make it orthodox.

Juan urged the religious person to withdraw his emotional
treasure from human and other earthly commitments and to
store it in God. Sister Catalina de la Cruz, a candid, simple soul
who cooked for the convent, asked why the frogs jumped into
the pond and swam to the bottom whenever she came near.
Juan said they found their security there. That is what you
must do, he said. Flee from creatures and plunge into the depth
and center—which is God—and hide yourself in him. The
depth and center was to be found within oneself. The center of
the soul was God.

Juan compared the contemplative soul to the solitary
bird—not a fancied creature but an actual species, the *pájaro
solitario* or solitary thrush. Known also as the *pájaro loco* or
crazy bird, it is described as eight inches long, dark brown

spotted with white, an eater of insects and grapes, nesting in ruined buildings, preferring solitude, having a sweet, agreeable song. Juan's Spanish will help us understand Castaneda's use of this simile:

> Las condiciones del pájaro solitario son cinco:
> la primera, que se va a lo más alto;
> la segunda, que no sufre compañía,
>   aunque sea de su naturaleza;
> la tercera, que pone el pico al aire;
> la cuarta, que no tiene determinado color;
> la quinta, que canta suavemente.

Castaneda translated these lines as a frontispiece for *Tales of Power*, attributing them to "San Juan de la Cruz," who many non-Catholic readers no doubt thought was another modern poet like César Vallejo or Juan Ramón Jiménez. My translation leans on that of Peers:

> The characteristics of the solitary bird are five:
> first, it soars as high as it is able;
> second, it can endure no companionship,
>   even of its own kind;
> third, it puts its beak into the air;
> fourth, it has no definite color;
> fifth, it sings softly.

Juan explains these lines as follows: The contemplative soul must rise above transitory things, paying no more attention to them than if they did not exist. She (the soul, the bride of God) must be so fond of solitude and silence that she will not tolerate (Peers says, cannot endure) the company of any other creature. She must put her beak into the air of the Holy Spirit—that is, she must seek God's inspiration to make herself more worthy of his company. She must not have a definite color— that is, she must not be intent on anything except what is the will of God. She must sing softly (or sweetly) in contemplation and love of her divine Husband.

Castaneda's translation departs from the above in three significant ways, which set limits on his imitation of the mystic saint. One of these departures is a definite error of translation, but since I am confident he knew how to translate *no sufre compañía* correctly, I take the apparent error to be an intentional change of meaning. Let me start with the least impressive departure.

Castaneda changed "the" solitary bird to "a" solitary bird,

thus replacing Juan's simile with his own metaphor. Juan says: The contemplative soul is like the solitary thrush. Castaneda says: I am a solitary bird. The metaphor is more personal, more centered on Castaneda, less subject to the authority and guidance of a dead saint—whom Castaneda deftly transmuted (for the general reader, at least) from Doctor of the Universal Church in Mystical Theology Writing Didactic Prose to Unknown Poet Seeking Himself. To adapt the saint's lines to his own purposes, Castaneda had to ignore the interpretation that follows immediately in the saint's text.

Castaneda rendered "puts its beak into the air" as "aims its beak to the skies," disregarding the saint's explicit, unambiguous intent, which was the submission of the soul to her divine Husband by seeking to breathe and be transformed by his purifying air. Castaneda seeks no inspiration from any guide, male or female, not under his control. Rather he rises by his own power (that is, by power accumulated from an impersonal source and temporarily at his disposal) to the highest point of self-development (whose height, uncalibrated by dogma, he will judge himself). As elsewhere, he rejects the Judeo-Christian separate God, preferring an Eastern or idiosyncratic absolute within, a That thou art. (The soul found her Husband within, but doctrine required the saint to think and speak of him as separate.)

Inserting the word *for*, Castaneda produced a new proposition: "It does not suffer for company." Where Juan says the soul does not tolerate or cannot endure the company of any creature, Castaneda says the accumulator of personal power does not miss having company, not even of persons like himself. In this line (though not elsewhere) Castaneda's solitude, unlike the saint's, costs him nothing. He whistles in the graveyard of friendship lost and love departed. (Altering the meaning, he also falls into ambiguity, since most idiomatically his line means: He has plenty of company, even of persons like himself. That could not be true from anyone's point of view.)

Castaneda adapts San Juan's dualistic mysticism to the monistic Way of don Juan. The solitary bird, who is Castaneda himself, soars alone to the highest achievement on wings of personal power, feeling no need for companionship. By having no reliable public characteristics, and by not raising his voice or being abrasive, he escapes the demands and controls of his fellows.

Some of San Juan's propositions fit into don Juan's teachings without change. Both teachers deprecate specific visions, which can mislead or distract the seeker, prescribing formless union instead, San Juan the oblivious union of the soul with her Husband, don Juan the sorcerer's metaphoric leap into the void. Don Juan prescribes a clean *tonal*, where ordinary thoughts have been thinned out and swept to one side. San Juan says:

> When thou thinkest on anything,
> Thou ceasest to cast thyself upon the all.

Carlos was touched in some undefined part of himself by the luminous coyote, after which indescribable warmth and well being exploded within him. The Beloved inflicted a most subtle touch upon the bride, inflaming her heart with love:

> Oh, living flame of love
> That tenderly woundest my soul in its deepest center.
> Oh, sweet burn! Oh, delectable wound!
> Oh, soft hand! Oh, delicate touch!

The soft, silky, furry paw of a giant rabbit seemed to touch Carlos's neck, nearly maddening him. The Beloved wounded the bride's neck, causing her senses to be suspended. Touched by the coyote, Carlos soon had no thoughts or feelings; he was floating free. The oblivious soul reclined her face on the Beloved.

In his euphoria, Carlos discovered a simple secret that encompassed everything but could not be put into words or even thoughts—an ineffable truth. Juan de la Cruz entered a place he did not recognize and heard great things so secret they could not be told. He was filled with understanding that drove out understanding. The more he knew about the all, the less he knew about particulars. The closer he came to God, the less of him remained. That closeness he felt as an act of God's compassion. Carlos could not put his illumination into words or thoughts, but his body—which is to say, his feelings—gave it substance and quality to be remembered.

Divest thyself of what is human in order to seek God, San Juan said. "After you become a sorcerer, you're no longer human," said Castaneda, but as if reluctant to pay the whole cost of sorcery, he added: "There's a stupendous sorcerer in central Mexico who's supposed to have remained a human being. I'm going to talk to him tomorrow."

Love to be unknown both by thyself and others, San Juan said. "Nobody knows who I am or what I do," said don Juan, "not even I." Both were sometimes seen to have luminous faces. On the other hand, San Juan said we should be ready to lose and see others win, while don Juan said Carlos was not bound by his promise never to win again. The saint lost himself in service to others; the sorcerer sought power to rise above human folly. The saint took refuge from his desires in the mountains, saying, "I have less to confess when I am among these rocks than when I am among men." The sorcerer loved the rocks and mountains for themselves and trod his path among them joyfully.

A bird caught in the lime, said San Juan, must free itself, and make itself clean. Likewise, he who is mired in desire must free himself, and purify himself from that which has clung to him. The undesirable, evil things that can attach themselves to a warrior are rubbed off, Castaneda said, when he squeezes through the narrow exit. To travel the road of perfection, said San Juan, the soul must enter by the strait gate, stripping herself of sensual things.

As before, we see the man of novels reworking someone else's ideas, undeniably in the lines about the solitary bird, plausibly in the other examples. More to the point here, Castaneda tells us as directly as he says anything significant about himself that he and San Juan are birds of a feather, which in this case do not flock together but fly in separate realities. Sharing the solitary condition with the saint as with Genaro, Carlos is alone but, he says, not lonely. As San Juan has the divine Beloved to comfort him, Genaro and Carlos have the beloved World. As the saint must purify himself by renouncing desires, the sorcerers must scrape off clinging entities, which may well be desires unacknowledged. Unlike the saint, the sorcerers count on their personal power, refusing to submit to any master except death, and to him only at the last minute. Unlike the saint, they have no obvious bonds with human beings.

Despite his determination to cast off human ties, Juan de la Cruz was deeply attached to certain women. The bride in him yearned for the divine Husband, but the man yearned for mother, sister, and daughter. Not for wife apparently. A young woman who hoped to seduce him was turned aside with kind, unruffled words.

While his patroness Teresa lived he often denied himself the easy delight of visiting her. After she died, he carried her picture constantly. To free the bride within for contemplation of a greater love, he destroyed Teresa's letters, saved for years.

At the first monastery, his mother had come to cook for him. Later he was offered an appointment that would have kept them together but refused it, partly to mortify his desire for the natural love that is ever alive among kinsfolk. "I do not understand saints who do not love their own family," commented Saint Thérèse of Lisieux, a holy flower child who had enough love for all. However much Juan de la Cruz loved and needed his mother, the bride within him loved and needed the divine Husband more. Loving a particular person, he felt, was stealing love from God. That rocky path with heart led him steadily away from his fellow creatures, but now and then he allowed himself to look back for a moment at human love forsaken.

A year after his mother died he wrote a touching letter to a dear friend: "Sister Catalina de Jesús, wherever she may be." Though I don't know where you are (it said) I want to write these lines. Far away, alone in exile, vomited out by that whale (prison) into this foreign port (Andalucía, a region he detested), I have not been found worthy to see you again. As darkness prepares us for light, this trial is a gift from God, but how many things I should like to say to you. Not knowing whether this letter will reach you, I do not say them.

Five years after that lonely, stifled cry, Juan's friend was prioress at Beas, while he was spending a week with the nuns at Caravaca. One snowy morning he startled them by declaring he was urgently needed at Beas, where he must go even if the storm worsened. When they begged him to stay the full week, he said: "If I stay you will see that they will come for me." That day a messenger came from Beas, saying Catalina de Jesús was dead.

Don Juan de Sonora had his own professional colleague Catalina, with whom he too had supernatural communication. Unlike Catalina de Jesús, she was a fearsome witch, but like Catalina de Yepes she was both impeccable and beautiful. Did the witch get her name from the saint's mother or from his dear friend? Only Castaneda could tell us, but there are other possibilities.

The year 307 saw the lecherous Roman emperor Maxentius carrying off countless virtuous wives and daughters of Alexandria for his own amusement until rebuked in the name of Christ by a noble virgin whose name was Purity—Catherine in Greek. Helpless, we are told, against her brilliant theology, the emperor summoned 50 philosophers to dispute her. Though only 18, she convinced them all, whereupon Maxentius burned them at the stake. Without a word to his wife Faustina, he offered beautiful Catherine a throne beside his and a place in his bed. She refused. Whipped and thrown into prison, she made converts of 200 imperial guardsmen—and of Faustina, who dropped in to size up the competition. Maxentius sent the new members of the Church to greet their Maker and ordered a great wheel set with knives for Catherine's final punishment. As the dread machine began to do its dire work, it flew into pieces, scattering blades through the crowd and wounding many an unbaptized gawker. Undaunted, the emperor cut off his worthy opponent's head, but was as surprised as anyone to see milk rather than blood flowing from her severed veins. A band of angels carried Catherine's body to Mount Sinai, but her learned head was taken to Rome. Today she is recognized as patroness of schools, philosophers, and students of philosophy.

The wheel that failed to slice up Saint Catherine of Alexandria returns in the names of various magical symbols and practical objects. Among the latter, the spinning firework is called a catherine wheel. In Spanish, the main wheel of a watch has the same name, *rueda catalina*, or simply *la catalina*. Dwelling on that, I see a writer's (not a sorcerer's) vision of little Carlos standing at his father's elbow staring mesmerized into the shining movement of a gold watch his father is repairing.

"This is *la catalina*," father Arana says, touching the slow main wheel with his slender forceps. Though Carlitos hears the name, his gaze has already been sucked into the whirlpool of the balance wheel, spinning and shimmering like a tiny ballerina. He reaches toward it, but his father warns him it is too delicate and precious to be touched by little boys or non-watchmakers.

One evening he sees another golden spinner, skating along the ground or clinging to a tree trunk. A flaming whirl, a sputtering hiss, an acrid smell—then suddenly it is gone again into the shadows. Creeping up to see what happened, he finds the lovely vision's body dead but still warm. A voice behind him asks, "Is there another *catalina*?"

Women, too, are mesmerizing beauties, fiery whirlers in their full skirts, sometimes too delicate and precious to be touched by little boys or non-watchmakers. At climactic moments they may go all to pieces and puncture graceless bystanders. Beloved women can be feared, especially "a woman so big that she reached up to the sky and eclipsed the sun," an angry giantess who picked a house up with one hand.

Of course other *catalinas* were available. The Chimu kings ruled a valley the Spaniards renamed Santa Catalina. The sec-

ond puppet Royal Inca married his sister Doña Catalina.
Spanish engineers call a gooseneck gin a *catalina*. A gossiping
woman who makes trouble and stirs things up is dubbed *la
Catalina*. Wherever the Sonoran Circe got her name, she is the
prime model of woman Castaneda gives us. We have to take her
seriously not only as a wicked witch of the West but as a vessel
charged with his feelings toward the women in his life.

'La Catalina' is young, beautiful, cold, dangerous, stocky,
strong, splendid, and evil, a bad mama if ever there was one.
You dare not turn your back on her. When you want to get away
from her, she follows you around. When you want to get close,
to press your face into her clothing, she jumps away like a big,
black flea. In dreams she soars above you like a silent bird of
prey. When you flee a noisy party where everybody thinks you
are a misfit, she hops out of the shadows and chases you all the
way home. When you hope for a word of condolence, she howls
at you like a wild animal. Her direct stare paralyzes your limbs
with fearful cravings. Her icy smile invites and forbids you at
the same time. The scarier she is, the more you want her.

Older, more experienced, somewhat cynical men tell you
how to deal with her, how to conduct an affair with a witch.
You must take your blunt, split-end instrument in your hand,
your ugly, bristly, revolting boar's foreleg, and ram it right into
the middle of where she lives, no matter how sick it makes you
feel. Give her one hell of a time, but don't say a word to her
while you are doing it. Leave your calling card in her belly,
something she can't get rid of though no one else can see it. She
won't bother us men after that. Whatever you do, don't fail to
pierce her, or she will cut you dead from then on, and she may
even tell her male relatives you tried to take liberties with her.
When you meet her again, be sure not to move from your spot.
Don't give an inch in your feelings about her, for if you do she
will take your soul and keep it, and you will waste away and be
no good any more as a sorcerer or a man.

Pablito's oldest sister had a look so mean it killed lice.
Stronger than he, she pulled a handful of his hair out like
chicken feathers. Pablito lived in fear of his beastly sister until
don Juan took pity on him and magically transformed her into a
saint. Don Juan's satanic benefactor had only to set eyes on a
woman to see her wane away. Don Juan magically caressed a
hungry puma's tits from a distance of several feet until she
relaxed and let him escape. In the separate reality, sorcerers
dominate females by raping them symbolically or casting

spells on them. How does a sorcerographer deal with women in the ordinary reality?

Though Castaneda told the Irvine students he had never heard of a woman apprentice—"Maybe it's because sorcerers are chauvinistic male pigs"—he was charming, graceful, and attentive to the women around him, noted John Wallace. He told funny stories in New York about Carlos's failures with women, Eric Todhunter remembered. He showed up with a bunch of girlie magazines in his hand, Roy Buzza "seemed to recall." He could've got laid easy at the party, Warren Farley rued, he just wasn't trying.

A sorcerer needs a cubic centimeter of luck in his dealings with women, Castaneda said at Irvine. He does not deliberately seek women out but waits for them to come to him—the women he needs to protect him. Margaret Runyan sent him "an open invitation." Six months later, he sought her protection. In her mid-thirties like 'la Catalina,' she was no fiery witch but a decorous lady. Though he sometimes called her "Margarita," most of the time he called her "Miss Runyan," even after they were married. No house-upsetting giantess, she sat easily on his shoulder as he carried her playfully about. Like him she preferred ideas to feelings. "I did not fall in love with Carlos," she wrote. "I simply loved him completely and spiritually from our first meeting—as I do today." A year after the divorce—14 years after the separation—she said: "We are married spiritually and always will be." "He has a girl friend," *Time* reported, "but not even his friends know her last name." For 13 years her last name was Castaneda.

"You don't like the heat," said don Juan at sunset, "you like the glow." Careful not to cross the scorchline, Castaneda gets close enough to women to see the light of curiosity in their eyes or feel the glow of their friendly, often helpful interest. He likes to talk to women, even strangers, about himself, but presently grows restless, begins to tease, and then withdraws. The two Sacramento bookwomen heard complaints about Carlos's parents, disparagement of his students, and at last a solemn confession that his one remaining ambition was to travel the whole world in the footprints of Margaret Mead.

"Why are you laughing?" Booklady asked me.

"It's ridiculous," I said.

"He was insulting us!" she bristled.

One night in April 1962 Sue Parrott dreamed she found an abandoned baby on the stool next to her in a restaurant. Opening the blanket, she was horrified to see a man's head on the tiny body and a familiar face leering at her. *Now I've got you!* his expression said. Her sympathy for the helpless infant gave way to revulsion at the adult's trick.

No, Carlos, she said, *you'll not pull this on me!* Unwilling to mother or protect a grown sorcerer, she laid the bundle down and walked away. She was not the first.

Raised from the start by his Brazilian grandparents, Carlos lost his 15-year-old mother before knowing her. When he was only six she died or (in another version) left home. Peruvian Susana died in Lima when her son was 24. Refusing to attend the funeral, he locked himself in his room, where he stayed three days without eating. Coming out, he announced he was leaving home. Twenty years later he still carried the "horrendous burden" of her love.

Daring to speculate on this skimpy and suspect evidence, we see a man whose strongest bond in life was with his mother—not a bond of joy and contentment but one of worry and longing. From the start (he felt) she let others take care of him, and when he was only six (it seemed) her love for him went elsewhere. Until the age of 24 he waited near her, not knowing he was waiting, to feel her love come back to him. At her death he returned 18 years into the past to comfort the motherless six-year-old Carlos. Man and boy they fasted three days together, mourning the love that was somehow unbearable or had been lost and not regained. Then they left home forever.

In his adopted country the twice-abandoned son dreamed of finding the enveloping, protecting love he could not remember but had always wanted. "You have looked for her everywhere," don Juan told Carlos. Margaret was more like her than anyone else, but no living woman could satisfy a formless craving born in childhood and buried alive at 24. Though rarified, the demands of marriage proved too heavy to bear, and after six months he turned away to a companion who knew just what he was ready to give and never asked for more.

Don Juan *saw* Carlos had lost a very dear blond woman, who had left him because he made himself too available to her, because he hung around day after day until they both got bored, because everyone knew about the two of them. Righting this topsy-turvy romance we get a more plausible version. The husband left his very important brunette woman because he could not be as open as she wanted, could not enjoy her company very long without getting bored, could not share friends or colleagues with her, could not endure her attempts to get more of him.

She was a fine person, don Juan said. You should speak no ill of her. She was weak, Carlos retorted. What was her weakness? No doubt like everyone she needed to be the baby part of the time, but he wasn't ready for that. You cling out of desperation, don Juan said, exhausting both yourself and your partner. A hunter deals intimately with his world, yet is inaccessible to that world. That's a contradiction, Carlos objected. Don Juan explained the inaccessible intimacy.

A hunter does not squeeze his world or his beloved out of shape. He taps lightly, stays as long as he needs to, then swiftly moves away leaving hardly a mark. What kind of love taps lightly, stays as long as it needs to, and moves away swiftly leaving hardly a mark? Love in a separate reality, love for Mother Earth, love for an unpopulated biosphere. In the world of men and women love penetrates, inflames, absorbs. Water to seed, spark to tinder, mercury to gold, it stays not as long as it needs to but as long as it can, moving away not swiftly but with grateful sloth, from a beloved not unmarked but wounded, pierced like the lover, sundered and rearranged. Such catalytic love a warrior does not seek and could not tolerate. Love suffered by the child does not delight the man. Nevertheless, a warrior needs women—four at a time.

As the Mother of God visited Juan de la Cruz in prison, showing him a remote window through which he would escape, teaching him to loosen the hinges of his door, cushioning perilous falls and leaps, guiding him with glorious light and voice, and lifting him over an unscalable wall, so when they are needed four benevolent women are blown to a sorcerer like four winds—not to join their lives to his, not to touch or hold him close, not to exchange pleasures with him, but to stand with him for a little while against the assaults of the ally, the specter that returns from exile or comes from an unknown part of him to test his defenses. Either he wrestles the ally to the ground and takes its power, or the ally whirls him up and away from the prison of this world into worlds beyond. The sorcerer who hopes to come back to the ordinary world is foolish indeed to confront the ally without his amazon retinue, but he cannot actively seek them. They must come to him voluntarily, subtly drawn by his aching need and charismatic power. More charming than Carlos and less disconcerting, young Pablito had already attracted three volunteers and if he could get a fourth would not have to face the ally by himself.

The four and one journey together to a nameless Sonoran plain, where the ladies man their positions at the cardinal points. To the north, facing the sorcerer, stands the shield and protector. To the south, behind him, stands the warm wind, the joker, she who relieves the sometimes oppressive solemnity of the northwind woman. To the west stands the introspective spirit catcher, to the east the weapon, the foremost authority, the wind of illumination. One by one these noble altruists are "flattened" or otherwise knocked out of the fight, leaving the ally presumably weakened for the final wrestling match with the one who counts.

The characters of the women and the details of the struggle had not been all worked out when the Irvine students heard this parable in 1972, but one thing was clear: the selfless women a sorcerer expends against psychic or occult forces neither desert him in his hour of need nor ask any reward beyond the privilege of serving him. Though a rumor spread at Irvine that his teaching assistant had found him a volunteer coed, Castaneda admitted not a single wind had blown his way and said he expected to stand on that fateful plain alone. Lacking his shock troop he would most likely be no match for the ally. As it had spun don Juan and Genaro, the ally would spin Carlos out of this world forever, permanently exhausting his human feelings and setting his feet on a road that would lead him perpetually homeward but never bring him home.

Though Thomas Wolfe said you can't go home again, he proved you can bring home with you. Most people carry enough along to satisfy them, remembering what they like and forgetting the rest. Proust and Anaïs Nin remembered practically everything. Of course the past we carry with us is our own particular version of what happened, the one we care about. Thomas Wolfe grew up in Ashville, North Carolina but wrote about Eugene Gant of Altamont, Old Catawba; that was his version of home. Carlos Arana grew up in Cajamarca. Like other sorcerers, he keeps trying to go home, fully aware that he can't. Since anyone can go to Cajamarca when the road isn't washed out, I take it his destination is really Caxamalca—an archaic spelling sounding much the same, signifying Castaneda's private version of home. Why does he want to go there when he could bring it with him?

Sorcerers blame their homesickness on the ally. Spinning into other worlds, they say, redefines everything, dims the old memories, dessicates the past, dulls the familiar scenes making them unreal. New people seem no more real than the old. To get their special knowledge, sorcerers say, they willingly pay this tragic price.

I am not ready to swallow the sorcerer's explanation whole. Some visionaries keep memories bright and ties unbroken. Lame Deer reminisced with great feeling. María Sabina and Ramón Medina were not homeless in either past or present. Though the Señora was a far out lady whose conversation seemed to refer to worlds apart, she sang to her son, was assisted in ceremonies by her daughter, and enjoyed the company of her neighbors. Though Ramón had learned his shamanic destiny as a little boy from Our Father Sun who spoke to him in dreams, he had a loving wife and was the leader of his people. These shamans bridged two worlds and two conditions, human and superhuman. As superhuman beings they visited the spirit world. As human beings they took pleasure in the ordinary relations Castaneda said sorcerers would find no longer real. They were not solitary birds who could endure no company, not even of their own kind.

Castaneda compared himself by implication to Saint John of the Cross, but we don't have to believe the two arrived at the solitary condition in the same way. Juan Yepes was called to serve the Virgin early in his life; we have no evidence young Carlos heard from Inti or Saint Catherine. Padre Juan would rap sharply on the wall of the cloister as he walked along, to keep himself from ecstasy; he was reluctant to say the mass, fearing the Beloved might speak to him and interrupt the proceedings. Carlos's yearning for the absolute seems wholly intellectual, not a cause of his separation from mankind but an excuse and compensation for it. San Juan's renunciation of human love cost him dearly. When he allowed himself to turn to a friend, he told her how he really felt, and he signed his name. Castaneda did not reveal himself or his name to his most intimate companion.

I suspect those sorcerers and quasi-sorcerers who keep trying to go home are like other nostalgic people. Their Ixtlan or Caxamalca does not satisfy now because it never did. They can't enjoy it and they can't get rid of it. They want to improve it but they don't know how. Sometimes they dream of going back and starting over—adoring her more intensely who sang the lullabye about a lost apple, running faster to keep up with a grown man in a hurry, accepting a first-grader's awkward hero worship, weeping openly at unexpected approval, speaking out the words of love a father couldn't hear unspoken, saying a sorrowful goodbye at the harbor instead of talking only about good times and cracking desperate jokes.

A sorcerer abandons those he has loved, don Juan told Carlos. Never can he go back to them. Was there no way, Carlos pleaded, to retrieve them? Couldn't he rescue them and bring them along? No, he couldn't, don Juan said firmly. Even fellow sorcerers had to say goodbye.

At the northwest corner of ancient Cuzco just beyond the House of Inti rises a great round channeled rock called the Sliding Place because the playful used to slide down in the grooves. As we stand gazing up at it, do we not spy our playful benefactor waving to attract our scattered tourist attention? Now he begins to slide, gets stuck in midcourse, plummets down, holds his behind, pretends the rock has pinched him— the sort of trick one might expect from a 70-year-old-by-now sorcerer who "looked like a small child with shiny mischievous eyes," laughed uncontrollably shaking his body and kicking his legs "like a child," rolled on the ground, lay on his stomach, began to swim on the floor, pretended to fly his hat like a kite, imitated driving a car. In the back seat while Carlos was driving Gerancho giggled with Juancho.

"Are we getting closer?" Juancho whined.

"We're about to get there," muttered Papa Carlos.

If imaginary playmates surrounded Carlitos Arana, some of whom were rescued and brought to a new land, Genaro and don Juan may not be the most important members of the troupe. As Joseph Margolis hints, Pablito and Nestor may go back a lot farther. Pablito is the sunny side of Carlos, small-boned but wiry and strong like Genaro, nearly thirty but acting like a teenager, flashing a winning but devilish smile. Nestor is the shadow side, taller, heavier, and much older, so gloomy and withdrawn he would have died, Pablito said, if Genaro had not turned him younger. Eternal childhood may be the secret of a sorcerer's survival.

Whoever the unseen companions are, I count them Castaneda's true and only intimate friends. To them he reveals himself, on them he depends for consolation. Yet sometimes he regrets their insubstantiality and longs for love whose arms he can feel around him. When don Juan sent him out into the wilderness alone, Carlos felt suddenly abandoned, as if the only point of reference, the sole origin of the separate reality had always been Carlos himself, "as if don Juan had never really been there," as if when Carlos looked for him "he became what he really was—a fleeting image that vanished over a hill."

"Don Juan has no real compassion for me," Castaneda said. "He can only approximate true human feelings." Perhaps not a harsh judgement of an imaginary being who has been spun by his ally, and yet somewhat unfair. Until the rest of us heard about him, don Juan spent every waking minute entertaining Castaneda. Many of their best conversations went unreported to the outside world because Carlos couldn't take notes while driving. We are told, for example, that he brought don Juan within 50 miles of Los Angeles.

"I'm not going in *there*!" don Juan said. "Too many evil spirits." Carlos had to turn the car around and take him back to Yuma—but what did Castaneda do? Drove straight on to Malibu, in my opinion. During Tucson's Earth Week Carlos attended an ecology lecture, where the speaker punctuated his condemnations of pollution with puffs on a cigarette. A dignified old man in the seat next to Carlos leaned over and whispered: "I cannot imagine that he is concerned with other people's bodies when he doesn't like his own." I'll give you one guess who that old man was.

Castaneda travels the ordinary reality alone, but he travels the separate reality with his comrades by his side. Their love may not be truly human, but it is better than no love at all. Like the loneliness of a child whose playmates are imagined, a warrior's loneliness is real but not complete.

Tales of Power put an end to both apprenticeship and story—that was Castaneda's solemn promise. The apprentice no longer needed don Juan as master, the man of novels was done with him as character. Declaring they would become again what they had always been, dust on the road, the dons left Carlos and Castaneda more alone than they had been for 13 years.

New public companions are needed now for the separate reality, but the Sonora Spoofers will be a hard act to follow. What will happen to Carlos next? Various possibilities loom: Carlos's double captured by a worthy opponent and held for psychic ransom. Carlos influencing the dreams of UCLA volunteers, one of whom turns out to be a witch. Carlos-Sorcerer, arrived at last, instructing his own apprentice in the mountains of Malibu, or on Wilshire Boulevard in a building ornamented by a sculptured goddess. Carlos retracing the footsteps of Margaret Mead. Carlos in primal therapy. Castaneda writing his autobiography, telling it like it was—names, dates, places, facts, history restored.

Come to think of it, that last would be a winner. Could he do it? I don't think so, but I wouldn't sell him short. He is bold and determined, a man of surprises. What is left to do that could top what he has done? Only to deal with a new reality, the ordinary reality, where rocks do come back from the moon, where the most common event is an ultimate mystery, where a man like Carlos Castaneda can live in the flesh as well as in books. Don Juan said the best work in Carlos's life would be done towards the end of the day.

In the midst of the sad goodbyes, Genaro slipped in a joker as usual. "We will now be like dust on the road," he echoed don Juan, then added: "Perhaps it will get in your eyes again, some-day." What did he mean by that?

One day in winter (the story will go) Carlos Castaneda was driving down a pretty smooth stretch of the road to Caxamalca, when he saw a familiar figure trudging along. Screeching to a stop, he jumped out of the bus.

"Genaro!" he shouted. "I thought you would be dust on the road!"

Genaro sauntered up to him with a big grin. His step was as springy as ever.

"This part of the road is oiled," he said, unslinging his carry-ing net. "How far you going?"

"Caxamalca."

"Good!" Genaro climbed into the bus. "I'll go with you."

Carlos was elated. He took his seat and they got rolling.

"Glad to see you again, Carlitos." Genaro patted him on the head. The gesture filled Carlos with an overwhelming sadness.

"Why do you want to go to Caxamalca?" he asked.

"I don't." Genaro took out a knife and began to pare his toenails. "I'm still on my way to Ixtlan. You know that."

"This road won't take you to Ixtlan. I have the map right here."

"Let's see it." Genaro snatched the map out of his hand.

"I thought you couldn't read Spanish," Carlos objected.

"When you're in love with the world, all maps are Mazatec," Genaro retorted. Humming a Huautecan tune, he traced the tortuous route with his knife. "Just what I thought," he said. "There's a dead end further on, a permanent washout. This road won't take you to Caxamalca."

"It won't take you to Ixtlan either," Carlos reminded him.

"I know that." Genaro sighed. "So we may as well travel together."

"I just wish . . . " Carlos choked up and couldn't continue.

"You wish old Juancho was riding with us, don't you?"

"Yes," croaked Carlos. He peered down the sunbaked road, fighting back the tears.

"You know, your friend Al Egori sent him a copy of *Tales of Folly.*"

"Sent *who* a copy?" Carlos nearly drove off the road.

"Take it easy! Don Juan, of course."

Carlos was thunderstruck. "Don Juan is alive?" He stared at Genaro with open mouth.

"As alive as I am!" Genaro chuckled.

"That's wonderful!" Carlos was bursting with excitement. "What did he think of the book?"

"He said the cover looked great but the pages weren't very soft."

Carlos's face flushed. "He said that *again?*"

Genaro laughed. "I'm just kidding. You can ask him yourself when we catch up with him."

"What do you mean?" Carlos was confused.

"He's on his way home too, you know, but he started earlier."

"Don Juan wasn't born in Caxamalca."

"Neither was I, but here I am!"

Carlos shook his head. "I don't understand," he said.

Genaro pounded him on the knee. "By golly, Carlitos! You haven't changed a bit. You're just as dumb as you were in 1968!"

"Please explain it to me!" Carlos begged.

"Okay. It doesn't matter where don Juan was born. He can't get back there anyway."

"But why would he travel the road to Caxamalca? Just tell me that."

Genaro laughed till the highway rippled. "I can't believe what an idiot you are!" he wheezed. "What makes you think there's another road? What would we need another road for?"

"To go different places!" Carlos was getting annoyed.

"Sure, to go different places. But this road doesn't."

"Doesn't *what?*" Carlos was exasperated. He thought Genaro must be losing his marbles.

"Doesn't go places. This road doesn't go to Ixtlan, doesn't go to Caxamalca, doesn't go to every place somebody wants to go. This is the road sorcerers go home on, and sorcerers can't go home, so it doesn't."

Carlos began to smile. "That's how we can all travel together!"

"You got it, my boy!" Genaro ruffled his friend's coyote-grey
hair. "That's called the sorcerer's compensation."

"I never heard of it before," Carlos admitted.

"You didn't need it till now," Genaro said softly.

"What made you think me a bird?" he asked.

"You looked a raven, and I saw you dig worms out of the ground with your beak."

"And then?"

"Toss them into the air."

"And then?"

"They grew butterflies and flew away."

"Did you ever see a raven do that? I told you I was a sexton."

"Does a sexton toss worms into the air and turn them into butterflies?"

"Yes."

"I never saw one do it."

"You saw me do it."

"I see a pigeon!" I said.

"Of course you see a pigeon," said the raven, "for there is the pigeon. I see a prayer on its way."

"How can a pigeon be a prayer?" I rejoined. "I do understand how it should be a fit symbol for a prayer—but a live pigeon to come out of a heart!"

"It must puzzle you."

"A prayer is a thought," I pursued, "a thing spiritual."

"Very true. But if you understood any world besides your own, you would understand your own much better. When a heart is really alive, it can think live things. All live things were thoughts to begin with." He pointed his beak downward.

"That is a prayer-flower," he said.

I looked and saw a little flower of gracious, trusting form, its color as of a new world that was yet the old, like an anemone of pale rose hue, having a golden heart.

"I never saw such a flower before," I said.

"No prayer-flower is quite like any other."

"How do you know it is a prayer-flower?"

"By the expression of it."

"Could you teach me to know a prayer-flower when I see it?"

"And if I could, what better would you be? Why know the name of a thing, when the thing itself you do not know? Whose work is it but your own to open your eyes? Indeed, the business of the universe is to make such a fool of you that you will know yourself for one, and so begin to be wise."

—George MacDonald
Lilith

Logical or chronological errors in the narrative constitute the best evidence that Castaneda's books are works of fiction. If no one has discovered these errors before, the reason must be that no one has listed the events of the first three books in sequence. Once that has been done, the errors are unmistakable.

Though I call them errors, I do not mean they are inadvertent slips of the typewriter. On the contrary, they are massive, systematic, and apparently deliberate transpositions needed when the author changed his thematic emphasis and invented additional incidents that had to be back-dated to find accommodation in ordinary time and to show that don Juan had been on the right track all along while only his thick-headed apprentice had been wandering. Our impression that the author knew very well what he was doing comes from seeing how boldly his rationale for the change contradicts the events it purports to explain and how smoothly his anachronistic flashbacks are folded into an otherwise straightforward story line to hide logical conflicts from any reader who does not undertake the tedious chore of plotting the sequence of events. Needless to say, very few readers will have done that.

In his second book, Castaneda began to shift his emphasis subtly from drug experiments to non-drug experiences. Table 1 lists Carlos's 22 drug experiments in sequence. The first column in the table identifies the three classes of experiments—eating peyote (P), drinking infusions or applying paste of the Jimson weed (J), and smoking the mushroom mixture (M). Each experiment is numbered within its class, so that we find peyote experiments numbered 1-6, Jimson weed 1-4, mushroom 1-12. The three books are identified as *The Teachings of Don Juan* (J), *A Separate Reality* (R), and *Journey to Ixtlan* (I). The page numbers come from the Pocket Book paperback editions. Each experiment is dated according to the text. Minor conflicts with Castaneda's dates arise from his dual dating system, which mixes dates of events with dates of writing up field notes, and from verbal refinements in the text, as when the author says something like: "Two days later I smoked the mushroom mixture again."

The 22 drug experiments occupy a narrative period of eight years. Carlos's learning progresses in an orderly fashion from one experiment to the next, with just enough false starts and wasted effort to imitate the imperfections of ordinary life. No inconsistencies are evident. In contrast, the non-drug experiences are logically disordered.

Table 2 lists 34 non-drug nonordinary events occurring from January 1961, when Carlos had known don Juan (dJ) only six months and had not yet entered the formal apprenticeship, to October 1970, when don Genaro (dG) leapt ten miles to the mountain tops. During those ten years other non-drug nonordinary events may have occurred, depending on the reader's judgment of what is a nonordinary event and what is a mere illusion or mistake, but the 34 listed events are the most vivid and least mistakable ones from that period. (Part Two of *Journey to Ixtlan* is excluded, because it treats events occurring in May 1971, too late to have a bearing on this argument.)

Numerous metaphysicians have told us that in the nonordinary reality, in the *nagual*, or in some absolute realm time can stand perfectly still, can bring past and future into an eternal present, or can run in any direction. One theory of subatomic particles holds that matter going forward in time equals antimatter going backward. I would certainly not dismiss these propositions.

TABLE 1
Sequence of Drug Experiments

Expt	Book	Page	Year	Month	Day	Experience
P 1	J	36	1961	Aug	4	Plays with Mescalito-dog
J 1	J	61		Sep	7	Sees red spot, good omen
P 2	J	100	1962	Jun	28	Sees Mescalito as green man
J 2	J	113	1963	Apr	17	Hears lizard speak. Sees book-thief and girl who may go mad
J 3	J	125		Jul	4	Flies. Comes to rest half a mile from dJ's house
M 1	J	132		Dec	26	Wipes face off. Penetrates pole & wall. Rises by will alone. Enters dJ's chest
P 3	J	144	1964	Sep	3	Begins first mitote
P 4	J	144			4	Sees Mescalito
P 5	J	145			5	Sings his own peyote song
P 6	J	146			6	Sees Mescalito & father. Weeps. Kelp threatens to devour him
J 4	J	154		Dec	20	Lizard-sewing. Sees book-thief again
M 2	J	163	1965	Jan	19	Falls asleep too soon
M 3	J	166			31	Head turns into crow. Sees like crow
M 4	J	168		Mar	18	Flies with silvery crows. Gone 3 days
M 5	R	115	1968	Nov	9	Giant gnat, wings hit Carlos's eyes
M 6	R	121			11	Dissociated talking. Rises by will
M 7	R	127	1969	Jan	18	Escapes gnat-guardian
M 8	R	154		Jun	28	Cries about little boy. dJ's face glows
M 9	R	163		Jun	30	Seeing the water
M 10	R	170		Aug	9	Rides on a bubble
M 11	R	182		Sep	3	Sees man in plowed field. dJ's face glows. Next day a flashback
M 12	R	221		Nov	10	Hears sounds. Sees ally

In fact I am devoted to them. All the same, when we try to determine whether a book is a novel or a factual report, we do not probe its subatomic structure or visit the writer in our dreams. We examine the text, judging it by common-sense rules of time and tide, clock and calendar. Marked anachronisms or logical conflicts in Castaneda's work must argue that his text is an imaginative fabrication rather than a factual report.

Applying the ordinary rules to Castaneda's narrative does not, of course, prevent us from sharing don Juan's sense of magical time, as when we saw the same leaf fall four times. It merely directs our attention for the moment to the normal temporal context of those magical events. And that context is not negotiable. Castaneda uniformly maintains that the timeline of his story is the familiar progress of events in the practical world, where people go to work, sign up for classes in anthropology, and meet or fail to meet their publisher's deadlines. In these three books he makes much of the exact dates on which things happen, and his conventional chronology helps us to accept his unearthly adventures. Having enjoyed this narrative benefit, Castaneda must now pay the cost by following the rules he has imposed. Wherever his *ordinary* acts violate the rules of conventional time, his story turns into fiction before our eyes.

Carlos's 22 drug experiments are confined to the first two books. Introducing the third book, Castaneda begs the reader's pardon for having erroneously assumed that drug states were the only avenue to don Juan's knowledge. The mistake, he says, was forced upon him by the fact that Carlos's drugged perceptions had been "so bizarre and impressive." Though don Juan had actually tried to give Carlos the core of the teachings in the first two years through non-drug techniques, and though Carlos had doggedly written those non-drug lessons into his field notes along with the drug lessons, he had neither found them so unusual nor been so impressed by them that Castaneda could not systematically eliminate them while writing *The Teachings*.

Before one has read *Journey to Ixtlan*, this rationale sounds quite reasonable. Afterwards, the reflective reader may notice a contradiction. Despite the rationale, some of the non-drug experiences have been strange indeed, and Carlos has certainly been impressed by them. But while the Carlos of *Ixtlan* finds these lessons intensely moving and wholly relevant to don Juan's teaching, the Carlos of *The Teachings* apparently did not. (*A Separate Reality*, the transition volume, describes 15 such incidents without calling attention to their non-drug character.) It seems we are dealing here with two different Carloses, who lived through 1961 and 1962 in the same places with the same teacher but felt and understood it all quite differently.

Carlos-Two, of *Ixtlan*, the Carlos we met second, saw a falcon in don Juan's features (Event-1), saw a bridge and slept in a cave that did not exist in the ordinary world (E-6), spied a bush on one side of a hill whose ordinary location was on the other (E-7), had a fleeting vision of a vast world in the surface of a rock (E-12), saw a range of mountains as a web of light fibers (E-13), and attended a magical demonstration where don Juan appeared simultaneously to five apprentices in five different guises (E-14). Reacting to these extraordinary events, Carlos-Two felt his heart had stopped, stared dumbfounded, was nearly paralyzed by the shock of seeing his surroundings, went through a moment of unparalleled confusion, refused to believe what he was witnessing, grappled for any kind of an explanation, felt a chill run up his spine, felt a hand grabbing his stomach, and screamed involuntarily. Carlos-One, in contrast, found these events so commonplace that Castaneda felt no need even to allude to them in *The Teachings*.

The Teachings seldom mentioned nonordinary seeing, only once without linking it to drugs. *Ixtlan* mentioned it at least a dozen times, identifying it as an important aspect of don Juan's non-drug teaching. Carlos-Two was formally introduced to *seeing* on 28 December 1961, when don Juan said: "Look without blinking until you *see*." Carlos-One first encountered it on 2 April 1968, when don Juan said: "The little smoke will help you to *see* men as fibers of light." "Fibers of light?" The phrase came unfamiliar to Carlos-One's ear, though Carlos-Two had seen a range of mountains as fibers of light in 1962 after don Juan had instructed him at some length in that particular kind of seeing.

On 8 November 1968 don Juan said to Carlos-One: "There is something in you that resembles *seeing* but isn't." On 29 January 1962 don Juan had told Carlos-Two: "This morning you *saw*." Though these discrepancies are sugar coated by Carlos-Two's frequent protestations that he does not understand what don Juan is telling him, don Juan insists that telling and understanding are not the point; *seeing* is the point. In *seeing*, Carlos-Two is seven years ahead of Carlos-One. The uncoated pill has a sharp taste of contradiction.

Manifestly, these books are describing parallel universes, one inhabited by Carlos-Two, the other by Carlos-One. The conventional rules, by which

TABLE 2
Sequence of Non-Drug Nonordinary Events

Event	Book	Page	Year	Month	Day	Description
1	I	29	1961	Jan	25	Sees falcon on dJ's face. dJ's ESP
2	J	28		Jun	23	Finds power spot on dJ's floor
3	I	61			29	Wind searches for Carlos
4	I	67			30	dJ's ESP about blond girl
5	I	101		Aug	19	Sees branch as monster
6	I	126		Dec	28	Visions of bridge and cave
7	I	145	1962	Jan	29	Sees displaced bush. dJ's ESP
8	I	161		Apr	8	Feels heat from leaves
9	I	175			8	Menaced by entities of the night
10	I	182			11	Suspended in air by bed of stone strings
11	I	185			12	Mountains move, yellow cloth illusion
12	I	197			13	Fleeting vision of vast world
13	I	202			14	Sees mountains as web of light fibers
14	I	207			14	dJ shows magic to four young Indians
15	R	11		May	14	Sacateca's will stops Carlos
16	R	204		*O/N		Fires shotgun at Catalina-blackbird
17	R	210		*O/N		Boar's foreleg to pierce Catalina
18	I	216		*O/N		Stalks Catalina with car
19	I	218		**Dec	11	Catalina sails slowly overhead
20	I	224		**	12	Catalina hops along road
21	I	229		**	13	Catalina stands in doorway
22	J	182	1965	Oct	1	Female soul-stealer (Catalina) impersonates dJ (the "special" event)
23	R	19	1968	Apr	2	dJ's ESP, knows Carlos has come
24	R	55		Jun	16	Hears & sees mother at second mitote
25	R	102		Oct	17	dG tumbling & perching on waterfall
26	R	134	1969	Apr	24	dJ's ESP about childhood promise
27	R	200		Sep	5	dJ prevents car from starting
28	R	231		Dec	15	Carlos's hand grows warm
29	R	231			15	Moth as big as a man
30	R	244			17	Moth taps back of Carlos's neck
31	R	253	1970	Oct	16	Sees sound of dG's great boulder
32	R	256			16	dG leads/follows Carlos on trail
33	R	260			18	Same leaf falls four times
34	R	261			18	dG leaps ten miles to mountain tops

*Page I-215 places Events 16-18 in October or November of 1962.

**Events 19-21, dated in *Journey to Ixtlan*, were left undated in *Sorcery: A Description of the World*.

Castaneda bound himself when he dated Carlos's field notes, tell us these two universes cannot both be our daily world, where graduate students do tangible field work and become doctors of anthropology.

Compelling as this evidence is, a more startling anachronism remains to be described. In October 1965 (E-22) Carlos-One went through an ordeal so unexpected and disturbing that he sadly withdrew from his apprenticeship and avoided don Juan for more than two years. The ordeal was a night-long confrontation with a powerful enemy who had assumed don Juan's bodily form though not his accustomed gait or speech. It disturbed Carlos deeply because for the first time he entered a vivid and extended state of nonordinary reality that did not result from using a drug. This unique event confirmed his growing suspicion that the nonordinary reality could, without drugs, break through his comfortable daily certainties and flood his sober consciousness. Rather than be overwhelmed by that other world, he fled in terror back to Los Angeles, where Castaneda wrote a book featuring the special event not only as the climax of its story but as the crowning exhibit in an academic analysis of "special consensus."

The reader of *The Teachings* found this development disappointing but plausible. In contrast, the reader of Table 2 discovers that the "special" event was not so special after all, since it was preceded by 21 earlier non-drug nonordinary events, in many of which even stranger visions or more menacing confrontations had invaded Carlos-Two's sober consciousness. Reacting to these earlier events, Carlos-Two had been terrified, angered, saddened, horrified, dumbfounded, deprived of speech, suffocated, born up by exquisite warmth and supreme well being, or gripped by abdominal pains. He could hardly have forgotten about them, but if he had, his field notes would have reminded Castaneda.

Curiously, when Carlos-One begged don Juan to explain what had happened during the "special" event, "the conversation began with speculations about the identity of a *female* person" (italics in the original) who had snatched Carlos's soul and borrowed don Juan's form. The lady was not named, and the reader was left to wonder whether the galvanizing impersonatress was in fact a certain "fiendish witch" called 'la Catalina,' who had been mentioned briefly on 23 November 1961, four years earlier. At that time don Juan had said he was harboring certain plans for finishing her off, about which he would tell Carlos-One "someday." Poor Carlos-One had to wait ten years to learn about those plans in *Tales of Power*, but Table 2 reveals that Carlos-Two, traveling on a parallel time track, carried out those plans with moderate success in the fall of 1962, when he met the magic lady six times in a row (E-16-21), once as a marauding but indistinct blackbird, once as a sailing silhouette, and four times face to face "in all her magnificent evil splendor" as a beautiful but terrifying young woman. Reacting to those encounters, he felt his ears bursting, his throat choking, his hands frozen, his body chilled, and his arms and legs rigid. The hair on his body literally stood on end. He shrieked and fell down to the ground. He was paralyzed. He began to run. And he lost his power of speech.

Here we are asked to believe that a flesh-and-blood anthropologist who enjoyed this tumultuous supernatural affair with a glorious witch in 1962 did not recall her name in 1965, did not make the connection between the last meeting and the previous six when sorting through his field notes in the safety of his apartment, did not put it all together when naming her in his first book, but found the memory "as vivid as if it had just happened" on 22 May

170

1968, a few pages into his second book. Even if we could credit this uncharacteristic amnesia, we would still have to account for don Juan's equal failure to name 'la Catalina' in 1965. The puzzle is easily solved by switching from the factual to the fictive model. The abrupt, unsatisfying ending of *The Teachings* is not a symptom of ethnographic battle fatigue, for our campaigner has already survived six such battles with colors flying. It is only a serialist's preparation for the next episode, a cliffhanger that makes us hungry for another book. Tune in to my next nonordinary volume and hear 'la Catalina' say: "*Oye muchacho!* If you theenk thees blackbirding, boar-dodging, car-stalking, sky-sailing, road-hopping, doorway-standing stuff ees bad, just wait three years till I eempersonate don Juan."

On these showings, one thing is certain. *The Teachings of Don Juan* and *Journey to Ixtlan* cannot both be factual reports. One of them at least is fiction.

At this point one may well ask why Castaneda did not save himself a lot of trouble by telling his story in a straight line right from the beginning. Why did he start off with drug experiments if he or don Juan thought that was the wrong way to go? Having made the false start, why couldn't he change his course gradually, as he was doing in *A Separate Reality*, without going back to Day One?

I don't know what Castaneda's explanation will be when he writes his confessions, but my theory runs like this. Many people who have known Castaneda describe him as consistently opposed to the use of drugs, and his four books taken together support that judgement. The 1960s, however, were not the right time for a non-drug visionary book. The market belonged to Timothy Leary. If Castaneda wanted to teach young people a better way, or even if he just wanted to sell them a lot of books, he had to meet them where they were, which was dropping acid in strawberry fields. As soon as he got a firm grip on his readers, or the market veered away from drugs, he could alter his course. By 1970, when the market was looking better for non-drug books, Castaneda realized he had unwittingly torpedoed his message by allowing many of his readers to believe nobody could get high enough to enter the other world without a powerful boost from the psychotropic rockets. To rescue the teachings, he had to go back over the old ground, illustrating in convincing detail don Juan's distaste for drugs and his capacity to teach any but the most inept apprentice how to *see* without them. To accomplish that rescue, *Ixtlan* had to be backdated.

Or did it? Carlos "had the feeling don Juan was capable of arguing his way out of anything." Why not let him argue his way out of the mess Castaneda had gotten him into? He could blame everything on Carlos's stupidity or stubbornness, and *Ixtlan* could follow *A Separate Reality* in narrative time as well as calendar time. That way, the contradictions would have been avoided, and this analysis could never have been written. But that option was closed, because the author had run out of calendar time.

In the flush of first success, Castaneda had been grinding out magical events faster than the earth was turning, and his readers (and presumably his agent and his publisher) were already howling for more. *A Separate Reality* had carried us all the way to October 1970, narrative time. *Ixtlan* would be published just two years later, calendar time. That left a two-year credibility gap in which somebody had to experience 17 of the events listed in Table 2 (as well as the events of May 1971, not listed), and Castaneda had to write a book

171

about them, saving out at least six months and more likely a year for the publisher's manufacturing and premarketing. To make matters worse, during the first of those two years Castaneda was actively enrolled as a student at UCLA, presumably doing visible things on campus. In the spring of the second year he was lecturing regularly at UC Irvine. Even for a sorcerer that's a pretty tough schedule. Anybody who did not believe a flesh-and-blood anthropologist could pop back and forth between UCLA and Mexico in the blink of a lizard's eyelid would not buy it.

(A systems analyst may warn me this argument is going to founder when I get to *Tales of Power*, which was not backdated. That won't happen, because *Tales of Power* does not pretend to be the log of an apprentice slowly accumulating extended lessons requiring many long absences from Los Angeles. It is a climactic revelation, told in great detail but occupying only a few days spent with the masters. And there are no dates. To justify it, the author had to disappear from public view seldom, briefly, and never on any particular day. Even if the book had been factual, he would have had a year or more to write it. By that time, school was out anyway. The author was sure of his Ph.D. He could drop the narrative devices that had imitated factual reporting and write an unashamed romance.)

Summing up my theory, the vicissitudes of the literary market, the pressures of success and commercialism, the author's productivity, and the passage of ordinary time (which don Juan told us was relentless) combined to trap Castaneda, compelling him to leave in his books some well hidden but ultimately discoverable clues that would someday betray what he had been up to. I don't suppose he worried much about leaving them. A warrior does not wait around to be clobbered. Though he *saw* that I would find his clues in 1975 and publish them in 1976, he also *saw* that he would be flying much too high by that time to be brought to earth again by mere twelve-gauge conclusive proofs of fictioneering.

GO TO THE BLACKBIRD AND WRITE

THE WORD FOR CHANATE

Scanning the first six sections (but not the rest) of *The Teachings of Don Juan*, I picked out every phrase that was given in both of Castaneda's languages. Table 3 shows these bilingual entries classified into four categories: Spanish-to-English (italics on the left), English-to-Spanish (italics on the right), Justifiable (above), and Unjustifiable (below).

I call an item justifiable when the two parts of it supply different information the reader needs. The ten items in the upper part of the table can be justified without difficulty. The Spanish, of course, gives us the ring of don Juan's speech, but what counts here is that the items also name particular unfamiliar plants, introduce sorcerer's terms, distinguish Yaqui Spanish from Mexican Spanish, or employ Spanish idioms and plays on words that must be translated or explained. These items resemble the bilingual entries in ethnographic works, where the original language keeps breaking through to inform us more fully or to provide us with a more efficient vocabulary for describing the culture.

TABLE 3
Bilingual Entries in *The Teachings of Don Juan*

Page*	Text	Translation or Explanation

Justifiable Entries

Page*	Text	Translation or Explanation
14	*brujo, diablero*	sorcerer, black sorcerer
23	*maís-pinto*	red-streaked corn kernels
44	*mamá; tu chingada madre*	(substitution explained)
49	*escogido*	(sorcerer's term) chosen man
52	*la yerba del diablo*	(*Datura*) devil's weed
53	*humito*	(mushroom mixture) little smoke
56	*su nombre de leche*	(idiom) her temporary name
80	All Soul's Day	(Yaqui) *ánimas* (for Mexican *difuntos*)
89	*cielo*	(ambiguity) heaven, sky
106	*cantidades de caminos*	(idiom) a million paths

Unjustifiable Entries

Page*	Text	Translation or Explanation
29	spot	*sitio*
38	This is to be chewed.	*esto se masca*
	Chew it, chew it.	*Masca, masca*
49	There are some secrets I know.	*Tengo secretos* (I have secrets)
58	the only thing that grabs or hooks onto it	*lo unico que prende*
59	portions	*partes*
60	the night air	*el sereno*
63	plant shoot	*brote*
66	to frighten the Indians	*para asustar a los indios*
67	blackbird	*chanate*
70	the bond has been established	*la amistad esta hecha*
71	the little mushrooms	*honguitos*
79	mound	*pilón*
89	He shows things and tells what is what	*enzeña las cosas y te dice lo que son* (tells you what they are)
91	*honguitos*	mushrooms
121	crevices made by running water	*zanjitas*
124	fat from the intestines	*sebo de tripa*
129	a man who has taken the devil's weed flies as such/As birds do?/ No, he flies as a man who has taken the weed.	*el enyerbado vuela así/Así como los pájaros?/ No, así como los enyerbados.*

*Page numbers from Pocket Book paperback edition, 1974.

173

I call an entry unjustifiable when either part of it can be derived from the other simply by opening an abridged dictionary and looking up the common meaning. The 17 items in the lower part of the table fit this definition. Every one is an easy exercise from first-semester Spanish. Having encountered a few of the items from the top of the table, any reader who understands Spanish will pause when he sees an item from the bottom of the table to ask, Why has this been translated into Spanish? He feels a complete, unnecessary redundancy between the two halves of the item. These items do not resemble bilingual entries in ethnographic studies. If we try to explain their presence, we see right away how they serve illustratively to strengthen our belief that the original language was Spanish, particularly if we do not know Spanish and do not feel any redundancy.

Novelists, of course, sometimes make us feel we are reading one language when we are actually reading another. "The woman of Pablo" hispanicizes "Pablo's wife." "I took them to my lips and their taste jumped in my mouth" Washoes our English. But novelists do not randomly parenthesize translations into supposed languages of origin any more than ethnographers render native terms in sprung English. To each his own technique. Castaneda stands oddly between the two.

His compromise may be understood if we consider the alternatives. Hemingway or Sanchez can write sprung English successfully because English is their language and they feel its seams. For Castaneda English is a foreign language. Though he handles it well much of the time, occasionally he writes quaint things like "I did not give a fig," or slips out of the idiom into "Clarity has loomed upon you" or "That statement had clinched me." The added burden of distorting the idiom on purpose may have seemed too great. Moreover, many readers don't like sprung English. Lastly, those who spring it are known to be novelists, while Castaneda said he was writing a factual report.

The ethnographic technique, on the other hand, would here have required him to generate 17 additional justifiable entries—not so easy if the indigenous informant is in one's head. Worse yet, a flesh-and-blood don Juan would have used some Yaqui words. Granted, most Yaquis speak Spanish, but they also speak Yaqui, and don Juan was living in home territory. A writer intending to give the flavor of an actual encounter could hardly have resisted the exotic Yaqui words even if don Juan habitually used only half a dozen of them. They would have erupted into the text. But if don Juan was imaginary, such eruptions would have to be counterfeited. A maneuver both laborious and risky. Easier and safer to stick to the compromise technique and the intermediate language.

In the table, the nearly perfect correlation between language-order and justifiability suggests that the justifiable items entered the text in one way, the unjustifiable in another. One can easily see the justifiable items arising naturally in the course of composition, the unjustifiable items being inserted later to add artistic verisimilitude, perhaps at the urging of a canny editor.

For appendix "The Chicken or the Huevo," including Table 4, see the first edition, pages 175-176.

NOTES

Each note is identified by page number and key word or phrase, as in the example: **55** false skepticism. Some notes refer to passages occupying consecutive pages, though only the first page number is given.

The four don Juan books (References: Castaneda-a, -c, -d, -f) are coded in the notes as: J, R, I, P, signifying *The Teachings of Don JUAN, A Separate REALITY, Journey to IXTLAN,* and *Tales of POWER.* Pages are cited (from the editions specified in the References) as follows: J11; R12, 22, 44; Iviii, 154; P44-45, 101-2.

Other works are generally cited by putting all or part of the citation in parentheses, as follows: (Castaneda-b, 100); (M. Castaneda; Parrott; *Time*, 43); Wasson (-i); MacDonald (210); (Peers, II-27). A work not listed in the References will be fully identified in the citation, as follows: (Frederick B. Pike, *The Modern History of Peru,* Praeger, 1967).

Works by more than one author are cited by the name of the first author only. For letters that distinguish works of one author (-a, -b, -c, -d, etc.) see References introduction.

Don Juan and don Genaro will often be abbreviated dJ and dG. Additional notes are on page 196.

11 In Dr. Wills'. Nandor Fodor reporting on the Thornton Heath poltergeist in the *Journal of the American Society for Psychical Research,* 1938(May), 32(5), 152-160; quote from page 154.

11 Rumbling. William Roll (135) reporting on the Olive Hill Demon.

11 Margaret. (M. Castaneda). Castaneda's former wife.

12 four best sellers. (Castaneda-a, -c, -d, -f), hereafter coded as J, R, I, P.

12 *Mushrooms.* (Wasson-j).

14 D. D. Home. A famous levitator (Roll, 3).

14 Tiger & Fox. Prominent social scientists.

16 Polanyi. (123). Irreversible discovery P228.

16 *hupa.* (Kurath, 43). "On a stump" should be "in a mesquite tree."

17 shamans' vocabulary. (Cravens-b). For the sound of shamans, see: Wasson (-i); Henry Munn, The mushrooms of language (Harner-e, 86-122); Furst (-a); Myerhoff (179-188); Johannes Wilbert, Tobacco and shamanistic ecstasy among the Warao Indians of Venezuela (Furst-b, 55-83).

18 Garfinkel. Mandell (67).

19 merchandising voice. *American Anthropologist,* 1968(June), 70(3), back cover.

20 reviewer. (Ash).

20 *Lophophora.* Peyote plant.

22 What else can a man have. R96. Mothering Matus J137; R88-89, 247; I25, 182, 184; P212, 254.

22 San Juan de la Cruz. Peers (II-27).

24 Testing the Tonal. These nine synthetic answers fairly represent the range of reaction I found in reading and talking to people.

25 In those days. M. Castaneda (74). For Castaneda's biography, I have depended mainly on (M. Castaneda; Parrott; and *Time*). Though some of *Time's* inferences are naïve or illogical, my limited checking with Peruvian and domestic sources generally confirms *Time's* facts. *Time* did swallow Castaneda's non-existent M.A., misspell his grandmother Novoa's name, and get a couple of his textual complications wrong, but most seriously *Time* repeated unfounded allegations against writer John Wallace and failed to publicly correct its mistake. One of *Time's* misstatements could have been avoided simply by examining Wallace's article.

25 Oswaldo Aranha. *Current Biography*, 1942(Mar), 1-3; 1960.

25 Atau Huallpa. Later spelled *Atauhuallpa*; *atau*, success in war; *huallpa*, turkey; the former spelling *Atahuallpa* means chicken and is to be avoided (Brundage, 371; W. H. Prescott, *Conquest of Peru*; W. W. Johnson & others, *The Andean Republics*, Time Inc., 1965).

26 names. Though Arana (ahRAHna) is not a very common name, it is almost as common in Peru as Castañeda; the Lima telephone book had 191 Aranas, 243 Castañedas; in contrast, Mexico City had 141 Aranas, 680 Castañedas. Arana cannot be transliterated into the Portuguese Aranha (ahRAHNya). "Uncle" Oswaldo had blue spiders embroidered on his shirts, pajamas, and underwear because *aranha* (Spanish, *araña*) means spider. Spanish-speakers generally shun the name Spider; the Madrid telephone book listed only two Arañas. Portuguese-speakers don't seem to mind the name Spider, though slang meanings of *aranha* are fumblefoot, nitwit, and sap. Castañeda (CahstahnYEHthah; hard *th* as in *the*) means chestnut grove; Castaneda (without the *ñ*) means nothing in Spanish and, like Araña, was not listed in the telephone books of Mexico City, Lima, or Santiago, Chile. Some people have surprising difficulty with the name Castaneda; I have several times seen it repeatedly spelled Casteneda or Castenada and have often heard it pronounced CastenYAHda; Vine Deloria (see Note: **140** mesoamerican-European wise man) wins the Castaneda-misspelling prize with: Castenada, Castanada, and (in the index) Casteneda, but never Castaneda.

26 heritage. Mestizos, however, may have completely Spanish names.

26 Margaret. (M. Castaneda). Margaret Runyan told me her great grand-father was the brother of Damon Runyon's father; she did not comment on the difference in spelling. Margaret will tell her story in a book co-authored by Wayne Slater which, she said, will reveal that Carlos was actually born in Italy. Tentative title: Solitary Bird.

27 UCLA career. Undergraduate: Sep 1959 to June 1961, Jan to July 1962. BA anthropology 7 Sep 1962. Graduate: Sep 1962 to Dec 1964, Jan to March 1969, Jan 1970 to Dec 1971. PhD anthropology 23 March 1973. No master's degree. Source: Stanley Chin, Registrar.

27 Irvine appointment. (Rueger).

28 Spaniard. Castaneda has not claimed to be an Indian. dJ was baffled by Mescalito's ready acceptance of Carlos, because Carlos was "not an Indian" (I90). Castaneda told Cravens (-a, 97) that he could not live "like an Indian" and that he was "the first European" to follow the path of Indian sorcery.

28 presumptive facts. A presumptive fact is a datum giving reasonable grounds for belief. Though I cannot guarantee other people's observations cited here, I expect most readers to find my exposition reasonable and generally credible. I hope Castaneda and the other actors in these events will correct any errors, providing evidence as persuasive as mine. It is my intention to be fair both to them and to the reader.

28 jobs. Margaret's reports that Carlos worked as cab driver, delivery boy, and women's wear accountant seem to depend entirely on Castaneda's unsupported, vacillating word (M. Castaneda, 75; Parrott, 80). Let me add a rumor of my own. Carlos (R87) "used to talk at great length" with a rich lawyer who had struggled ten years against the New Deal (the National Industrial Recovery Act was first broached 17 May 1933), then exiled himself for 25 years (1943 to 1968 at the earliest), returning at last to live in a home for the aged. He was 84 when Carlos met him. The most likely place for long, repeated conversations with such a person would be the residents' quarters or grounds of the home for the aged. Carlos could have known the old man only between 1968, before which the old man was in exile, and 1970, when the story of the encounter had been written for *A Separate Reality,* published May 1971. Was Castaneda working as a nurse or an attendant in a retirement home between 1968 and 1970? As a youth, his apparent model, San Juan de la Cruz (P7), "spent all his leisure in nursing the patients in the hospital with the utmost zeal, patience, and gentleness" (S. Baring-Gould, *Lives of the Saints*).

28 cousin Sue. Wanda Sue Parrott.

29 as Gordon Wasson was told. See Note: **47** fully and frankly.

29 Carlos's childhood. R45, 136-141, 249. (Cook; Cravens; Keen; *Time*).

29 César Vallejo. P116.

30 glosses. (Cravens-a, 97).

30 similarities. picking plants (Wallace, 142). beach house: *Time* (36,45) allowed Castaneda a Malibu beach house, a Volkswagen minibus, a Master Charge card, and an apartment in Westwood.

30 Carlos E. Castañeda. (The corregidor in Spanish colonial administration. *Hispanic American Historical Review,* 1929, 9, 446-470).

31 Enrique Arana. (*Quién es Quién en la Argentina,* 1955, 46.)

31 interviewers. (Cook; Cravens; Hughes; Keen; *Time*; Wallace).

31 Kastaniebaum. German: chestnut tree.

31 Goanananda. Pronounced Go-ON-an-ON-da.

31 Ossian McFingal. Scottish poet James Macpherson (1736-96) pretended to have translated his own English works, including *Fingal,* from Gaelic originals by the legendary poet Ossian.

31 Ferdinand Maximilian. Austrian emperor of Mexico, 1864-67.

32 only a reporter. Keen (92).

33 Margolis. (231).

33 Nogales. My best guess at the location of the bus station.

33 tape recording. R58-59.

34 anthropologists. Hsu, Ochoa (*Time,* 38). (Leach; La Barre-c; Harris-c, 251).

34 Wasson. (-f).

34 Noel. (67).

36 got into my car. R93, 99. Pablito lives nearby P195.

37 seeing before he saw. R25, 36; I134, 149.

41 happened to Castaneda. "These thing[s] Castaneda writes about *could*

179

have happened. I just don't think they did. . . ." (Kleps).

41 A friend of mine. Metaphysician J. W. Nicholas.

42 lizards. J153-4. Don Juan showed Carlos two small lizards he had prepared (J112), but he did not demonstrate the stitching technique or tell how to
punch a wide hole in a narrow cactus spine to allow a thick, rough fiber to
pass through. if lizards had died J158-9.

43 *Handbook.* (Rowe, 314).

43 Wasson. (-a, -b, -c, -j; V. Wasson). The Blake and muleteer quotes may be
found in (-c). Superscripts—*shi³tho³*—indicate voice tones; Mazatec is such a
tonal language that the Huautecans talk to each other across canyons simply
by whistling (Budd Schulberg. The night we ate magic mushrooms. *Esquire,*
1961(Dec), 56(6/337), 129-30, 312-6).

45 psilocybin experimenters. "The employment of psilocybian fungi, at
one time completely restricted to Mexico for magico-religious purposes, has
mushroomed in the twentieth century to become a worldwide transcultural
phenomenon" (Pollock, 80).

45 gratified and disappointed. Edward Spicer felt a corresponding disap-
pointment when comparing *A Separate Reality* with *The Teachings* (letter 17
Nov 1975): "I can only sigh and wish that a sensitive young man had
continued his efforts to understand the reality which he was beginning to get
in touch with at first."

46 Newton. (Westfall).

46 mash the chunks. J81.

46 puma charges. R152; (Wasson-f).

46 original language English. (Wasson-f).

47 fully and frankly. (Wasson-f, -g). Wasson writes (letter 23 April 1976) that
Castaneda said his father's name was Castaneda, his mother's name Aranha,
that his paternal grandfather had been Sicilian, and that he had been born in
Brazil and schooled in Buenos Aires.

47 automatic writing. J18; R215; P22; Iviii; J25.

48 slang. J67, 117; I62, 97, 160, 97, 91, 219, 172; P174, 170, 187, 31, 43.

48 editorial errors. R84; P181, 258; J178.

49 weird. R215, 67; (Tovar-b, 248, 79).

49 quirks. I59. Tovar (-c, 94) rendered quails as *perdices,* which means
partridges, and which loses Castaneda's English alliteration.

49 evil splendor. R202.

49 *Touché. Mais en garde.* Your point. But watch out.

50 pulling your leg. P102, 84. See Added Notes on page 196.

51 formal discourse. The European formality of the 15-April passage may
have commended it also to a prominent anthropologist who reproduced it as
an example of Indian wisdom in his college textbook, under the heading, "A
Yaqui Man of Knowledge" (Goldschmidt, 187-190).

52 dJ's daughter-in-law. J67.

52 *es bonita su casa.* (Kurath, 40).

52 Yaqui dJ. J18; R5, 30, 58, 71, 136. Wasson-e said dJ spoke the Yuma
language; Wasson-f said dJ's mother was a Yuma Indian; La Barre (-b, 271)
evidently picked this up from Wasson. Failing to find the Yuma datum
anywhere in Castaneda, I queried Wasson, who answered (letter 23 April
1976) that Castaneda had written him (6 Sep 1968) dJ was born in Arizona to a
Yuma mother, spoke Yaqui, Yuma, and Mazatec, but Spanish better than any
other language, and also (Castaneda believed) understood English perfectly.

53 Yaqui words. *yori* R60; *torim* R65; only for Yaquis R71.

53 three Genaros. Genaro-1 was "a very old man" in Sonora (J17); Genaro-2, dG, "a Mazatec Indian" (R20) "in his early sixties" (R93); Genaro-3, "a tall, husky, middle-aged" Yaqui (R61). R. G. Wasson writes (letter 15 Nov 1975): "The name 'Genaro' is common in every Mesoamerican Indian community that I know; not common like Juan and José but common enough not to arouse comment. It is the same as Jenaro, the same as Yanario; it is 'January.'" If the name is common, a factual reporter might meet three Genaros in eight years, but if he did he should take more trouble not to confuse his reader with them than Castaneda took. Having borrowed the name from someone else's book, an undeclared novelist might in his preoccupation have used it several times inadvertently, while a craftier crypto-fictioneer could have repeated it to mimic natural coincidences a frank fiction writer would shun to preserve clarity. Narratively, "don Genaro" was an assumed name, R92.

53 shotgun friend. R204.

53 met Lucio 1966. R58.

53 Talking Tree. (Giddings).

53 names of plants. J81; R94.

53 kinship charts. I10-11.

53 Yaqui vocabulary. (Johnson; Kurath; Beals). bunch of crap. R194.

54 returners from death. R195-6.

54 Navy diver. Grosso (65-66) cites this non-evidential story to illustrate the non-skeptical reaction of a typical person whose belief system (like Carlos's) had *not* prepared him for any paranormal experience.

55 false skepticism. drugged meat I135. teaching assistants I178. In Table 2, Events: 6, 9, 7, 14, 17, 20, 19, 24, 25, 27, 29, 31, 33, 34.

56 being tricked. P28, 43-44.

56 never occurred to me. P56.

56 stupendous look. I2.

56 don Indian. (Wasson-h; -e); J58, 132

56 Reichel-Dolmatoff. (Wasson-h).

57 whatever we perceive. R147.

57 six sources. R193, 195; (Keen, 92, 95). Nonspecifically, Castaneda wrote (I2-3): "I became acquainted with every work available [on] the peyote cult of the Indians of the plains."

57 ebony. (Keen, 92). The treasury of power objects described to Sam Keen is not consistent with an earlier statement about dJ (J21): "he himself had no respect for power objects . . . frequently used as aids by lesser brujos."

57 don Parvenu. P161-2.

58 publication of *The Teachings*. R7, 19-20; P11. (University of California Press, Berkeley, letter 9 Feb 1976).

59 narrative and calendar time the same. A passage about the bubble of perception, published late in 1974, contains the following sentence (P267): "I understood then that it would have been of no consequence if he had told me everything fourteen years before." Fourteen years before what? Carlos met don Juan in 1960. Add 14 years and you get 1974. Carlos's bubble of perception must have opened just when Castaneda was writing about it, early in 1974 or late in 1973.

59 *Psychedelic Review*. (Swain). R157; P256; R118; J165; P246-9; J136.

60 Wasson-Castaneda parallels. (Wasson-j, 245-310—particularly: 251-5, 261, 295, 304). a whole year J14, left eye P231, free to see J82, where God is J89, sweeten the smoke J80, as many times as he could J141.

61 smoking mushrooms. "In Popayan [in the Colombian Andes] it was learned that some people occasionally smoke dried mushrooms, usually after elaborate preparation with other agents. The idea to utilize them in such a manner may well have come from Castaneda's 'humito,' the smoke resulting from combustion of magic mushroom dust plus special botanic sweetening agents in a ritual pipe. 'Humito' has never been encountered by ethnobotanists, mycologists, or other investigators of ritualistic mushroom use in Mexico [the center from which mushroom use has recently spread through the Western Hemisphere]. Furthermore, with Castaneda's very own admission [J215] that the mushroom dust did not burn but was ingested, it seems 'humito' was really a symbol or literary device to intrigue the reader. Dried samples of the mushrooms so employed at Popayan appeared to be *Stropharia cubensis.* It is said to take a larger quantity for effect and the duration of action is considered very much shorter than by the oral route. . . . I later gave the smoking method a trial but received only a headache" (Pollock, 77). Good thing dJ didn't say, "Stick 'em in your ear."

61 María Sabina's face. Photographs of María Sabina may be seen in (Wasson-a, -b, -i, -j) and at the beginning of this chapter, the last taken 24 May 1960 at Huautla de Jiménez by Frederick A. Usher.

62 Carlitos and Don Juan. This apocryphal Yaqui folktale follows English models in (Giddings) and Yaqui models in (Johnson). The Yaqui vocabulary was mostly picked out of (Johnson; Kurath; & Beals) or constructed from Yaqui roots. Vocabulary and syntax are reasonably correct. I am grateful to John M. Dedrick, of the Summer Institute of Linguistics, for his generous and helpful advice (letters 10 Mar, 15 Apr 1976); he is not responsible for errors and booby traps that remain. The latter include the following non-Yaqui interpolations: 1) *karpokaps asaltitans = carpocaps asaltitans,* Latin for the moth whose wiggling larva makes the jumping bean jump, 2) *untsoweiter = und so weiter,* German for etcetera, 3) *akad'emic puton* = academic or emic put-on. The story was conceived as a startling though brief immersion in the Yaqui language, to show that Yaqui is completely alien to the English- or Spanish-speaker and to make the point that if I could learn this much Yaqui in about two weeks, an accomplished linguist like Castaneda should have learned more than two words in nine years.

64 native genius. (*Time,* 38).

64 type of student. (*Time,* 44). power takes care of you (*Time,* 45).

65 Gate of Power. Compare (Eliade, 482-6), the strait gate, the shaman's paradoxical passage to the otherworld.

65 academic analysis appended. (Rueger, 74).

65 no way to escape. I214.

65 *Tales of Folly.* true or untrue I191, pimp I57, clobber me I67, crush him like a bug I177.

66 stubbornly indifferent. (Sukenick, 118). affected to be unfamiliar. (R. Stafford, seminar student, telephone 5 Sep 1975).

67 abstract. A jarring note in the abstract was Castaneda's statement: "I was not permitted to tape-record or photograph any event that took place during that time"—that is, 1961 to 1971. What happened, I wondered, to the tape recording (R58-59) made on 4 Sep 1968? Did don Juan confiscate it?

67 Xerox statistics. (Helen Greenway, University Microfilms Vice President, telephone 13 Nov 1975, letter 9 Jan 1976).

67 *Visions of Hermas.* (*The Apocryphal New Testament.* London: Printed for William Hone, Ludgate Hill, 1820. Pp. 194-208).

68 dissertation. *Vita:* Submitting his dissertation before *Time's* exposé was published, Castaneda said he was born in Sao Paulo, Brazil, 25 December 1935. He recorded his 1962 B.A. from UCLA and listed stints as teaching assistant at UCLA in 1963-64 and lecturer at UC Irvine in 1972. *Publications:* Only J, (Castaneda-b), R, and I. *Editorial changes:* One tiny but provocative discrepancy between *Ixtlan* and *Sorcery* affords a fascinating vignette of Coyote's dealings with the defenseless academy. Though all other narrative dates from *Ixtlan* are reproduced in *Sorcery*, two have been deleted. Dissertation pages 292 and 300 omit the dates (11 & 12 December 1962) that tell us just when 'la Catalina' sailed, hopped, and stood in the doorway (see: "Carlos-One and Carlos-Two," Table 2, Events 19-21; Event 21 is dated by textual inference only). Removing these crucial dates, Castaneda markedly reduced the risk that a skeptic, if there was one on his committee, might notice and be troubled by the stark logical conflict between Carlos-One's first meeting with 'la Catalina' (Event 22, published with faculty approval in 1968) and Carlos-Two's narratively prior meetings with the same sinister lady (Events 18-21) described in the dissertation. Having read an early draft of the dissertation without the telltale dates, a skeptic would hardly look for those dates in his autographed personal copy of *Ixtlan* received later in the year. Deleting the dates also lightened the responsibility of permissive or credulous committee members, who presumably were not at all troubled by Castaneda's fiction but might eventually be called to account for having either condoned it or accepted it as fact. *Circulation record:* In the two years this copy had been on the shelf five faculty members (or graduate students) and four undergraduates had borrowed it; estimating an equal number for the second copy, we have 18 persons inspecting the dissertation at UCLA. The only other transaction was a loan to the public library at Gettysburg PA, which implies that no scholar at any other university had seen *Sorcery*. Prospective borrowers outside of California need to remind the UCLA librarian that *Sorcery* (call number: LD 791.9 A6 C275) is not available on microfilm.

68 *Ixtlan* on sale. Simon and Schuster published *Journey to Ixtlan* on 23 October 1972, and Castaneda correctly listed it in his dissertation as a prior publication. His Ph.D. was granted as of 23 March 1973, the day after the end of the 2nd quarter, which ran from 2 January to 22 March. Even if *Sorcery* was officially approved by the committee on the first day of that quarter, Castaneda could not have written his restrictive instructions to University Microfilms until ten weeks after *Ixtlan* went on sale, which rules out the commercial and perfective motives. University Microfilms received the document from UCLA in February 1973. Though it is a 1973 dissertation, it bears a 1972 copyright notice, carried forward as the law requires from Simon and Schuster's 1972 first edition.

68 Riesman. An apparently psychic typesetter for the *New York Times Book Review* subtitled *The Teachings, "A Yanqui Way of Knowledge."* (Letter to Riesman 14 Aug 1975; reply 1 Dec 1975, from Djibo, Upper Volta.)

71 Yaqui subtitle rejected. (Spicer-d; Kelley in Moisés, xxxiv; La Barre-c; Leach; Madsen, 80).

71 "A Structural Analysis." J189-256. Compare (Lévy-Strauss).

71 parody. (Oates-b, 10).

71 became obvious. J20.

73 emic. Well known for years to anthropology students, the term has not spread much outside of anthropology.

73 Berreman. Spoke on 8 May 1965 (Berreman).

74 emic-etic. (Harris-a, 133-150, especially 138-141; Harris-b, 568-604). Castaneda (-e, Abstract) said he had gained "membership" as a sorcerer by becoming "intimately familiar" with dJ's alien "perceptual reality." The claim answers the wish to get inside the native's head, a wish Harris (-a, 141) called futile. Like any other scientist, the social scientist must build an explicit theory by which to interpret established classes of observations. The more general the theory, the more widely it can be applied, but the greater the risk of arbitrary interpretation. At one extreme, the scientist imposes a quite inappropriate theory on alien behavior, wallowing in complacent ignorance of what certain acts mean to the actors themselves. My favorite non-scientific example finds some Spanish explorers meeting a Southwest tribe who call themselves *A'a'tam*, "the people." "How do you call yourselves?" the Spaniards ask. *"Pimatc,"* reply the *A'a'tam*, thereby acquiring the name *"Pima,"* by which we call them today. In the language of the *A'a'tam, pimatc* means, "I do not understand [the question]" (Russell, 19). At the other extreme, the traveler insists on knowing the native reality solely as the natives know it, thereby acquiring quasi-nativehood and abandoning science. No one seriously proposes the practice of either extreme. Theories are built by alternating between observations that already fit the theory and unexpected or outlandish observations that do not fit and may cause the theory to change or grow. Whatever his intentions or illusions, the scientist or traveler cannot fully adopt his informants' point of view. Either he relies on an explicit theory established in his own culture, or he relies (perhaps without realizing it) on his personal conceptual system, his unique life experience, his implicit cultural background, his internal thesaurus. Neither explicit theory nor personal thesaurus is likely to match the conceptual system or world view of the people he is observing or joining. The best he can do is achieve a synthesis of his view and theirs that will be fair to both. If he is a Basquish-Peruvian-Spanish intellectual, he is not going to become a Yaqui or even a Yaquiless Indian no matter how hard he tries, but he might learn that when a Yaqui says, "The world wishes to end," he is not predicting the collapse of a subjective world Susanne Langer says is held up by language (Pearce-a, 51, 168) but watching an eclipse of the sun, which he will cure without fail by throwing live coals at the sky (Beals, 47). For a balanced application of the emic-etic dichotomy in a study of modern mysticism, see (Bharati).

74 Carlos-Emic. cross eyes I49, hands I98, leaves I161, plants J80, gait I169.

74 Carlos-Etic. kinship I10-11, coarse ways I38, pimp I57, wind I65, suit I89, dumb I78, food I263, greasy (Cravens-a, 91). Professor Volpe comments: "Plant names, geneologies, and kinship terms are the stock-in-trade of ethnoscientists. Castaneda may here be urging broader humanistic concerns on fellow emicists."

74 Etic-Procrustes. Volpe: "Structuralism is often considered a form of emic analysis, so Castaneda may again be trying to humanize emicism. To get your ethnoscience straight from the horse's mouth see: Stephen A. Tyler, *Cognitive Anthropology* (HRW, 1969), especially the introduction. I would say the one good book to come out of ethnoscience is: Brent Berlin & Paul Kay, *Basic Color Terms* (U. Calif., 1969)."

75 from the very moment of our birth. Sapir: (Mandelbaum, 546). Castaneda: "from the moment I was born," Iviii; "from the time we are born," I254; "from the moment of our birth," P247.

75 *Oye, Carlitos*. Hey, little Carlos! Look at your mama's face. Here the eyes. Here the nose. Here the mouth.

75 rebel and reality. Sapir (Mandelbaum): rebel 572, existence 572, individual 574, Two Crows 569, 572. dJ: making this room I211-212, not as birds J129, rocks P270, whatever we perceive R147. Incidentally, I would not argue that spatial perception is not at all learned, but that convention affects the learning of space less than the learning of an alphabet. While we are on the subject, another of Sapir's ideas set off a Sonoran echo in my head: "Perhaps," wrote Sapir (Mandelbaum, 549), "there is a far-reaching moral in the fact that even a child may speak the most difficult language with idiomatic ease but that it takes an unusually analytical type of mind to define the mere elements of that subtle linguistic mechanism which is but a plaything of the child's unconscious." "The very fact that we are thinking and talking," the Indian don told Carlos (P270), "points out an order that we follow without ever knowing how we do that, or what the order is."

76 Press spokesman. (Los Angeles office, letters 14 & 18 Aug 1975).

78 ethnography. To publish *The Teachings* as ethnography (or ethnology) was to present it to scholars as a scientific work based on factual, cultural field observations. In fact, it was neither scientific, factual, nor cultural. If the UCLA pundits meant to redefine ethnography, they should have done so explicitly, in the book and in the advertising. Volpe comments: "Since ethnoscientists don't care much about culture, the spurious Yaqui subtitle probably wouldn't bother them as much as it would a genuine ethnographer like Spicer. On the other hand, ethnoscientists care a lot about language, so a Yaqui informant who spoke not one word of Yaqui in the hearing of the fieldworker should have given them pause." Lévi-Strauss (3) distinguishes ethnography, the grass-roots description of how people in one group live together, from ethnology, the comparative use of data from ethnographic studies of two or more groups. Both concepts imply culture, fact, and scientific treatment.

78 review of *The Teachings*. (Young).

79 closing the village gate. I am not saying Castaneda can't walk around on campuses, lecture at the invitation of students, visit other teachers' classes, participate in research projects, or engage in various other peripheral activities, only that he will presumably not be appointed to a "ladder" position in any faculty of social science. In my theory, though physically present or visible, he is academically absent or invisible.

80 Garfinkel. (*Time*, 44; Mandell). Schaefer spoke 26 Oct 1971 (Noel, 182). Professor Garfinkel did not accept an invitation (letter 5 Nov 1975) to contribute to this discussion, confirming, correcting, or refuting my theory as he wished.

81 disclaimed cultural milieu. J18.

82 nonsense. I wrote to Professor Goldschmidt (14 Oct 1975) that since I took ethnography and allegory to be mutually exclusive categories, roughly equivalent to fact and fiction, I wondered if his first paragraph could mean: This book is *part* ethnography and *part* allegory. (Which would still have been misleading but no longer nonsense.) He declared himself bemused (21 Jan 1976) at a scholar who could not see that something could be ethnography and allegory at the same time. I protested (23 Jan 1976) that ethnography might well treat allegoric material or be interpreted allegorically by poets, but allegory could hardly constitute or replace ethnography. He declined to say more.

82 analogy. My reading of "allegory" as "analogic world view" is based on the fact that Goldschmidt's discussion of cultural constructs and "worlds other than our own" comes right before his conclusory statement: "Hence the allegory as well as the ethnography." An alternative reading would skip back to the previous paragraph, which laments the inadequacy of our language to render the sorcerer's world; Castaneda could then be describing *that* world under the guise of *this* world, which come closer to the common meaning of "allegory." Perhaps Goldschmidt confounded these two meanings (one conventional, the other idiosyncratic or jargonic) but the order and terms of his argument fit my reading best. For my own conception of mental content as analogs, see (de Mille).

82 Pearce. (-a, 138).

82 fallacy. Don Juan said *seeing* shows you things "for what they really are," R37, 149. Oddly, *The Teachings* barely hints at this Platonic reality. In his Foreword, Goldschmidt anticipated—perhaps even inspired—Castaneda's later Platonism (see Note **121** true reality).

83 roared. P50.

83 swelled the rolls. According to Volpe's impression.

84 condemned. P277-282.

85 *Disagi-ki.* Condensed from (Thord-Gray, 555).

86 A warrior. R220; I81, 267.

86 The quality. C. S. Lewis in (MacDonald, 12). For discussion of Lewis and Williams, see: (Hillegas).

86 talking animals. Lewis Carroll buffs should compare dJ's meeting with the magical deer (I76-78) and Alice's conversation with the Fawn (*Through the Looking Glass,* Chapter 3). For the deer's sweet whistle, see (Furst-a, 55).

88 dG spins with ally. I260, 266, 264.

88 Oates. (-c).

89 C. S. Lewis. In (MacDonald, 8).

89 Pearce. (-b, 233).

89 psychotherapists. (Hendlin; Pulvino).

89 parodists. "The Teachings of Don B." is the best parody, frequently funny (Barthelme). "The Teachings of Joe Pye" brightens only for an instant, when Mescalito becomes Muscatelo (Tomkins). "Don Long Juan" thrice saves the Furry Freak Brothers from disaster and shows them pre-Aztec ruins beneath Mexico City (Shelton). A mexiphile lesbian claims in passing to have done "gynecography feel work under a gorgeous Yakkity Indian witch, doña Juana." "I wanna," confesses Callista (McAllister, 42).

90 Ixtlan fable. I257-268. Urashima (Seki, 111-114).

90 aphorisms. twilight P286, J115. survivors P194. death I33. die alone P281. prisoners P280. crap R66. lion R191. mountains R98.

91 stylistic manure. masterful R98, 103. glass shreds R47. each rock I197. sprung I95.

91 dG clue. R19-20, 93; P187, 245.

91 anonymous entries. friend Bill J13; R1; I1, 7, 18, 27; (Keen, 92; *Time*, 43). sinologist P278. botanist (Wallace, 142). Husserl student (Keen, 92). rodents I115. folk song I21. exclamations I182.

92 a bona fide termination. Ivii.

92 Wittgenstein. (Margolis).

93 ineffable. dG I259. dJ J185; P30.

93 inexplicable *tonal* & *nagual.* P269-271. dJ actually said "indescribable *tonal*," but that was Castaneda's error. The *tonal* is both description and describable. dJ describes it for pages, draws a diagram of it (P98), and makes a model of it on a table top (P125-9).

94 admired Huxley. (Wayne Slater, telephone, 5 Dec 1975).

94 Heard. (196, 200). brief instant J83, 87.

94 luminous egg. (Atkinson, 58). R23. (Klüver, 37).

94 published by the dozen. Atkinson's book *Personal Power* was published in 1922 by the Personal Power Company, of Detroit.

94 oval aura at Irvine. (Rueger, 76). Of course, many other parallels between Siberian and American Indian shamanism do *not* depend on William Walker Atkinson; see: (La Barre-a).

95 luminous blobs. P39-42. dG P43. golden aura (Atkinson, 65).

95 Klüver. (53, 27, 28). By an inspiring coincidence, I found myself working with Paul Radin's personal copy of Klüver's *Mescal*, autographed: "Dem Peyotekultforscher Paul Radin zugeeignet! Heinrich Klüver, Chicago, April 1929," which seems to say that the book is an appropriate gift for peyote-cult researcher Paul Radin.

95 left and right minds. (Bogen). People in many societies associate the left side of the body with mythical and supernatural forces, including death (Katz; Myerhoff, 88). P183-4, 191, 200.

95 ethnobotanist. (Wasson-a, 109). great gates (Wasson-j, 295); though the "paradoxical passage" between worlds is nearly universal in shamanism (Eliade, 482-6; Furst-b, 161-6), the similarity of dJ's and Wasson's language and imagery suggests direct influence. crack J185. like dying P266; compare Blake on "little death" (Pearce-a, 172). decide whether to return P276.

96 psilocybin users. (Swain, 237, 226, 227, 225). soar J126, 168-9. child P224. Italian J40.

96 Juan Matus. I37. Bandera & Maldonado (Spicer-b, 27-31); Yaqui Rolling Stone is *Tetabiate*. Luis Matus (Spicer-c, 83; Moisés, xix). In the narrative, both "Juan Matus" and "Genaro" were assumed names, R92.

96 *hikuri*, Tarahumara. (Thord-Gray).

96 omens. jet I6, rock I22, percolator I8, crow I20, wind I61, sunbeams I144, 155, dreams I92. (Moisés, xxxi-xxxiii). dreaming I92, 113, 150; P19.

98 loss of soul. Ideas of vision quest, guardian spirit, soul-loss, soul-capture, and personally acquired impersonal power are held in many societies (Harner-a, 268).

98 Harner-Castaneda parallels. (Harner-a, -b, -c, -d; respectively published 1962, 1963, 1968, 1972; respectively abbreviated in the rest of this note *only* as: A, B, C, D). waterfall A260; R99. Datura A261, 271; J21, 64, 161. danger B113; R184, 193, 214, 234. secrecy A261; J73, 78, 150. accumulate power A262; J86; I91, 122, 159. give or sell it B104; I164; see also: (Bennett, 256). spirit helpers and shields B112; R216-8, 225. power objects collected B105; J21-22, 108, 123. hurled B106; J22, 23, 178; P61; see also: (Kluckhohn, 34). disdain B103; J66. rub B104; R166. follows teacher B104; J65-66; R98, 214. tell visions A261; I209. creatures A261; B109; R117; P259. moth B106; R231, 235; P24, 97, 211; the Jívaro butterfly sang to the visionary with its wings (C28) as Carlos's ally-moth sputtered its song (P211). chest A261; J138. fog A267; R90. bird B107, 113; R204-7. steal soul A262; J177. guess assailant A263; J177. lies C28; I200. quartz D154; I204-6; J23 mentioned crystals but not quartz and not particularly powerful; shamanic use of rock crystals is well known (Eliade; Furst-a, 42, 90), but the wording and timing here suggest direct influence. corpse D113; Ixii. out of the ordinary D90, 134; Ixi; for bogeyman, compare: (Matthew W. Stirling, *Indians of the Americas*, National Geographic Society, 1955, p. 45): "Both the Iroquois and the Algonquians believe in a masked cannibal called 'Long Nose,' who kidnaps children. Youngsters are never disciplined by corporal punishment. Fear that Long Nose will carry them off in his huge pack basket usually insures their good behavior."

99 Pearce. (-a, 2-3, 5-6, 132).

100 shrug. "What must Carlos Castaneda think of the immense popularity of his works?" asks Mexican poet Octavio Paz. "Probably he shrugs his shoulders" (Tovar-a, 10).

100 Pearce-Castaneda parallels. (Pearce-a, abbreviated in this note *only* as: A). hill intervenes A127; I144-5. unreal men A130-1; I264; in contrast, the previous volume called Vicente's *allies* "not people" R38-39. unpredictable A157; I75. find crack as child A173; P224, 247, 197. balance A154, 184, 185; P13, 248. clearing in forest A15-17, 150; P125-127. our notions A13, 189; P243. collapse A51, 168; I136, 253.

101 extensions of dJ's Way. Though Pearce's eight ideas were available in some form before *The Crack in the Cosmic Egg* was published, their absence from Castaneda's pre-*Crack* books and presence in his post-*Crack* books suggests *Crack* influenced Castaneda. Langer's language-supported world was present before as "collapse of certainty" (J252), maintaining the world with internal talk (R218), and "undoing" the world by stopping the internal talk (R219), but the formula "collapse the world" had not appeared. Castaneda's friend Barbara Myerhoff had presumably shared her interest in Langer with him before 1968 (Myerhoff, 24).

101 Littlechap. I244. (*Time*, 1962(Oct 12), *80*(15), 67; Henry Hewes, *Saturday Review*, 1962(Oct 20), *45*(42), 37; *Life*, 1962(Nov 30), *53*(22), 117).

101 stop the world. Wasson (-h, 245) noted a striking similarity between don Juan's "Stop the world" and María Sabina's "Woman who stops the world am I." Since the latter was not published anywhere until 1975 (Wasson-i), the coincidence promised the first bit of evidence that Castaneda had actually met an authentic shaman. The evidential balloon was punctured when translators agreed (Eunice Pike, letter 9 Dec 1975; Florence Cowan, telephone 14 Jan 1976) that "Woman who *supports* the world am I" would be a better translation of the Mazatec, Chjon^{42} se^{1}nqui^3 te^3 nia^{13}. The idea of support finds no place in Stop the world, which Castaneda renders also as Collapse the world (I136, 253). "Whenever the dialogue stops, the world collapses," don Juan says (P40). Historian Alfredo López Austin writes from Mexico (6 Jan 1976) that although the term One who knows (*el conocedor*) is much used in mesoamerican shamanic texts, he has not found a single epithet referring to the shaman in his capacity to Stop the world (*detener el mundo*).

102 dream writing. (Cravens-a, 97; Nin-a, 312, 266, 312; Sukenick, 110-1). "It was Nin who helped Castaneda publish 'The Teachings of Don Juan' when he was having publisher troubles" (Sukenick, 110); according to Rupert Pole (Nin's husband, telephone 8 Jan 1976) Nin provided some New York publishing contacts for Castaneda before the University published *The Teachings*; her friendly gesture had no evident practical consequences. Pole recalled that Castaneda met Nin for the first time when poet Deena Metzger brought him and Barbara Myerhoff to Nin's house. See Added Notes on page 196.

102 radically different uses. "The definition of a dream is: ideas and images in the mind *not under the command of reason*" (Nin-b, 5). As dJ dreamed to divine undreamlike facts and accumulate practical power, Castaneda purportedly dreamed to get his undreamlike rational dialogue and discursive narrative. Often borrowed from other writers, the ideas and images filling Carlos's dreams, visions, and drug trips continued to be tightly commanded by Castaneda's wide-awake reason. See Added Notes on page 196.

102 false separation. (Sukenick, 114). About the need to separate imagination from reality, Kung-Fu say: Man with both legs in one pant fall down.

103 writer. (Parrott, 80; *Time*, 45) P156, 275. A good standard against which to judge the don Juan books for authentic mystery, depth of feeling, and literary expression is Haniel Long's faithful though brief and interpretive retelling of Cabeza de Vaca's eight-year walk from Florida to Mexico in the 16th Century. For the original, see: (Nuñez). For Long's retelling, try library or bookstore for any of seven out-of-print editions, under any of three titles: *The Power Within Us* (Duell, Sloan and Pearce, 1944); *Interlinear to Cabeza de Vaca* (Frontier Press, 1969—a beautiful edition); or *Marvellous Adventure of Cabeza de Vaca* (Ballantine, 1973—which includes *Malinche,* another wondrous tale, though withouts its Epilogue). Like Castaneda, Alvar Nuñez Cabeza de Vaca assumed his mother's name without explaining why.

104 Alexander. (227). Radin (168).

105 coyote not reliable. dJ I254-5. everything to every man (Radin, 169).

105 Trickster. For trickster myths I depend chiefly on (Radin), slightly on (Alexander) and (Joseph Campbell, *The Masks of God,* Viking, 1959, pp. 275-7). (Blackburn) tells many fine tales of *xuxaw,* coyote trickster and culture hero of California's Chumash Indians.

109 Trickster parallels. pranks R141. inadequacy I109, 200. horse R97. warrior used I214. bones walk (Parrott, 81). take off clothes P254. loneliness into art (Keen, 96). rewrite thesis (*Time*, 44).

111 Rorschach man. occultists (Globus). Greens (Doug Boyd, *Rolling Thunder,* Dell, 1976, p. 272). hypnotic subject (Globus): though Globus adduces appropriate evidence for hypnotism, the hypothesis fails to account for Castaneda's systematic fictioneering; if dJ had actually lived, fictioneering would have been neither necessary to Castaneda nor plausible as part of dJ's plan of instruction. Nancy Wood (Letter, *Time,* 1973(Mar 26), *101*(13), 8). Harris (-c, 243-258). Gott (*New Statesman,* 1972(Jan 14), *83*(2130), 51-2). James W. Sire (*Eternity,* 1975(Nov), *26*(11), 40-41). Hal Lindsey (*There's a New World Coming,* Vision House, 1973, pp. 146-7). professional helpers (Hendlin; Pulvino). For further Christian comment, see: Joseph Grange (*Commonweal,* 1971(Sep 17), *94*(20), 482-3); Mark Imhoff (Fuller Graduate School of Psychology, Pasadena) Castaneda, Christianity and psychology on the nature of man (Christian Association for Psychological Studies, 1976, paper); Martin E. Marty (*Christian Century,* 1973(Mar 21), *90*(12), 351); David Nelson (*Inside,* 1974(Jul-Aug), *5*(4), 22-28).

112 Ramón and dG at waterfall. (Furst-b, 152-3) R99-104. Bolivian somersaulting (Furst-b, 132). "Carlos Castaneda and I often talked about shamans and sorcerers, and his deep understanding of these matters contributed greatly to my own thinking," wrote his fellow graduate student Barbara Myerhoff (24), whose mother had wisely taught her a rather unusual idea— that dreams were real—and who had been present that day in 1966 when Ramón balanced on the waterfall. Myerhoff's photo of Ramón's birdlike stance (45) shows the shadow of a semicircular cloud like the one Castaneda describes (R99). Myerhoff's field notes from 1966 contained other likely models for persons and events in Castaneda's books: a Pablo was younger than a Carlos (120); an old man named Francisco was quite as impish as dG (119-120, 146-7, 168); Ramón, like dG, knew of ten levels of knowledge (101;

R99); and Huichol shamans were materially poor but spiritually rich (98-9, 263), as the urchins Carlos felt sorry for were just as well off as he because any one of them could become a man of knowledge (R20-22). Myerhoff's dissertation on the Huichol peyote hunt was accepted at UCLA in 1968 (*Dissertation Abstracts International*, 1969, *30*(02), B-475).

113 Siskind. In (Harner-e, 28-9).

113 Sharon. In (Furst-b, 116).

113 When I first undertook. (Harner-c, 28-29; reproduced in -e, 16-17).

114 Yaquis fly with *Datura*. (Harner-e, 140). Carlos did fly J126-7. dJ hints about flying: with *Datura* J66, 106; with peyote J105.

115 Spicer. (Letter 17 Nov 1975).

115 coyote sees shadow. (Russell, 251).

115 under the world. (Radin).

115 Trickster. The original version of the Spanish Don Juan myth was Tirso de Molina's play, *El Burlador de Sevilla, The Trickster of Seville* (D. G. Winter, *The Don Juan Legend by Otto Rank*, Princeton U., 1975).

116 Plato. After Jowett, condensed from *Symposium* 211, *Phaedo* 109-111. The Greek words, *he alethos ge*, mean "truly the earth" or "the true earth."

117 The world is. dJ: I165.

117 other writers trace wisdom. (Boyd; Keen; La Barre-a; Margolis; Rueger; Wilk). Added References: (Gill; Silverman).

117 *nagual* and *tonal*. P121, 125, 131, 157, 243, 248, 265-6, 270-1.

118 *Tractatus*. (Ludwig Wittgenstein. *Tractatus Logico-Philosophicus*). Compare (Margolis, 236-238).

118 Why is there something and not nothing? Leibniz.

118 returns to its potential state. Compare (Margolis, 234).

118 the only experience we have. Castaneda's distinction between *tonal* and *nagual* is not consistent. In one place, the *nagual* is an unknown void (P271), in another it is a world that can be visited, perceived, or witnessed (P173), in yet another it is personified, dJ being called "the nagual" (P216). In this chapter I adopt the first use, intensifying it to make the *nagual* not only unspeakable or unknown but unknowable. The *nagual* can then be hypothesized as an unknowable source of events witnessed in the (specially prepared, naguallian sector of the) *tonal*. All events are ultimately inexplicable; some may also be proximately ineffable, or unspeakable. In science, the unexplained is often held to be proximately explicable but never ultimately explicable. Would-be sorcerers who despise science as the enemy of mysteries have science confused with scientism, which holds all things to be ultimately explicable. For every explanation science gives, it generates a new mystery. As dJ told us, there is no shortage of mysteries. There never will be.

119 alternative realities. flying J127-130. losing body J139-142. others would not see him as a crow J175. separate reality grows familiar J234. shift at will from one reality to another J235. the other world R113. it was not a gnat when it hit you R120. the guardian will take you away R131. whatever we perceive, in any manner we choose R147. they become nothing and yet they are still there R160. if you have no feeling toward it, the guardian will become nothing R170. for the first time I did not believe in the final reality R189. dreaming also takes place I92-3. warrior can tell one reality from another, Carlos can't I99. it is also as you picture it, but that's not all there is I165. making this room, agreement I211-2. world is not the same for a beetle I249. coyote was not talking the way you and I talk I253. dG did not take car away but forced Carlos to see world of sorcerers I255. reality depends on agreement with others P28—which contradicts R147, above, and the general idea of a separate reality, but perhaps dJ was only exaggerating Carlos-Skeptic's social conformity. rock is rock because we attend to it as such P234. perception went up and down cliff P267. no rocks from the moon P270.

120 no more ineffability. Compare (Bharati, 60): "the mystic may simply be a clumsy speaker or writer."

121 Carlos's psi powers. J116; I144, 181; P162. dJ also acknowledges hauntings and poltergeists R233.

121 serious psi literature. (Rhine; Roll; *Parapsychology Review*; *Journal of the American Society for Psychical Research*; *Journal of Parapsychology*) for example.

121 true reality. a plane above the ground J186. see things for what they really are R37, 149. *seeing* is sneaking between the worlds I254. neither you nor I will ever know what really took place P30. neither of us is correct P34. essence of tree P200. weasel between views to arrive at the real world; true excursions into the *nagual* P240. dJ purports (P240) to clarify an earlier statement (I254) about sneaking between worlds to arrive at *seeing* and knowing: "I meant that one can arrive at the totality of oneself only when one fully understands that the world is merely a view, regardless of whether that view belongs to an ordinary man or to a sorcerer." This non-Platonic formula is surely an improvement, but ten lines later dJ falls back into Platonism with his "true excursions into the *nagual*." In an earlier Note (**82** fallacy) I said Goldschmidt had anticipated Castaneda's Platonism. Perhaps Castaneda grasped the true reality firmly for the first time while reading Goldschmidt's Foreword to *The Teachings*, then glimpsed its fallaciousness while reading Pearce's 1971 finding (-a, 138) that Goldschmidt was in error—the author, in each case, instructed by his critic (compare pages 82-3, 100-1, above).

122 sophistical. Castaneda (P29) says Carlos had come to understand *seeing* as intuitive grasp, instant understanding, or penetration of motives. This is blatant revisionism. Over and over Carlos had known *seeing* as visualization—of lights, forces, structures, and events.

122 bubble of perception. P246-9.

123 diagram. P98, 270. *tonal* doesn't know P243.

123 will. R84, 146-9, 197-8; P13. Castaneda (Keen, 100): "The body has a will of its own. Or rather, the will is the voice of the body."

123 body. learns, knows, feels friendship I180. practices not-doing I188. receives instruction I194. detects ally I199. recognizes crisis I232. makes decisions I247. knows the ineffable I253. realizes it can *see* I256. is the non-intellectual part of the mind P45. exudes will from navel I178.

123 feelings. avoided by shifting from looking to *seeing* R83-4, 90-91. by disrupting mood R89. are only self pity I111. my sadness was so intense that I began [—to weep, to cry, to sob? No—] to think P37.

124 Sapir-Whorf. J. B. Carroll in (Whorf, 27).

124 Langer. I continue to cite Pearce (-a, 51, 168) instead of the original (Added Reference: Langer, 148, 150)—which Pearce correctly quoted but incorrectly cited—because I suspect Langer's influence was thus indirect.

124 I've smoked you. J28. falcon I32.

124 power. (La Barre-a). power inferior to knowledge J66, 55, 161, 69; R199; J87; R239-40; J86. power equal or superior to knowledge J21, 24, 53; I122-4, 157; J86; P193, 280. Pearce (-b, 176) comments on the longing for power: "*ME*-God (you Jane)."

126 twilight. P286. Among the Incas, vision time was "the first glimmering of dawn when the eye could not distinguish between a ghost and a solid person" (Brundage, 194).

126 warrior. as to war J51. death J172-3; R47, 49, 150, 196, 197; I33-36, 40, 81, 88, 153-6; P283. Though a warrior consults death, he does not play chess or badminton with him as we have seen in Ingmar Bergman's *Seventh Seal* or its parody *The Dove.*

126 four enemies. J82-87; R198.

126 path with heart. J11, 160, 185; R217-8;, 225; I266. On a parallel path with heart, Coyote sang to Earthmaker: "My world where one travels by the valley-edge; my world of many foggy mountains; my world where one goes zigzagging hither and thither; range after range, I sing of the country I shall travel in. In such a world shall I wander" (Alexander, 218-9). Carl Oglesby (Noel, 184) recognized the voluntarism in dJ's path with heart.

127 folly. R77, 79, 82, 85, 88, 150-1, 153, 168, 170, 219; I197, 200, 214. Compare Wittgenstein: "all propositions are of equal value" (Margolis, 239).

127 erasing personal history. J150; I11-17. Brazil R178. unspecified life goal R225. dJ assured Carlos (P236) that erasing personal history would not make him shifty or evasive, because he would not feel himself more important than a beetle, would take responsibility for his acts, and would consult his death about decisions. I do not see how those provisions would keep him from being shifty and evasive. Compare note: **122** sophistical.

127 truth. J105; R28; I15, 191.

127 warrior. takes responsibility I39-42, 110. cannot be surprised P155. in control R181. neither remorse R34. nor self-pity I110-1. familiar stranger R189, 251. orderly life I92. unpredictable I75. clobbered R182. never idle or in a hurry R191.

127 double. dJ says (P52): "The sorcerer that finds himself face to face with himself is a dead sorcerer." Otto Rank says: "The double who catches sight of himself must die within a year" (50); "the double-projection . . . was among the most popular motifs in Romantic literature" (9); Goethe survived a precognitive vision of meeting himself; Guy de Maupassant took dictation from his double, who sat opposite him at his writing desk (39). Lévy-Bruhl (203) mentions "bi-presence" in primitive societies, the same living individual being observed in two different places at the same moment.

128 isolation dJ's flaw. (Pearce-a, 172). Castaneda's myth of don Juan denies human reciprocity and community and deifies the isolated self, wrote Peter Marin (The new narcissism. *Harper's*, 1975(Oct), *251*(1505), 45-50, 55-56). "He who loves, sees," said C. S. Lewis (MacDonald, 7).

128 warrior's beloved. P283-6. choice (predilection) and secret P283.

129 Prescott. (W. H. Prescott. *History of the Conquest of Peru.* Modern Library, no date, p. 1095. First published 1847).

130 Trust your personal power. dJ: I167. back against the wall, Castaneda to Sam Keen (98).

130 Cajamarca. For Peruvian background, I depend mainly on (Brundage), slightly on (Frederick B. Pike, *The Modern History of Peru*, Praeger, 1967; J. H. Steward, editor, *Handbook of South American Indians*, volume 2, *The Andean Civilizations*, Smithsonian Institution, 1946; W. W. Johnson & others, *The Andean Republics*, Time Inc., 1965).

134 false portrait of father. (Cravens-a, 94; Cook). R5; I40-43.

134 Catholic religion. God as tablecloth P127. confession I206-7. medallion I259. Trinity P218. cathedral P105.

135 José. (*Time*).

135 childhood. helpless, lonely, and afraid R136-7; I109-10; P87. summers R45. violent fellow I29. anger and embarrassment R237-8. Joaquín R141.
136 Carlos like dJ. I2, 56, 157.
136 rebel. lxii; R141; I179.
136 self-condemnation. I183, 200. man and burro P218. whanger I5. father's opinion I12. no longer a war P156.
137 restricted feelings. suffering only a thought R142. laughing R84. don't look at body R91. callous I109. poet P282. a bit crazy I27. plugged up R104.
138 boredom. where to go P285. empty days P242-3. lies for excitement I16. depression, suicide (Keen, 102, 100).
138 no other way to live. R125.
139 rite of passage. (Eliade, 482-6). infant P87. Wallace (142).
140 no *nagual*, not rich. Antonio de Herrera y Tordesillas (Foster, 90).
140 Vallejo. P116-7.
140 mesoamerican-European wise man. Indian spokesman Vine Deloria, author of *Custer Died for Your Sins*, found dJ rather unIndian: "A substantial number of young people took up the Carlos Castenada books as if they were the final word on Indian religion, [yet] Few Indians recognized anything having to do with Indian religion in the books. Where were the sacred mountains, the healing ceremonies, the tales of creation and historical migrations? ... It was only with Castanada's *Journey to Ixtlan* that the books began to take on a discernable Indian shape" (Vine Deloria Jr, *God is Red*, Grosset & Dunlap, 1973, pp. 52-53, 307, 368).
141 Burton. (*Time*).
142 meet by accident. Roy Buzza met Castaneda *both* in an elevator *and* in a coffee shop, a dual encounter Castaneda called an omen. Adam Smith (*Powers of Mind*, Random House, 1975) met Castaneda or his double in a stairwell at Simon and Schuster's. Smith perpetuates the story about Mexican students scouring Sonora for signs of dJ, but academician Roberto Pirineo B. writes from Mexico (19 Aug 1975): "Neither I nor any of my colleagues have heard of a single Mexican student engaging in such a venture. Our students can easily go to Huautla for the mushrooms or find a local Guru if they want to. Research indicates peyote is practically unknown in big cities of Mexico, the only ones with college populations (see studies from: Centro Mexicano de Estudios en Farmacodependencia, Insurgentes Sur 1991-B, 7° Piso, México 20, D.F.)."
142 telephone in closet. (Wayne Slater, telephone, 5 Dec 1975).
143 Lévi-Strauss. (174). To be fascinated by another kind of illusionist who lives to feel his power over his listeners, see a study of swindlers, off-shore bankers, advance-fee racketeers, Tennessee land mongers, corporate shell gamers, phony mutual funders, bogus insurers, and Bankers of Sark (Kwitny).
143 shaman not lying. (Harner-c, 32-33). shaman faking (Lévi-Strauss, 178). The shaman pretends, says La Barre (-a, 267), but not with any intent to deceive.
144 Jesus. (Pearce-a, 182).
145 Wasson. (-j, 295), reproduced by permission of R. Gordon Wasson.
146 Lest flesh and blood. St John of the Cross (Peers, III-221). We are all alone, dG P281. Yet they keep trying, Castaneda (Cravens-a, 97).
146 Juan Yepes. For the background of St John of the Cross, I depend on (Peers; Bruno; Baring-Gould, *Lives of the Saints*; Butler, *Lives of the Saints*) and others to be cited.

147 Upon my flowery breast. (Peers, I-10). There he gave me (Peers, II-28). Where hast thou gone, translated from (Bruno, 173).

147 frogs. (Crisógono de Jesús, *The Life of St John of the Cross*, Harper & Bros, 1958, p. 134). center of the soul is God (Peers, III-25).

148 *Las condiciones.* (Crisógono de Jesús and others, *Vida y Obras de San Juan de la Cruz*, Madrid: Biblioteca de Autores Cristianos, 1964, p. 967).

148 translation of Peers. (III-253-4).

149 dJ and San Juan. deprecate specific visions J118; I90, 112; (Peers, I-149-58). leap P287. When thou thinkest (Peers, I-63). Carlos touched I252-3. Oh, living flame (Peers, III-18). most subtle touch (Peers, II-97). furry paw R244; "Sometimes you just feel a furry hand, soft as a kitten, on your shoulder and neck" (Fire, 194). bride's neck (Peers, I-10). secret things (Peers, II-448-50). Divest thyself, love to be unknown, ready to lose, service to others (Peers, III-255). no longer human (Cravens-a, 97). nobody knows who I am I14. luminous faces R157 (Peers, III-372). not bound by promise R141. less to confess (Butler, *Lives*). bird in lime (Peers, III-243). strait gate (Peers, I-87, 383).

151 women of San Juan. seducer (Butler, *Lives*). Teresa (Bruno, 232). refused appointment (Bruno, 171-2). Thérèse (Bruno, 228). letter to Catalina (Peers, III-264-5; Bruno, 230). death of Catalina (Peers, III-373-4; Crisógono de Jesús, 1958, pp. 167-8).

152 Catherine of Alexandria. (Baring-Gould, *Lives*; Butler, *Lives*).

153 angry giantess. P203.

154 'la Catalina.' See Table 2, Events 16-22. felt her clothes on my face R210. mixed feelings about her P241-2.

154 more experienced men. dJ tells Carlos to dominate 'la Catalina' by piercing her R207-8. Is it only by chance don Juan shares his name with the Spanish seducer? De Rougemont (101-7) tells us the mythic Don Juan cannot live with a woman but must dominate women by violating and rejecting them. Ever pursuing an ideal of perfect woman, he need never commit himself to a real woman. His love is eternally distant. Enjoying intellectual as well as carnal rape, he gains power by deceiving, believing truth cannot endure and contradictions do not matter. Castaneda's violation of academic standards and Carlos's hostile intercourse with a witch have the flavor if not the form of the Spanish myth.

154 don't move from your spot. J187.

154 sorcerers dominate females. P216; I122; R153.

155 Todhunter, Buzza, Farley. Pseudonyms.

155 luck with women. (Wallace, 86).

155 don't like the heat. I155.

155 Sacramento. The bookwomen identified their customer (the date was recalled as some time in 1973) when he bought a copy of *The Teachings*, autographed it, asked them to mail it for him, and admitted he was Carlos Castaneda. Booklady's recollections of his appearance and mannerisms are consistent with other accounts. In response to their interest in him, he returned later, went into a back room, and talked to them about himself for an hour or so.

156 death of Susana. (*Time*, 44). horrendous burden R56.

156 let others take care of him. R140.

156 looked for her everywhere. I68. blond/brunette, hunter's love I67-70.

156 could not share. "As a couple we did not form social friendships. I had my own friends and Carlos had his" (M. Castaneda, 75). Margaret told me (letter 22 Oct 1975) Castaneda had never said anything to her about Michael Harner, Jívaro Indians, or *Mushrooms Russia and History.*

157 her attempts to get more of him. "I was so jealous of him! I would follow him to see if he were going out with other women" (M. Castaneda, 77). Of course, she couldn't *see* don Juan.

157 Juan de la Cruz escapes. (Bruno, 179-184; Peers, I-xxvii).

157 parable of the four wind-women. (Wallace, 140-1). I suspect this vivid, self-contained allegory was intended to be an episode in *Tales of Power*, possibly the climax, until Wallace's article prematurely disclosed it in December 1972.

157 ally. wrestle ally to ground R234; I206. spun by ally into other worlds I259-268.

158 not a single wind. Though Carlos got no women at all and Pablito got three he had to leave behind when he went to face his ally, wily old dJ had a good thing going inArizona with "a lovely young social worker." On one occasion, dJ hid Carlos under the mat when the mothering lady came calling. There Carlos spied on the two of them as a child spies on its parents, until his tittering gave him away. "Sorcerers have a lot of fun together," John Wallace commented wryly (140).

159 Lame Deer. (Fire).

159 María Sabina. (Wasson-a, -c, -j).

159 Ramón. (Myerhoff, 33-34, 145-6).

159 bridged two worlds. (Eliade, 486). Traditional shamans seem to *add* superhumanity to their humanity, while Castaneda's sorcerers must *lose* their humanity to achieve superhumanity.

159 San Juan reluctant to say mass. (Peers, III-372).

159 most intimate companion. Margaret.

159 starting over. lullabye J137. man in a hurry I25. first-grader R141. approval P191. words of love unspoken J147. talking about good times P273. desperate jokes P282.

160 rescue them. I265.

160 imaginary playmates. *suchona,* the sliding place (Brundage, 224); dG slides down rock P211-2. mischievous eyes P55. kicking legs etc. I231. kite I244. imitates driving I237. names: Juancho, Gerancho P185. in the back seat I245. Margolis (232). Pablito and Nestor P195-6, 224. dJ a fleeting image R237. no real compassion (Wallace, 141). Los Angeles (Wallace, 85). Tucson (Keen, 102). dust on the road P100, 287.

161 solemn promise. "This is the last thing I will ever write about don Juan" (*Time*, 45).

162 end of the day I155.

163 haven't changed a bit. R23, 263; I47.

164 compensation. Compare dG about dJ: "This is the only one who is real. The world is real only when I am with this one" I265.

165 *Lilith.* Condensed from MacDonald (210, 206-7).

168 *Ixtlan* mentions *seeing* in 1961-2. I39, 104, 119, 125, 134, 136, 149, 156, 183, 188, 194, 202.

171 dJ argue his way out of anything. I54.

174 Sanchez. (Thomas Sanchez, *Rabbit Boss,* Knopf, 1973, p. 247).

174 I did not give a fig. P283. clarity has loomed upon you R115. that statement had clinched me R193.

175 smoothly translated. (Wasson-h, 246).

ADDED NOTES

See also ADDED REFERENCES on page 201

13 controlling dreams. Krippner (300-2) describes a UCLA dream study whose reported results do suggest a psi effect, but the actual agent could as well have been anthropologist investigator Douglass Price-Williams as intended agent Castaneda.

28 not an Indian. Also J49.

61 Mazatec Genaro. An Indian pumping Pemex at Ixtlán de Juárez told me on 10 October 1976 there was indeed a local Don Genaro, of many but uncounted years and no visible occupation. "Does he speak Mazatec?" I asked breathlessly. "Nobody here speaks Mazatec," the young man replied. Nor is Mazatec spoken in Ixtlán del Río or Ixtlán de los Hervores. Villa (1955) or Weitlaner (1969) could have suggested a better home town for dG. Cerro Rabón, magic mountain of the Mazatecs, rises at Jalapa, for example. Mazatecs live in Chilchotla, Soyaltepec, and Ixcatlán. Come to think of it, maybe dG told Carlos—who wrote it down wrong—about his journey to Ixcatlán.

102 Nin's help. Nin believed her interest in *The Teachings* had worried UCLA into publishing it (Hinz, 227)—which sounds to me like a flattering illusion fostered by Trickster.

102 different uses. Question, March 1973: "Are you interested in the Carlos Castenada method of exploring the unconscious?" Nin: "No, it's not my method to use drugs" (Hinz, 134).

ILLUSTRATIONS

Cover drawing by Frederick A. Usher. **vi** 'La Catalina,' hotel in 1962, woman redrawn (fh) by Linda Trujillo. **vii** Guatemalan mushroom stone. **32** Ayesha, She-who-must-be-obeyed. **33** María Sabina. **62** Yaqui dance mask. **64** Smiling face, Mexico. **85** Huautecan fabric design. **86** Peyote. **104** Huave fabric design. **105** Mimbres Coyote-Trickster, New Mexico. **116** The true earth—literally: truly (*alethos*) the earth (*he ge*). **177** *Tonal* welcoming *nagual*. **125** Eight points on the fibers of a luminous being. **129** Peruvian Spaniards uncovering an Indian woman, Huaman Poma. **130** Chimu mask. **145** Mushrooms of vision, Psilocybe mexicana *Heim*. **146** Mochica messenger, Peru. **164** Pima basket design.

ACKNOWLEDGMENTS

Proprietary permissions and other explicit contributions are acknowledged in particular notes or text above. Here I wish to thank those whose help, though often crucial, remains invisible: A.J.O. Anderson, Michael J. Buckley S.J., José Luis Byr, Margaret de Mille, Ned Divelbiss, David Dolan, Donald Dozer, Marie Ensign, Tomás Loayza, J. Raúl Martínez, Mary Moon, Joanna and Robert Morris, Zoltan Pazmany, Silvio Spigno, Rhea White, and others who remain anonymous. In the second edition, special thanks to Marcello Truzzi and William Madsen for mentioning the Piltdown parallel and to David Christie for pointing out the Catalina connection on page 232 of La Barre's *Peyote Cult.*

PRODUCTION CREDITS

To Camera-ready Composition for typesetting; Santa Barbara Photo Engraving for camera work; R.R. Donnelly & Sons, Crawfordsville, Indiana, for printing and binding; Rood Associates for covers and jackets.

With few exceptions, these references have been specifically cited in the text or notes. Additional references, not listed, will be found in the notes.

Where alternative editions are listed, cited pages are from the edition marked with an asterisk (*). Works beyond the first listed for one author are identified by letter (b, c, d, etc.). For such authors, the letter -a may or may not be used to cite the first work. When no letter appears, the first work is intended. For example: Cravens = Cravens-a, Pearce = Pearce-a.

Castaneda's four don Juan books (Castaneda-a, -c, -d, -f) are respectively coded in the notes as: J, R, I, P—standing for Juan, Reality, Ixtlan, Power.

Alexander, Hartley Burr. *The Mythology of All Races,* volume 10, *North American.* Marshall Jones, 1916. Macmillan, 1944. Cooper Square, 1964.*

Artaud, Antonin. *The Peyote Dance.* Farrar, Straus & Giroux, 1976.

Ash, Lee. [Review of *A Separate Reality.*] *Library Journal,* 1971(May 1), 96(9), 1630-1.

Atkinson, William Walker (Pseudonym: Yogi Ramacharaka). *Fourteen Lessons in Yogi Philosophy and Oriental Occultism.* Chicago: Yogi Publication Society, 1909.

Barthelme, Donald. The teachings of Don B.: A Yankee way of knowledge. *New York Times Magazine,* 1973(Feb 11), 14-15, 66-67. Reproduced in D. Barthelme, *Guilty Pleasures.* Dell, 1974. Pp. 53-62.

Beals, Ralph L. *The Contemporary Culture of the Cáhita Indians.* Smithsonian Institution, 1945.

Bennett, Wendell C. & Robert M. Zingg. *The Tarahumara.* U. Chicago, 1935.

Berreman, Gerald D. Anemic and emetic analyses in social anthropology. *American Anthropologist,* 1966, 68(2, pt 1), 346-354.

Bharati, Agehananda. *The Light at the Center: Context and Pretext of Modern Mysticism.* Sta Barbara: Ross-Erikson, 1976.

Blackburn, Thomas C. *December's Child: A Book of Chumash Oral Narratives.* U. California, 1975.

Bogen, Joseph E. The other side of the brain. II: An appositional mind. *Bulletin of the Los Angeles Neurological Societies,* 1969(July), 34(3), 135-162. Reproduced in Robert E. Ornstein, editor, *The Nature of Human Consciousness.* Viking, 1974.* Pp. 111-125.

Boyd, James W. The teachings of don Juan from a Buddhist perspective. *Christian Century,* 1973(Mar 28), 90(13), 360-363.

Brundage, Burr Cartwright. *Lords of Cuzco: A History and Description of the Inca People in Their Final Days.* U. Oklahoma, 1967.

Bruno de Jesus-Marie. *St. John of the Cross.* Sheed & Ward, 1932.

Castaneda, Carlos. *The Teachings of Don Juan: A Yaqui Way of Knowledge.* U. California, 1968. Ballantine, 1969. Pocket Books, 1974*—code J.

b ———. The didactic uses of hallucinogenic plants: An examination of a system of teaching. Paper, 67th Annual Meeting of the American Anthropological Association, 1968, *Abstracts,* 21-22 (reference copied from La Barre-a).

c ———. *A Separate Reality: Further Conversations with Don Juan.* Simon & Schuster, 1971. Pocket Books, 1974*—code R.

d ———. *Journey to Ixtlan: The Lessons of Don Juan.* Simon & Schuster, 1972. Pocket Books, 1974*—code I.

e ———. Sorcery: A Description of the World (Doctoral dissertation, University of California, Los Angeles, 1973). *Dissertation Abstracts International,* 1973, 33(12 Part 1, Jun), 5625B. (University Microfilms No. 73-13,132—"For copies contact author at 308 Westwood Plaza, P.O. Box 101, Los Angeles, California 90024")

f ———. *Tales of Power.* Simon & Schuster, 1974—code P.

Castaneda, Margaret Runyan, as told to Wanda Sue Parrott. My husband Carlos Castaneda. *Fate,* 1975(Feb), *28*(2/299), 70-78.

Cook, Bruce. Is Carlos Castaneda for real? *National Observer,* 1973 (Feb 24), *12*(8), 33.

Crapanzano, Vincent. Popular anthropology. *Partisan Review,* 1973, *40*(3), 471-482.

Cravens, Gwyneth. Talking to power and spinning with the ally. *Harper's Magazine,* 1973(Feb), *246*(1473), 91-94, 97.

b ———. The arc of flight. *Harper's Magazine,* 1974(Sep), *249*(1492), 43.

de Mille, Richard. The perfect mirror is invisible. *Zygon,* 1976(Mar), *11*(1).

de Rougemont, Denis. *Love Declared: Essays on the Myths of Love.* Pantheon, 1963.

Dobkin de Rios, Marlene. *Visionary Vine: Psychedelic Healing in the Peruvian Amazon.* San Francisco: Chandler, 1972. Dover, 1975.

Eliade, Mircea. *Shamanism: Archaic Techniques of Ecstasy.* Princeton U., 1964.

Fire, John/Lame Deer & Richard Erdoes. *Lame Deer, Seeker of Visions.* Simon & Schuster, 1972.

First, Elsa. Don Juan is to Carlos Castaneda as Carlos Castaneda is to us. *New York Times Book Review,* 1974(Oct 27), 35, 38, 40.

Foster, George M. Nagualism in Mexico and Guatemala. *Acta Americana,* 1944(Jan-Jun), *2*(1 & 2), 85-103.

Freilicher, Lila. The Carlos Castaneda trilogy. *Publishers Weekly,* 1972(Nov 20), *202*(21), 50-51.

Furst, Peter T. Huichol conceptions of the soul. *Folklore Americas,* 1967(June), *27*(2), 39-106.

b ———, editor. *Flesh of the Gods: The Ritual Use of Hallucinogens.* Praeger, 1972.

Garfield, Patricia, Ph.D. *Creative Dreaming.* Simon & Schuster, 1974.

Giddings, Ruth Warner, collector. *Yaqui Myths and Legends.* U. Arizona, 1959.

Globus, Gordon G. Will the real 'don Juan' please stand up. *The Academy,* 1975(Dec), *19*(4), 11-14.

Goldschmidt, Walter. *Exploring the Ways of Mankind,* 2nd edition. Holt, Rinehart, & Winston, 1971.

Grosso, Michael. Plato and out-of-the-body experiences. *Journal of the American Society for Psychical Research,* 1975(Jan), *69*(1), 61-74.

Harner, Michael J. Jívaro souls. *American Anthropologist,* 1962(Apr), *64*(2), 258-272.

b ———. Machetes, shotguns, and society: An inquiry into the social impact of technological change among the Jívaro Indians (Doctoral dissertation, University of California, Berkeley, 1963). *Dissertation Abstracts,* 1963-64, *24,* 3497. (University Microfilms No. 64-2060)

c ———. The sound of rushing water. *Natural History,* 1968(Jun-Jul), 28-33, 60-61.

d ———. *The Jívaro, People of the Sacred Waterfalls.* Natural History Press, 3 November 1972. Doubleday Anchor, 1973.*

e ———, editor. *Hallucinogens and Shamanism.* Oxford, 1973.

Harris, Marvin. *The Nature of Cultural Things.* Random House, 1964.

b ———. *The Rise of Anthropological Theory.* Crowell, 1968.

c ———. *Cows, Pigs, Wars & Witches: The Riddles of Culture.* Random House, 1974.

Heard, H. F. (pseudonym of Gerald Heard). Dromenon. In his *The Great Fog and Other Weird Tales.* Vanguard Press, 1944. Pp. 156-204.

Hendlin, Steven Jeffrey. Toward a Converging Philosophy: Don Juan Matus and the Gestalt Therapy of Frederick Perls (Master's thesis, United States International University 1973). *Masters Abstracts,* 1973, *11*(3, Sep), 313. (University Microfilms No. M-4599)

Hillegas, Mark R., editor. *Shadows of Imagination: The Fantasies of C. S. Lewis, J. R. R. Tolkien, and Charles Williams.* So. Illinois U., 1969.

Hughes, Robert. The sorcerer's apprentice. *Time,* 1972(Nov 6), *100*(19), 101.

Johnson, Jean B. *El Idioma Yaqui.* México: Instituto Nacional de Antropología e Historia, 1962.

Katz, Solomon H. Toward a new science of humanity. *Zygon,* 1975(Mar), *10*(1), 12-31.

Keen, Sam. Sorcerer's apprentice. *Psychology Today,* 1972(Dec), *6*(7), 90-92, 95-96, 98, 100, 102.

Kennedy, William. Fiction or fact. *New Republic,* 1974(Nov 16), *71* (20/3123), 28-30.

Kleps, Art. [Letter] *New York Times Book Review,* 1973(Feb 4), 24-25.

Kluckhohn, Clyde. *Navaho Witchcraft.* Boston: Beacon Press, 1944.

Klüver, Heinrich. *Mescal, The 'Divine' Plant and It's Psychological Effects.* London: Kegan Paul, Trench, Trubner, 1928.* Reissued as: *Mescal and Mechanisms of Hallucination.* U. Chicago, 1966.

Kurath, William & Edward H. Spicer. *A Brief Introduction to Yaqui, A Native Language of Sonora* (University of Arizona Social Science Bulletin No. 15). U. Arizona, 1947.

Kwitny, J. *The Fountain Pen Conspiracy.* Knopf, 1973.

La Barre, Weston. Hallucinogens and the shamanic origins of religion. In Furst-b (261-278), 1972.

b ———. *The Peyote Cult,* 4th edition. Schocken, 1975. Cites comments, not cited here, by: H. Gregory, V. Howes, R.. Jellinek, & C. Simmons.

c ———. Stinging criticism from the author of *The Peyote Cult.* In Noel (40-42), 1976.

Leach, Edmund. High school. *New York Review of Books,* 1969(June 5), *12,* 12-13.

Lévy-Bruhl, Lucien. *The 'Soul' of the Primitive.* Praeger, 1966.

Lévy-Strauss, Claude. *Structural Anthropology.* Basic Books, 1963.

Lewis, C.S. *Till We Have Faces.* Harcourt, Brace & World, 1956. Eerdmans, 1964.

Lindsay, David. *A Voyage to Arcturus.* Macmillan, 1963. Ballantine, 1968.

McAllister, Callista. *Pornella.* Sta Barbara: Capra Press, 1975.

MacDonald, George. *Phantastes and Lilith.* Eerdmans, 1964.* Introduction by C. S. Lewis, first published 1946. *Lilith* first published 1895.

Madsen, William & Claudia Madsen. The sorcerer's apprentice. *Natural History,* 1971(June), *80*(6), 74-76, 78-80.

Mandelbaum, David G., editor. *Selected Writings of Edward Sapir in Language, Culture and Personality.* U. California, 1949.

Mandell, Arnold J. Don Juan in the mind. *Human Behavior,* 1975(Jan), *4*(1), 64-69.

Margolis, Joseph. Don Juan as philosopher. In Noel (228-242), 1976.

Moisés, Rosalio, Jane Holden Kelley, & William Curry Holden. *The Tall Candle: The Personal Chronicle of a Yaqui Indian.* U. Nebraska, 1971.

Myerhoff, Barbara G. *Peyote Hunt: The Sacred Journey of the Huichol Indians.* Cornell U., 1974.

Nin, Anais. *The Diary of Anaïs Nin, 1931-1934.* Swallow & HBW, 1966.

b ———. *The Novel of the Future.* Macmillan, 1968.

Noel, Daniel C., editor. *Seeing Castaneda: Reactions to the "Don Juan" Writings of Carlos Castaneda.* Putnam's Sons, 1976. Includes articles cited here: *Abridged—* Boyd; First; Riesman; *Time. Unabridged—*Leach; Keen; Oates-a,b; Spicer-d.

Nuñez Cabeza de Vaca, Alvar. *Relation of Alvar Nuñez Cabeza de Vaca Translated from the Spanish by Buckingham Smith.* University Microfilms, 1966. Translation first published in 1871.

Oates, Joyce Carol. Anthropology—or fiction? [Letter] *New York Times Book Review,* 1972(Nov 26), 41.

b ———. Don Juan's last laugh. *Psychology Today,* 1974(Sep), *8*(4), 10, 12, 130.

c ———. Letter to Daniel C. Noel. In Noel (69), 1976.

Parrott, Wanda Sue. I remember Castaneda. *Fate,* 1975(Feb), *28*(2/299), 79-81.

Pearce, Joseph Chilton. *The Crack in the Cosmic Egg.* Julian, 1971. Pocket Books, 1973.*

b ———. *Exploring the Crack in the Cosmic Egg.* Julian, 1974. Pocket Books, 1975.*

Peers, E. Allison, translator and editor. *The Complete Works of Saint John of the Cross,* volumes I-III. Newman, 1949.* First published 1933-34.

Polanyi, Michael. *Personal Knowledge.* Harper & Row, 1964, Torchbook.

Pollock, Steven Hayden. The psilocybin mushroom pandemic. *Journal of Psychedelic Drugs,* 1975(Jan-Mar), *7*(1), 73-84.

Puharich, Andrija. *The Sacred Mushroom.* Doubleday, 1959, 1974.

Pulvino, Charles J. & James L. Lee. Counseling according to don Juan. *Counseling and Values,* 1975(Feb), *19*(2), 125-130.

Radin, Paul. *The Trickster: A Study in American Indian Mythology.* Philosophical Library, 1956.

Rank, Otto. *The Double.* U. North Carolina, 1971.

Rhine, Louisa E. *Psi, What is It? The Story of ESP and PK.* Harper & Row, 1975, 1976.

Riesman, Paul. The collaboration of two men and a plant. *New York Times Book Review,* 1972(Oct 22), 7, 10-12.

Roll, William G. *The Poltergeist.* New American Library, 1972, 1973.*

Roszak, Theodore. A sorcerer's apprentice. *Nation,* 1969(Feb 10), *208*(6), 184-6.

Rowe, John Howland. Inca culture at the time of the Spanish conquest. In J. H. Steward, editor, *Handbook of South American Indians,* volume 2, *The Andean Civilizations.* Smithsonian Institution, 1946. Pp. 183-330.

Rueger, Russ. Tripping the heavy fantastic. *Human Behavior,* 1973(Mar), *2*(3), 73-76.

Russell, Frank. The Pima Indians. In *Bureau of American Ethnology 26th Annual Report, 1904-1905.* Pp. 4-389 + 47 plates.

Seki, K., editor. *Folktales of Japan.* U. Chicago, 1963.

Shelton, Gilbert & Dave Sheridan. The 7th voyage of the Fabulous Furry Freak Brothers, A Mexican odyssey. In their *Brother Can You Spare 75¢ for the Fabulous Furry Freak Brothers?* (Freak Brothers #4). San Francisco: Rip Off Press (Box 14158, San Francisco, CA 94114), 1975. 24 unnumbered pages.

Spicer, Edward H. *Pascua, A Yaqui Village in Arizona.* U. Chicago, 1940.

b ———. Potam, a Yaqui village in Sonora. *American Anthropologist,* 1954(Aug), *56*(4, pt 2, Memoir 77).

c ———. *Cycles of Conquest.* U. Arizona, 1962.

d ———. [Review of *The Teachings of Don Juan*]. *American Anthropologist,* 1969(Apr), *71*(2), 320-322.

Sukenick, Ronald. Upward and Juanward: The possible dream. In Noel (110-120), 1976.* First published in *Village Voice,* 1973(Jan 25).

Swain, Frederick & others. Four psilocybin experiences. *Psychedelic Review,* 1963(Fall), *1*(2), 219-243.

Tart, Charles T. Did I really fly?—Some methodological notes on the investigation of altered states of consciousness and psi phenomena. In Roberto Cavanna, editor, *Psi Favorable States of Consciousness.* New York: Parapsychology Foundation (29 West 57th Street, New York, NY 10019), 1970. Pp. 3-10.

Thord-Gray, I. *Tarahumara-English, English-Tarahumara Dictionary and Introduction to Tarahumara Grammar.* U. Miami, 1955.

Time. Don Juan and the sorcerer's apprentice. *Time,* 1973(Mar 5), *101*(10). 36-38, 43-45. (Prepared by Robert Hughes, Sandra Burton, Tomás A. Loayza, and others.)

Tomkins, Calvin. The teachings of Joe Pye (Field notes for Carlos Castaneda's next epiphany). *New Yorker,* 1973(Feb 3), *48*(50), 37-38.

Tovar, Juan, translator, & Carlos Castaneda. *Las Enseñanzas de Don Juan: Una Forma Yaqui de Conocimiento.* México: Fondo de Cultura Económica, 1974. Prólogo de Octavio Paz: La mirada anterior, pp. 9-23.

b ———. *Una Realidad Aparte: Nuevas Conversaciones con Don Juan.* México: Fondo de Cultura Económica, 1974.

c ———. *Viaje a Ixtlán: Las Lecciones de Don Juan.* México: Fondo de Cultura Económica, 1975.

Wallace, John. The sorcerer's apprentice: Conversations with Carlos Castaneda. *Penthouse,* 1972(Dec), *4*(4), 83-86, 139-142.

Wasson, R. Gordon. Seeking the magic mushrooms. *Life,* 1957(May 13), *42*(19), 100-120.

b ———. The divine mushroom: Primitive religion and hallucinatory agents. *Proceedings of the American Philosophical Society,* 1958(June), *102*(3), 221-223.

c ———. The hallucinogenic fungi of Mexico. *Harvard University Botanical Museum Leaflets,* 1961(Feb 17), *19*(7), 137-162.

d ———. *Soma: Divine Mushroom of Immortality.* Harcourt, Brace & World, 1968. Harcourt Brace Jovanovich, 1971, 1972.

e ———. [Review of *The Teachings of Don Juan*]. *Economic Botany,* 1969(Apr-Jun), 23(2), 197.

f ———. [Review of *A Separate Reality*]. *Economic Botany,* 1972(Jan-Mar), 26(1), 98-99.

g ———. [Review of *Journey to Ixtlan*]. *Economic Botany,* 1973(Jan-Mar), 27(1), 151-152.

h ———. [Review of *Tales of Power*]. *Economic Botany,* 1974(Jul-Sep), 28(3), 245-246.

i ———, George & Florence Cowan, & Willard Rhodes. *María Sabina and Her Mazatec Mushroom Velada.* Harcourt Brace Jovanovich, 1974.

j ——— & Valentina P. Wasson. *Mushrooms Russia and History,* volumes 1 & 2. Pantheon, 1957.

Wasson, Valentina P. I ate the sacred mushrooms. *This Week,* 1957(May 19), 1, 8-10, 36.

Westfall, Richard S. Newton and the fudge factor. *Science,* 1973(Feb 23), 179(4075), 751-758.

Whorf, Benjamin Lee. *Language, Thought, and Reality.* MIT/Wiley, 1956.

Wilk, Stan. [Review of *A Separate Reality*]. *American Anthropologist,* 1972(Aug), 74(4), 921-922.

Young, Dudley. The magic of peyote. *New York Times Book Review,* 1968(Sep 29), 30.

ADDED REFERENCES

Gill, Jerry H. The world of don Juan: Some reflections. *Soundings,* 1974(W), 57(4), 387-402. Cited here at 117n.

Hinz, Evelyn J., editor. *A Woman Speaks: The Lectures, Seminars, and Interviews of Anaïs Nin.* Swallow, 1975. Pp. 134, 227.

Krippner, Stanley & Alberto Villoldo. *The Realms of Healing.* Celestial Arts, 1976. Pp. 300-302.

Langer, Susanne K. The growing center of knowledge. In her *Philosophical Sketches,* Johns Hopkins, 1962, pp. 143ff. * First published in, Lynn White, editor, *Frontiers of Knowledge,* Harper, 1956, pp. 257-286.

Silverman, David. *Reading Castaneda.* London: Routledge & Kegan Paul, 1975. A textbook of sociological epistemology. Cited here at 117n.

Tovar, d ———. *Relatos de Poder.* México: Fondo de Cultura Económica, 1976.

Villa Rojas, Alfonso. *Los Mazatecos y el Problema Indigena de la Cuenca del Papaloapan.* México: Instituto Nacional Indigenista, 1955.

Weitlaner, Roberto J. & Walter A. Hoppe. The Mazatec. In, *Handbook of Middle American Indians,* vol. 7. U. Texas, 1969. Pp. 516-22.

204

RICHARD de MILLE is a writer, editor, and scholar, whose study of science, philosophy, and religion drew him to Castaneda's books. He has also been a television director, a university professor, and a research psychologist. In the 1950s he published in *This Week*, the *New York Post*, and *Astounding Science Fiction*. The 1960s found him in *Psychological Bulletin*, *American Psychologist*, *Journal of Abnormal Psychology*, *Journal of Nervous and Mental Disease*, *Teachers College Record*, *Educational and Psychological Measurement*, and *Multivariate Behavioral Research*. In the 1970s he branched out in all directions, publishing in *Zygon*, *Reason*, *Maledicta*, *National Review*, *Parabola*, *High Times*, *Adam*, and *Weird Trips*. His *Put Your Mother on the Ceiling* (now from Penguin) is an oft-quoted classic in the field of didactic imagination exercises. His *Two Qualms & A Quirk* (from Capra) is the world's most daring paronymous anagrapsikon. He has edited surveys, safety reports, and computerizing plans, social science dissertations, occult and metaphysical tracts, a text on drawing, an otherworld fantasy, the autobiography of a would-be suicide, lake monsters for children, and novels on volleyball and gay frenzy. Following the spoor of don Juan, he acquired a most peculiar anthropological repertory, joined the American Anthropological Association, spoke at its 1978 meetings, and reviewed *Second Ring of Power* for the *American Anthropologist*. He is a member of the American Society for Psychical Research, consulting editor to *Skeptical Inquirer* and *Zetetic Scholar*, and associate in *Current Anthropology*. He lives in Santa Barbara.